# THE SIEGE OF ACRE, 1189–1191

# THE SIEGE OF ACRE, 1189–1191

Saladin, Richard the Lionheart, and the
Battle That Decided the Third Crusade

## JOHN D. HOSLER

YALE UNIVERSITY PRESS
NEW HAVEN AND LONDON

For information about this and other Yale University Press publications, please contact:
U.S. Office: sales.press@yale.edu    yalebooks.com
Europe Office: sales@yaleup.co.uk    yalebooks.co.uk

Set in Adobe Caslon Pro by IDSUK (DataConnection) Ltd
Printed in Great Britain by TJ International Ltd, Padstow, Cornwall

Library of Congress Control Number: 2017957460

ISBN 978-0-300-21550-2

A catalogue record for this book is available from the British Library.

10 9 8 7 6 5 4 3 2 1

In memory of
Edward "Skip" Cox,
*Requiescat in pace.*

# CONTENTS

# PLATES AND MAPS

## Plates

1. The Toron, viewed from the north. © John D. Hosler.
2. Remains of the Tower of Flies, Akko Harbor. © Yuval Yosub.
3. Acre, as illustrated by Pietro Vesconte, from Marino Sanudo's *Liber secretorum fidelium crucis super Terrae Sanctae recuperatione et conservatione*. © The British Library Board (BL Add. MS 27376, f. 190r).
4. Matthew Paris' map of Acre, from *Chronica maiora*. © The British Library Board (BL Royal MS 14 C. vii, f. 4v).
5. Evidence of northern crusade-era walls in Akko. © John D. Hosler.
6. Old Akko, viewed from atop the Toron. © John D. Hosler.
7. The siege of Acre, from *Chroniques de France ou de St Denis*. © The British Library Board (BL Royal 20 C. vii, f. 24v).
8. The Scythian women attacking a castle, from *Histoire ancienne jusqu'à César*. © The British Library Board (BL Add. MS 15268, f. 101v).

9. A crusade-era western sword, Oakeshott Type XIa. © Royal Armouries (Sword, IX.1082).
10. Richard and Saladin, Combat Series Chertsey Tiles. © The Trustees of the British Museum.
11. Coin, Ṣalāḥ al-Dīn. © The Trustees of the British Museum (BM 1865, 0804.40.X).
12. Saladin captures the Holy Cross, from Matthew Paris' *Chronica maiora*. © Getty/Heritage Images.

## Maps

# ACKNOWLEDGMENTS

My work on Acre has benefitted from the generosity and expertise of numerous colleagues, acquaintances, and friends. I especially thank Marika Lysandrou at Yale University Press for her advice and assistance and Heather McCallum for her guidance and encouragement, as well as Kelly DeVries, who introduced me to her in the first place. He and John France have been extremely helpful and receptive mentors in too many ways to count. I am also grateful to my former professors at the University of Delaware, Daniel Callahan and Lawrence Duggan, for my early grounding in Crusades studies, as well as for their continuing support, suggestions, and ideas. For their assistance in answering questions or acting as sounding boards at conferences and through correspondence, I thank David Bachrach, Dana Cushing, Ilana Krug, Kenneth Madison, Alexander Pavuk, L.J. Andrew Villalon, Nicholas Paul, Joanna Phillips, Andrew Holt, and especially Daniel Franke, as well as the general membership of *De Re Militari*. I am indebted to my colleagues in Israel: Allon Klebanoff, the faculty and staff at the Zinman Institute of Archaeology at the University of Haifa, and Abdu Matta, my tour guide in Akko. For consistently locating my research materials, I thank the staffs at the Earl S. Richardson Library at Morgan State University, the Eisenhower Library at Johns Hopkins University, and the Library of Congress. My sister, Gina Lamb, applied her professional editing skills to the final draft. As always, I thank my wife, Holly, for her sacrifice of many hours to facilitate my writing, as well as my three young children, Gianna Marie, Michael Plantagenet, and Rocco Alexander, who freed up more hours for composition by going to bed on time and sleeping in late.

This book is dedicated to Edward "Skip" Cox, my good friend and seminar mate at Iowa State University, who died too young from complications from cancer in 2015. His memorial was held on the exact day I traveled to Akko to research this book.

# ABBREVIATIONS

*Anonymous1*     "De expugnatione civitatis Acconensis," in
                 *Chronica magistri Rogeri de Houedene*, ed. W.
                 Stubbs, 3 vols, Rolls Series (London, 1868–71),
                 3.cvi–cxxxvi.

*Anonymous2*     "Libellus de expugnatione terrae sanctae per
                 Saladinum," in *Radulphi de Coggeshall Chronicon
                 Anglicanum*, ed. J. Stevenson, Rolls Series
                 (London, 1875), 209–62.

*Anonymous3*     "Ein zeitgenössisches Gedicht auf die Belagerung
                 Accons," in *Forschungen zur deutschen Geschichte*, ed.
                 H. Prutz, vol. 21 (Göttingen, 1881), 449–94.

Ansbert          *Quellen zur Geschichte des Kreuzzuges Kaiser
                 Friedrichs I*, ed. A. Chroust, Monumenta Germania
                 Historica, Scriptores Rerum Germanicarum, New
                 Series 5 (Berlin, 1928).

Blasien          *Ottonis de Sancto Blasio chronica*, ed. A. Hofmeister,
                 Monumenta Germania Historica, Scriptores
                 Rerum Germanicarum (Hanover, 1912).

| | |
|---|---|
| Coggeshall | *Radulphi de Coggeshall Chronicon Anglicanum, De expugnatione terrae sanctae libellus, Thomas Agnellus de morte et sepultura Henrici regis Angliae junioris; Gesta Fulconis filii Warini; Excerpta ex Otiis imperialibus Gervasii Tilebutiensis*, ed. J. Stevenson, 3 vols, Rolls Series (London, 1875). |
| Devizes | "The chronicle of Richard of Devizes," in *Chronicles of the Reigns of Stephen, Henry II, and Richard I*, ed. R. Howlett, 4 vols, Rolls Series (London, 1886). |
| Eracles | *La Continuation de Guillaume de Tyr (1184–1197)*, ed. M.R. Morgan (Paris, 1982). |
| Estoire | *The History of the Holy War: Ambroise's Estoire de la Guerre Sainte*, ed. and trans. M. Ailes and M. Barber, 2 vols (Woodbridge, 2003). |
| Howden1 | *Gesta regis Henrici secundi Benedicti abbatis*, ed. W. Stubbs, 2 vols, Rolls Series (London, 1867). |
| Howden2 | *Chronica magistri Rogeri de Houedene*, ed. W. Stubbs, 3 vols, Rolls Series (London, 1868–71). |
| Ibn al-Athīr | *The Chronicle of Ibn al-Athīr for the Crusading Period from al-Mail fi'l-Ta'rikh*, trans. D.S. Richards, Crusade Texts in Translation, 3 vols (Reprint, Farnham, 2010). |
| Ibn Shaddād | *The Rare and Excellent History of Saladin by Bahā' al-Dīn Ibn Shaddād*, trans. D.S. Richards, Crusade Texts in Translation (Farnham, 2002). |
| 'Imād al-Dīn | "Les livres des deux jardins: histoire des deux règnes, celui de Nour Ed-Dìn et celui de Salah Ed Dìn," in *Recueil des historiens des croisades, historiens Orientaux*, vol. 4 (Paris, 1898). |
| Itinerarium1 | *Das Itinerarium peregrinorum: eine zeitgenössische englische Chronik zum dritten Kreuzzug in ursprünglicher Gestalt*, ed. H.E. Mayer (Stuttgart, 1962). |

| | |
|---|---|
| *Itinerarium2* | "Itinerarium peregrinorum et gesta regis Ricardi," in *Chronicles and Memorials of the Reign of Richard I*, ed. W. Stubbs, 2 vols, Rolls Series (London, 1864–5). |
| Newburgh | William of Newburgh, *The History of English Affairs*, ed. and trans. P.G. Walsh and M.J. Kennedy, 2 vols (Oxford, 2007–11); or "Historia rerum Anglicarum," ed. R. Howlett, in *Chronicles of the Reigns of Stephen, Henry II, and Richard I*, 2 vols, Rolls Series (London, 1884–5). |
| *RRRH* | *Revised regesta regni Hierosolymitani Database*, http://crusades-regesta.com |
| Rigord | *Œuvres de Rigord et de Guillaume le Breton, historiens de Philippe-Auguste*, ed. H.F. Delaborde (Paris, 1882). |
| *Ymagines* | *Radulfi de Diceto decanis Lundoniensis opera historica*, ed. W. Stubbs, 2 vols, Rolls Series (London, 1876). |

Unless otherwise noted in the text, English translations are taken from the applicable editions above, as well as the following:

*The Crusade of Frederick Barbarossa: The history of the expedition of the Emperor Frederick and related texts*, trans. G.A. Loud (Farnham, 2013) [for Ansbert and Blasien].

*The Chronicle of Richard of Devizes, concerning the Deeds of Richard I, king of England, and Richard of Cirencester's Description of Britain*, trans. J.A. Giles (London, 1841).

*The Conquest of Jerusalem and the Third Crusade: Sources in translation*, trans. P.W. Edbury (Aldershot, 1998) [for *Eracles*].

*The Annals of Roger de Hoveden*, trans. H.T. Riley, 2 vols (Reprint, New York, 1968) [for *Howden2*].

*The Chronicle of the Third Crusade: The Itinerarium peregrinorum et gesta regis Ricardi*, trans. H.J. Nicholson, Crusade Texts in Translation (Farnham, 1997) [for *Itinerarium2*].

*The History of William of Newburgh*, trans. J. Stevenson (London, 1856).

*Arab Historians of the Crusades: Selected and translated from the Arabic sources*, ed. and trans. F. Gabrieli (Berkeley, 1984) [for ʿImād al-Dīn].

1. Acre and its environment.

# INTRODUCTION

Richard the Lionheart lowered his lance and drove it into the shoulder of his jousting opponent, the celebrated Ayyubid sultan Ṣalāḥ al-Dīn (Saladin), knocking him and his horse to the ground. The force of Richard's charge was unstoppable. He pushed forward, swinging his battle-axe, to slay wave upon wave of Muslim fighters. His bloody attack was so audacious, so glorious, that it inspired his knights to join the charge. More than 60,000 Muslims lost their lives.[1]

Richard and Saladin's momentous clash has gone down in history as a shining example of English heroism in the face of an obdurate enemy. The joust, however, never actually happened: rather, it is a well-known legend in a mid-thirteenth-century text, the *Romance of Richard Coeur de Lion*. Nevertheless, that legendary encounter between the leaders is emblematic of the very real war in which they fought: the Third Crusade, which saw the armies of Saladin and Richard meet several times, most famously in the latter's great victories at Arsur and Jaffa in 1191 and 1192. And, despite Richard's inability to recapture the ultimate prize of Jerusalem itself, which has led many historians to dub his crusade a failure, his valorous

1

reputation was made – and has endured – on the basis of his military exploits in the East.

The fighting of the Third Crusade, however, began long before Richard the Lionheart ever arrived in the East. In the summer of 1189, thousands of Christian soldiers gathered before the walls of the city of Acre. Called Ptolemais in the Bible and Akko in modern times, the peninsular city was one of the principal harbors on the Levantine coast.[2] Acre had been captured by Saladin during his momentous campaign of 1187, during which the sultan not only destroyed the army of the Kingdom of Jerusalem at the Horns of Hattin, but also retook the Holy City itself. The kingdoms of Western Europe girded themselves for another crusade in response. In the meantime, the unraveling of Saladin's gains had to begin somewhere, and Acre was to be the starting point. It was there that the armies of the Third Crusade gradually assembled and set about the brutal business of holy war.

The siege of Acre was the central action of the Third Crusade and, at nearly two years in length, was also one of the longest western-led sieges of the entire middle ages. It was a complex, multi-stage affair. The besieging Christians soon found themselves under attack from a Muslim army led by Saladin himself, which encircled the crusader camp and threatened to end the operation in short measure. In response, the crusaders built ramparts and dug ditches to protect themselves, which consequently trapped them between the sultan and the garrison defending Acre. The Muslims responded to every crusader action in tandem and with clever and carefully coordinated attacks against the ramparts and repulses of hostile sorties. This forced the westerners to fight on two fronts while desperately straining their necks in the hope of spotting seaborne reinforcements from the Mediterranean. Those ships, a sporadic but vital lifeline to the outside world, provided enough succor that the crusaders were able first to endure the assaults, and then to survive disease, starvation, and despair. Finally, led by the late-arriving kings Richard and Philip II Augustus of France, the soldiers managed to break through Acre's walls and achieve an improbable victory in July 1191.

The siege of Acre is therefore not the history of a single event, but rather a singular phenomenon: an extended period of regular warfare between two sides, during which their respective communities fought, negotiated, suffered, persevered, and rejoiced. And all this in the context of the most famous religious wars in history, the Crusades, waged between tens of thousands of men and women and led by the most renowned warriors of the age. This book presents the story of Acre in the first-ever comprehensive study of the siege in any language.

Acre shared a common role with Jerusalem, for both cities served as capital for the kings of Jerusalem (Jerusalem itself from 1099 to 1187, Acre from 1191 to 1291). In any war, the acquisition of a capital is a notable event and worthy of study; but while there are numerous studies of Jerusalem's capture by the army of the First Crusade in 1099, similar studies of Acre are lacking. There are obvious reasons for this disparity. The biggest difference between the two cities, besides location, was the religious significance of Jerusalem and its symbolic ability to evoke piety and draw believers to the idea of holy war.[3] Moreover, the First Crusade holds chronological pride of place.

The taking of Acre, however, was of comparable political importance. It was more than just a long siege or the beginning of a famous, but ultimately unsuccessful, crusade. Rather, for a brief spell, Acre was the center of the European and Mediterranean worlds. It was a rare occasion on which four heads of state were together on the same field of battle. Acre was a flame to the moths, drawing in these and other leaders one by one and capturing their personal and financial attention for months or years. After its capture in 1191, it became the central rallying point for pilgrims and crusaders alike.[4] Christian rule there persisted for a hundred years after the siege's conclusion. As Christian-held territory in the Levant steadily folded in the thirteenth century, the last outpost to fall was Acre. Much like

Constantinople up to 1453, Acre's survival meant the kingdom's survival, the last flickering light of crusading dreams in the East. The siege of Acre was one of the central military events of the crusading era and needs to be recognized as such.

It is also a tale remarkably balanced by historical evidence, plentiful and diverse in both western and eastern sources. The story of Acre can be told to a considerable degree from both the Christian and the Muslim perspective, and many of the confusing elements can be resolved via a comparative analysis of the primary documents. Numerically, there are far more Christian accounts: because the crusade was called in the West, authors there were naturally interested in its generation, progress, and outcome, and the witness accounts were later excerpted and copied into local chronicles. The presence of the kings of England and France at Acre only increased this fascination. The Muslim sources, though fewer in number, are evocative and commendable for their proximity to the siege and access not only to participants in the fighting, but also to Saladin and his principal lieutenants. They become less verbose when the siege nears its conclusion and a crusader victory seems certain. With only one exception, none of the writers appear to have been actual combatants, but the close proximity of several witness accounts suggests a higher level of credibility.[5] Witnesses are by no means infallible, however, and I have tried to maintain a healthy skepticism when dealing with them.[6] Nonetheless, the dual perspectives add humanizing details to an already dramatic story. From either side, we catch glimpses of the labors and frustrations of medieval armies, tempered by their victories and defeats.

It is not my intention in this book to present a comprehensive narrative of the origination of the Third Crusade or even its first two years. That would necessitate exploring the full story of Saladin's advance across Syria in the 1180s, the debacle at the Battle of Hattin in 1187, and Jerusalem's subsequent capture that same year. One would need to consider the timing, manner, and contexts of the western leaders' taking the cross and then their mustering of armies in Europe and their respective journeys – all of which were fraught with problems and delays – to the East. One would also need to explore in a fuller manner religious enthusiasm, as John France has called it, which was an important driver of any crusading army. That is a complex topic that has been subjected to intense academic scrutiny and can easily overwhelm a narrative; this book, like France's, seeks primarily to explore the physical states of the armies and to reference religious elements when those altered or conditioned them.[7] In any case, there are numerous other studies in which readers can explore the wider context of the crusade. General histories of the Crusades contain adequate or even excellent analyses of the political interplay between the lords and heads of state, although most of them are narratives within books about the larger crusading period.[8]

Moreover, while Acre is consistently mentioned in general military histories of the middle ages, there is no single history covering the operational and technological aspects of the siege. No historian has tried to synthesize the siege with all the battles, skirmishes, and naval engagements that took place outside the immediate Acre peninsula. Acre seems to have received attention primarily because of the famous warriors present there; but this sort of celebrity treatment has obscured the fuller story of the siege and the contributions of lesser-known figures. Such a focus on the principals has actually served to blur the place of the siege itself in their respective military records: as this book will argue, neither Richard's nor Saladin's performance at Acre was particularly impressive, while Philip's has been unfairly diminished. Therefore, here I have privileged the military events over the political, situating the siege of Acre as a central event and a locus of conflict where different and competing forces traveled, lived, and waged war. As the first point of hostile contact between Christian and Muslim armies, and a long one at that, it deserves an extended treatment all of its own.[9]

The sheer cost and scale of the operation, along with its organizational dimensions, require a much more extended treatment than they have customarily received.[10] This book is based on the military narrative and surveys the entire array of land and sea engagements: these include no fewer than eight formal battles in the open field, twelve directed assaults against the city walls, sixteen sorties, ten naval battles, and dozens of skirmishes. Building on this narrative are considerations of the personalities of the warriors involved, particularly the generals, the complex political circumstances in both the Crusader States and Ayyubid territories, and the competing cultural and religious influences and motivations of the combatants. As much as possible, I have tried to incorporate into the story sources beyond the written documents. Acre has been a fertile site for archaeological study and has been called, along with Jerusalem, "the best opportunity for studying medieval urban topography in the Kingdom of Jerusalem."[11] Although the living quarters, roads, and churches within the city are tertiary, archaeological study of Acre's harbor, fortifications, and surroundings is crucial to an understanding of where different armies were located and the manner in which they were able to operate. Such an interdisciplinary examination of conflict zones reveals new facets of the action and suggests new questions about the practicalities of the military operations described in the extant documents. In this light, I hope the book sufficiently narrates the entire siege and, by focusing on many of its neglected aspects, usefully contributes to the landscape of crusading warfare in general and the Third Crusade in particular.

# I

# TARGET ACRE

*"Acre will certainly win eternal fame,*
*for the whole globe assembled to fight for her."*[1]

Acre had been in Christian hands for seventy-three years by the time Saladin arrived before its walls on 9 July 1187. This was just five days after his great victory at the Battle of Hattin, near Tiberias, where the sultan had smashed the army of the Kingdom of Jerusalem, killing a thousand knights and capturing King Guy of Lusignan and Reynald of Châtillon, the lord of Kerak. Reynald was executed when he refused to convert to Islam, and a holy relic, a piece of the True Cross upon which Christ was crucified, landed in Muslim hands.[2] Jerusalem itself now lay at Saladin's mercy, but he first sought to capture the ports along the Mediterranean Sea in order to ward off the Christian military response that would surely be forthcoming.

With no army to protect it, Acre was vulnerable. Its governor, the seneschal Joscelin of Courtenay, had fought at Hattin and escaped the carnage, but he quickly surrendered Acre to the Muslims. Many of the citizens felt betrayed and threatened to burn the city down from within. Saladin was able to quell their anxiety by allowing them to depart with their possessions.[3] According to Ibn al-Athīr, there was a tremendous amount of loot captured within, which the sultan distributed to his soldiers; subsequently, the governance of the city was given to his son al-Afḍāl ʿAlī and the possessions and revenues of the Templar quarter in particular were given to the lawyer ʿĪsā (ʿĪsā Ḍiyā al-Dīn al-Hakkārī).[4] After settling these affairs, Saladin took his army on a campaign that led to the capture of Sidon (29 July) and Beirut (6 August) in the north and then Ascalon in the south (4 September).

## Conrad and Guy

There was one coastal city, however, that had managed to resist Saladin's advance: Tyre, a well-fortified port located between Sidon and Acre.[5] Most of the survivors of Hattin had fled to Tyre, and on 14 July 1187 Conrad, the marquis of Montferrat, arrived there on a ship from Constantinople. He had intended to travel to Acre to join his father, William V. He soon learned that not only had William been captured at Hattin, but Acre was in Muslim hands. Upon discovering this, he sailed north to Tyre instead.[6] After landing, Conrad learned of the death of the count of Tripoli, Raymond III. With Guy in Saladin's hands, Raymond dead, and the other coastal cities under Muslim control, the marquis was able to emerge as the principal Christian leader in the Levant.

Conrad of Montferrat fancied himself a rival to Guy of Lusignan. Guy held the crown of Jerusalem by virtue of his marriage to Queen Sibylla, the sister of King Baldwin IV "the Leper King" (d. 1185). However, Guy was Sibylla's second husband: her first had been Conrad's brother, William Longsword, who married her in 1176 and then died in 1177, but not before siring a son, Baldwin V, who died in 1186. There was thus a Montferrat tie to the throne, but it was dashed when Sibylla chose Guy and crowned him king, an action then ratified when Patriarch Heraclius of Jerusalem anointed him.

Guy had had many enemies over his long career, but Conrad would turn out to be one of the most persistent.[7] In the meantime, Saladin continued his march. After the fall of Ascalon, the sultan finally moved on Jerusalem. He besieged the city on 25 September; it held out for only a few days before Balian, the lord of Ibelin (modern Yibna) surrendered. Saladin entered the Holy City on 9 October.[8]

## Preparing for the Crusade

The disaster of Hattin made a significant impression in the West and led to the calling of the Third Crusade. Drafting of a crusade bull was delayed, however, for, as information flowed in about events in the East, Pope Urban III abruptly died on 20 October 1187, purportedly from shock after hearing the news of Hattin and the loss of the piece of the True Cross. His successor, Gregory VIII, would thus be the one to issue the bull *Audita tremendi* nine days later.[9]

Those preaching the papal bull and pushing for crusading commitments found a receptive audience. There had been no comparable expedition eastward since the disastrous Second Crusade in the 1140s, but interest in the Holy Land had remained stout nonetheless. The king of England, Henry II, was involved as far back as 1166, when he proposed a five-year tax of two pennies in the pound for relief in the East. He twice promised to go on crusade himself, in 1170 and 1172, in either Spain or the Holy Land; failing that, he promised to provide further monies for military support. These promises were finalized in Pope Alexander III's "Compromise of Avranches," which detailed Henry's penance for the role he played in the murder of Thomas Becket, archbishop of Canterbury. In 1185, the king promised funds from a three-year income tax, but rejected Heraclius' request for his personal involvement. His son Richard, the future Richard I "the Lionheart," took the cross prematurely, before the papal bull had even been issued.[10]

It was not until 21 January 1188 that Henry II made a firmer commitment. Joscelin, archbishop of Tyre, had been traveling around

Europe with stories of the fall of Jerusalem, and on this occasion he gave a sermon on the crusade to both Henry and King Philip II Augustus of France. Both kings and Philip d'Alsace, count of Flanders, took the cross; moreover, both agreed to Henry's proposal of a massive levy, dubbed the "Saladin Tithe." In England, the cost, somewhere around £12,000, was mostly borne by the English Jewry.[11] Two months later, in Mainz, the Hohenstaufen emperor Frederick Barbarossa similarly took the cross. Henry's early funding indeed paid for soldiers and arms that were present at both Hattin and Jerusalem in 1187, but the king himself never went on crusade. He died on 6 July 1189, two years after the Battle of Hattin, but nearly two months before Guy of Lusignan's arrival at Acre. It would be left to his son Richard to lead the English contingent. Preparations began across the continent: monies were raised, troops were assembled, and political disputes were put on hold as the three most powerful secular leaders in medieval Europe, along with a host of lesser nobles, prepared to journey east on the Third Crusade.[12]

Those leaders who volunteered would be cooperating with what was believed to have been the will of God. *Audita tremendi*, which formally started the Third Crusade nearly two years before the siege of Acre even began, outlines the connection:

> It is certainly not new, nor unusual, that that land is persecuted by a divine judgment that, after being beaten and corrected, it may obtain mercy. Of course, the Lord could preserve it by his will alone, but it is not for us to know why he would do this. Perhaps he wished to experience and bring to the notice of others if someone is understanding and seeking God, who having offered himself embraces the time of penance joyfully.[13]

This notion of God desiring the cooperation of man in matters of war would appear, in fact, in both Christian and Muslim accounts of Acre. Saladin's illnesses, for example, which often prevented his engaging the crusaders in the manner he wished, were attributed to the will of Allah and were to be accepted without complaint. Saladin himself would try to focus on divine signs that foretold his enemy's eventual defeat.[14]

As preparations were made in the West, back in the Levant discord and disunity were the order of the day. The plight of Acre was, at first, only a small footnote in the much larger story of the fall of the Holy City, which had been in Christian hands since 1099. But it would soon become the focal point of the entire crusading enterprise. In the summer of 1188, Saladin released Guy of Lusignan from captivity, doing so, perhaps, in the hope that the rivalry between him and Conrad of Montferrat would further destabilize Christian control in the region. As a condition of his freedom, Guy was made to swear an oath never to take up arms against Saladin again. He thereafter gathered his family and supporters and made his way to Tripoli, north of Beirut, where Balian of Ibelin had led the refugees from Jerusalem. Back in Tyre, Conrad had smartly fortified the city, for in November 1188 Saladin arrived and commenced a siege that would last through the summer of 1189. While Conrad success-fully repelled the Muslim assaults, Saladin simultaneously traipsed all over Syria, capturing city after city and fortress after fortress.[15] Now, in the summer of 1189, Guy collected as many soldiers as he could, both in Tripoli and Antioch, and led his new army south to Tyre. Whereas Tripoli lay within the County of Tripoli, Tyre was part of the Kingdom of Jerusalem; naturally, Guy and Sibylla expected to take up residence there. However, Conrad rebuffed them and refused to grant entry to the royal couple, let alone their soldiers.[16]

## The march to Acre

In August 1189, sitting outside Tyre, Guy of Lusignan decided he could wait no longer and prepared to move south to Acre. He had few choices before him, save for leaving the kingdom entirely, and the coastal city provided an obvious first target in what was sure to be a grinding campaign to wrest territory away from Saladin. His force was between 400 and 700 knights in number and he had some 7,000 to 9,000 infantry, certainly large enough to besiege Acre if conditions were favorable. Still, he asked for God's grace, since Acre was well fortified and he would likely be outnumbered should Saladin bring his armies in relief. He was encouraged by Patriarch Heraclius and his brother Geoffrey, who reminded him that the leaders in Europe had all taken the cross and would eventually join in the endeavor.[17] Guy set out on 22 August, marching south along the Scandelion Pass (al-Iskanderūna), a coastal road that hewed away from the interior where Muslim scouts might be lurking. The western sources claim that Saladin was oblivious to Guy's movements, but the Arabic texts indicate otherwise: he was indeed aware of the time and direction of the march, which seems to have been revealed when the army stumbled upon a small group of Muslims and skirmished with them.[18]

This early contact marked a crucial moment in the campaign. Messengers relayed the position of the crusaders to Saladin. Given the narrow confines of the road and the element of surprise, he considered throwing his army against Guy and destroying his forces right then and there. Yet he hesitated. Saladin was at al-Shaqīf Arnūn (otherwise known as Belfort Castle), which lay east of Tyre and in a defensible spot on the Litani River, between the sea and Damascus.[19] He wondered if Guy's move was an elaborate ruse, designed to pull him away from his location and thereby open the way north and south. At least that is the version offered by Ibn Shaddād (Bahā' al-Dīn Ibn Shaddād), one of Saladin's personal judges (qāḍī), who accompanied the sultan during most of the siege and wrote down his recollections in *The Rare and Excellent History of Saladin*. The two men did not actually meet until 1188, and so Ibn Shaddād was present neither at the Battle of Hattin nor during the retaking of

12

Jerusalem in 1187, but he was an eyewitness at Acre, and seems to have left Saladin's side only once during the entire siege. His background was that of an *'alim*, a religious scholar, and there are frequent references to the Koran throughout the text. His view of Saladin is quite complimentary, perhaps because he was composing his text while the sultan was still alive, and intended it as a gift to him.[20]

This was but one view. The Mosul writer Ibn al-Athīr (Ali 'Izz al-Dīn Ibn al-Athīr al-Jazarī) presents a completely different story in his universal history, *al-Kāmil fī'l-ta'rīkh*, which includes not only the Third Crusade, but also Islamic history prior to the First Crusade.[21] Although its composition is contemporary, Ibn al-Athīr never served Saladin and was not an eyewitness to any part of the siege of Acre.[22] His physical separation from events and seeming antagonism towards Saladin, which often reads as notes of subtle criticism, was pointed out by Hamilton Gibb in 1950, and he is now considered the least reliable of the three major Arabic sources for Acre.[23] According to Ibn al-Athīr, Saladin convened his emirs in council and sought their advice. While he wished to stop Guy at the pass, the emirs argued that it was too narrow and treacherous to fully engage the crusader army; therefore, the troops should be let through and then met on the Acre plain instead. Ibn al-Athīr suspects that the emirs were simply lazy and Saladin knew it, but he took their advice anyway and declined to engage, choosing instead to shadow the crusaders on their eastern side. He moved towards Tiberias and sent a detachment to harass their vanguard and report on their movements. The reports streamed in: Guy reached 'Ayn Baṣṣa and then al-Zīb on 27 August, and finally Acre the following day. The opportunity to stop the crusaders had now passed, and so the sultan rejoined his main army with the forward detachment at Marj Saffurīyya, pausing there until his baggage train caught up, and then finally moved his entire army to al-Kharrūba, a hill southeast of Acre. He was also able to send reinforcements and supplies into the city.[24] Its garrison would not capitulate without a fight.

Saladin's hesitancy in attacking the crusader army directly was emblematic of his leadership style. Throughout the Acre siege, he would often defer to the wishes of his emirs, knowing full well that it was necessary to cultivate their loyalty, else his grand army might splinter apart. Local disputes in Syria weighed on the minds of the regional lords, and their inclination was to keep one eye on Acre and the other on home. Yet on this occasion, collaboration and deferment may have cost the sultan dearly. Writing with the benefit of hindsight, Ibn al-Athīr speculates that the Muslims could have eliminated the crusader threat at the outset. Saladin himself believed that once Guy made camp outside Acre, it would be very difficult to dislodge him. The sultan's words were prescient, and so the author could only write, perhaps with a sigh, "when God wills a matter, he prepares its means."[25]

# II

# THE SIEGE BEGINS
## *1189*

*"One way or another the time was fully occupied with fighting."*[1]

By August's end, Guy of Lusignan and his army had survived the Scandelion Pass and arrived before Acre, where they were eventually joined by other contingents, as well as by the Pisans, who had chosen to sail rather than march. They gazed upon a formidable challenge: a peninsula protected on three sides by water and also a ring of stone walls. Because Acre had been in Christian hands from 1104 to 1187, its defenses were well known; but after capturing the city in 1187, Saladin had ordered its garrisoning and had strengthened the walls.[2] Taking it would be difficult.

A visitor to the modern city, today called Akko, is immediately struck by the fortifications which, although not of the crusader era, nonetheless provide an unforgettable image of how the peninsula could be protected and defended (see Appendix A). The old city of Acre sits on a 40-acre peninsula that is connected to the land on its north side and juts southward. To the west is the Mediterranean Sea, to the south Haifa Bay, and to the east a portion of that bay that

15

forms a harbor. In time, the early medieval settlement grew beyond the immediate peninsular area and onto the mainland, eventually encompassing about 62 acres, and defensive walls were built along a perimeter that surrounded this pocket of expansion, as well as all approaches to the peninsula itself. The land there lies at sea level, with one portion of the northern city rising to 6 meters above the rest.[3] Farther north and close to the Mediterranean coastline is the suburb of Montmusard, which is first mentioned in the year 1120 and grew slowly until 1187. After the city fell to the crusaders in 1191, it grew even more, eventually acquiring its own set of walls.[4] In other words, the crusader city was bigger than the walled portion of the city that stands today. Fighting was heavy at the city gates during the siege, but these are rarely identified in the sources or maps. Although the early maps show a double wall around the city, during the Third Crusade there was only one circuit. Several gates and towers studded the length of the wall, and it was fronted by a lower forewall and a deep ditch.[5]

## The blockade

The principals and their respective locations are marked by different sources. Guy of Lusignan, along with his wife Sibylla, her daughters Alice and Maria, his brother Geoffrey, and Patriarch Heraclius, camped upon the ancient hill of the Toron, otherwise known as Tel al-Muṣallabīn or Tel al-Fukhkhār (today, Tel Akko), climbing it by night to avoid detection. From this vantage point they could look down into the fringes of the city, and it provided an expansive view of the Acre plain. The eastern edge of the Toron drops steeply and would have given Guy a highly defensive position immune from cavalry charges (see Plate 1). Around and in front, between the Toron and the city walls, were Guy's soldiers. There was not much distance between the two positions, for archaeological finds suggest that the city's eastern wall was much closer to the Toron than previously thought. Moreover, the Christian army did not frighten Acre's defenders: the garrison outnumbered its attackers and could have swallowed them up, "just as a sparrowhawk takes a small bird."[6]

It likely did not frighten Saladin either. Marching from Belfort, the sultan had spent late August sending summonses for additional soldiers throughout his domains, and he refused to move against the crusader camp until the bulk of them had arrived. Men from Mosul, Sinjār, Diyār Bakr, and elsewhere soon flocked to the area. The Christians were acutely aware of the flow of Muslim reinforcements and watched them arrive, contingent by contingent, from the heights of the Toron. The flood of enemies inspired the Christian warriors to pray for God to succor them.[7] The first principals named in the Arabic sources were Taqī al-Dīn (al-Malik al-Muẓaffar Taqī al-Dīn 'Umar, Saladin's nephew and the lord of Hama) and Muẓaffar al-Dīn (Muẓaffar al-Dīn Kūkbūrī ibn Zayn al-Dīn, lord of Harran and Edessa). Saladin moved from al-Kharrūba on 30 August and made his camp on Tel Kaysān, closer to the city. His grand army then spread itself out in a crescent that surrounded the entirety of Guy's army. The Muslim left wing stretched west to the River Belus and the right wing to Tel al-'Ayyāḍiyya. In front of the main ranks was a stationary advance guard, whose orders were to harass the crusader perimeter on a daily basis and prevent anyone from escaping the encirclement. They would be in a good position to attack the enemy camp and to lob arrows upon Guy's forces atop the Toron both day and night. Trapped between Acre's walls and Saladin's ranks, "those who had come to besiege were themselves besieged."[8] Fear abounded, and the crusaders prayed for the Holy Spirit to come because he "knows our needs both militarily and bodily."[9]

The crusaders had managed to carry out only one attack upon Acre before Saladin arrived, probably on 1 September. Because his catapults were not yet assembled Guy was forced to attack solely with infantry, who rushed forward with ladders in an attempt to scale the city walls, and melees broke out along its line. The attack was quickly aborted when a messenger brought news that Saladin's main army was approaching. That report was misleading, because the Muslims arrived in waves, not all at once. The writer Richard of Templo seems convinced that the crusaders would have entered Acre and ended the siege that very day, had they not panicked so easily.[10] Richard was the prior of Holy Trinity in London, an Augustinian house, who arrived at Acre with the English contingent in 1191. His *Itinerarium peregrinorum et gesta regis Ricardi* is a major source for the Third Crusade, but for Acre it is mostly original for the last part of the siege, with the rest drawn from other sources. The first was the principal Old French account of the siege, the *Estoire de la Guerre Sainte*, a verse account of the Third Crusade written by Ambroise, a Norman, who may have been a jongleur or cleric, or both.[11] Richard's second source was a similarly named *Itinerarium peregrinorum*, which was probably written by a monk at Tyre but covers only events in the East up to 24 November 1190.

As it was, this was to be the only moment for the next two years when the Christians would have the luxury of besieging the city without simultaneously defending against Muslim attacks upon their camp. Saladin's first attack on the crusading army came the very next day. Despite wanting to wait for his brother al-ʿĀdil (al-Malik al-ʿĀdil Sayf al-Dīn Abū Bakr ibn Ayyūb) to return from a diplomatic trip to Baghdad, the sultan assented to his emirs' desire to move forward.[12] A letter to Pope Clement III written by two Italian crusaders, Theobald the Prefect and Peter, son of Leo, records the details of this very first combat between Guy and Saladin's soldiers. The Muslims moved their left flank forward towards the harbor, to the southwest of the Toron, attacking the camp of the Knights Hospitaller and Guy's brother Geoffrey of Lusignan, who happened to be with the Brothers at the time. The crusaders were thrown back and then squeezed north between the city walls and the Toron. This resulted in a brief opening of a pathway to the city, along the shoreline of the bay; worse, the Muslims partially trapped Guy and his men on their hill in the process. Looking down from the Toron, the king saw Muslims operating to the east, south, and west. Now defending his hilltop position and realizing his sudden plight, Guy pleaded to God for reinforcements. It was a desperate prayer, because he had no idea if Conrad of Montferrat, who had treated him so poorly just a few weeks beforehand, would be keen to help.[13]

Fortunately for Guy, more soldiers were indeed on their way, and not just from Tyre. In mid-September, a fleet arrived from the west, led by the lord of Condé and Guise, James of Avesnes. Fifty ships strong, the fleet carried between 12,000 and 14,000 Flemings, Frisians, Germans, and Bretons. A second fleet carrying Danes, Welsh, and Cornish seems to have arrived the day before. James himself is called "a Nestor in counsel" and an Achilles in arms, better and more worthy than Alexander or Hector; he had mortgaged all his properties in order to pay for the ships and men.[14] It seems that James took control of the army's field operations after his arrival, sometimes directing the flow of battle himself and at other times sharing the responsibility with Ludwig III, the landgrave of Thuringia.[15] Near the end of the month, reinforcements from Tyre arrived as well, brought by the marquis Conrad and Gerardo of Ravenna. The letter of Theobald and Peter claims that these latest troops numbered 20,000 infantry and 1,000 knights.[16] Ibn Shaddād put the full size of the crusader army, after the arrival of all the ships, at 2,000 cavalry and 30,000 infantry, and perhaps more. The additional ships served to tighten the naval blockade of Acre's port, as they joined with the fifty-two Pisan ships that were already in the area.

The port and harbor area feature prominently in the siege narrative. Acre's fortifications extended into the bay and served to protect the city's port. A prominent feature in the harbor was the Tower of Flies, built atop a Hellenistic foundation and constructed of ashlar stones joined by metal clamps. The remains of the tower can still be seen both from the shore east of the city and from the road that runs down the modern breakwater (see Plate 2). From the Tower of Flies, a mole once ran northwest to the eastern city wall. Built of marble and ashlar stones, the mole barred the city port from the natural harbor in the bay.[17] During the siege, there are periodic references to crusader ships landing beyond it and being offloaded. South of the peninsula, a quay ran from the land's edge east towards the Tower of Flies, serving as a breakwater. It ended in a second tower, and between it and the Tower of Flies hung a massive chain that guarded the port entrance.[18] With the chain withdrawn, ships could enter the port and dock safely: they likely approached the entrance from the southwest, entered, then turned sharply left (west) to dock. It seems that larger ships had trouble maneuvering in the tight confines, and instead dropped anchor in the bay, ferrying their cargo to shore in smaller vessels. This is because the entrance was only 85 meters wide, and the port itself was shallow and only 90,000 square meters.[19] After disembarking, sailors would move through the Iron Gate (*Porta ferrae*) and pay customs duties in the Court of the Chain.[20]

Sealing off the port entrance was a vital element of the crusader blockade. In the initial stages, however, the Christian captains did not always coordinate their movements and Muslim ships periodically ran the blockade to access the port. And as Christian cargo ships landed on the bay shoreline, they were attacked by Muslim detachments, and so the Christians near the shore, joined by soldiers coming down from the Toron, rushed forward to beat off the attacks and protect the newly delivered goods and men. Skirmishing between the reinforcements and Muslims continued even once the landings were complete.[21]

The arrivals set up camp outside the city. The area southwest of the Toron, flanking Acre's harbor and Haifa Bay, had been the scene of all the early fighting: there encamped men from the empire and Genoa, as well as the Knights Templar and Hospitaller. They were led by James of Avesnes and Ludwig III, and the Genoese by their acting consul Guido Spinola and six other nobles.[22] To the north and along the Mediterranean, in and near the suburb of Montmusard, were the Pisans; Conrad of Montferrat would join them there after his arrival.[23] The physical separation of Guy and Conrad was later noted by the historian William, canon of Newburgh. William wrote in northern England and relied heavily on witness accounts for information, to which he added more commentary than description. He attributed the lackluster opening stages of the siege to the two men's antagonisms.[24] This and other rivalries were a persistent feature of the crusades in general. Acrimony, petty grievances, and old grudges were commonplace in any mustering of soldiers in the period, but on crusade such disputes could be elevated and compounded. This was due not only to the diversity of the soldiers, the lands from which they hailed, and the variance between their motivations for fighting, but also to the absence of strong, central command.[25] At Acre, similar issues led to disagreements over strategy, long periods of inaction, and periodic missteps that resulted in combat losses. At other times, however, the crusading host was able to operate fluidly via an articulated division of command; maneuvering and fighting in tandem, it could perform quite well in the field.

In any case, the crusader army had now tripled in size and was able to invest the city walls with deeper ranks. In the mind of the western authors, these reinforcements were the direct result of divine intervention. Richard of Templo describes the joy and weeping of the men on the Toron as they first spotted the ships and their Christian standards, and one by one they praised God for his assistance:

> No one should doubt that it was God who sent this aid and comfort to those who trusted in His mercy.
>
> Now you will hear how God looks upon those whom He takes into His care.
>
> While they were in these straits, the Dayspring from on high visited them.[26]

In Richard's reading, the western reinforcements served two immediate purposes. First, they preserved the crusader presence at Acre. Guy's position was extremely precarious: he had initially been trapped on the Toron, but even once his reinforcements arrived he was presented with the challenge of fending off Saladin's full army. This meant defending against dual attacks from the city and Saladin on a daily basis – attacks that were coordinated by smoke signals.[27] Only some heroic efforts by the Knights Hospitaller and Templar (vaguely described, unfortunately) prevented the Muslims from penetrating the camp. Second, the new soldiers allowed a closer investing of Acre itself. The besiegers posted guards and patrols at each of the city gates, in order to prevent major sorties and easy communication between the Muslim contingents.

But the eventual human toll would be great indeed. Richard of Templo reveals that of the thousands of men who disembarked from the newly arrived ships in September 1189, only a hundred survived to see Acre fall in 1191.[28] This is a shocking number if true; but even allowing for exaggeration, the death rate was apparently extremely high.

## Probing the lines

The Arabic sources pick up the story once the Christian reinforcements had settled into camp. Saladin sent his emir Qāraqūsh (Bahā' al-Dīn al-Asadī Qāraqūsh) into the city to organize its defenses better.[29] At dawn on Thursday, 14 September 1189, the Muslims began their first full-on assault against the besiegers. It was a coordinated affair, as was to be the norm for the duration of the siege: the Acre garrison sallied out of the city gates on the southern and western sides of the Christians, while Saladin's army attacked from the east and north. This was the first formal battle at Acre in which armies drew up regular ranks, and it lasted for several days.

The operation had been determined in council the night before. Saladin's objective on this occasion was not necessarily to destroy the enemy army, but rather to break the crusader blockade and open a permanent route into Acre, in order to ensure its resupply. If successful, such a link would render the blockade fruitless. As was their wont, the Muslims attacked with light cavalry armed with bows, spiked clubs or swords, spears, and daggers. Richard of Templo describes their famous and customary tactic of the "feigned retreat":

> It is the Turks' habit, when they realize that their pursuit has stopped following them, to stop running away themselves – like an infuriating fly which flies away if you drive it off and returns when you stop. As long as you chase it, it flees; as soon as you stop it is there again. The Turks are just like that. When you stop pursuing and turn back, then the Turk follows you; if you pursue, the Turk flees.[30]

The plan was three-fold: Saladin's men assembled their ranks on Wednesday night and slept in position; *salat* prayers were said on Thursday morning (presumably *fajr*), and immediately after prayer concluded, the attack began. The army was divided into three divisions of left, center, and right, with the left division against the River Belus and the right against the Mediterranean, north of Montmusard. In this way, the sultan engaged the entire crusade camp at once.[31] This was the customary arrangement of a Muslim army in the period and was employed by Saladin throughout the siege. Although we lack details on the depth at Acre, the ideal sort presented in the later military manual by the writer al-Ansari was five lines: advance guard/vanguard and a second line behind it, both cavalry; a third line to protect the light baggage in front; a fourth line to protect the baggage at the back; and a rearguard.[32] On this occasion, the right wing seems to have had the most success, with Taqī al-Dīn nearly breaking through to the city along the Mediterranean coastline; but by the end of the day, the fighting concluded without result.

The next day, Friday, saw the latent fruits of the lord of Hama's efforts: the scattered crusaders facing Taqī al-Dīn had bunched together for protection, leaving open a slim seaside route to the city.[33] Here, the close proximity of the Arabic authors is invaluable because they were with Saladin and could see the next phase of the action. The sultan sent reinforcements to Taqī al-Dīn on the right flank, so that he might exploit the gap. There was only a sparse camp infrastructure, and it is doubtful that any wooden buildings had yet been constructed, and so the area was ripe for penetration. Saladin was personally involved at every point in this engagement, hardly stopping to eat and behaving "like a bereft mother in his great anxiety and abundant care."[34]

Taqī al-Dīn's attack commenced on Friday morning. His men first drove south, pushing the crusaders towards the city wall. He then pivoted his forces left and pushed again, sending the enemy sliding along that wall to the east, running towards the safety of their tents and comrades down the line. The result was a clear path to Acre along the sea. The Muslims then oriented into a defensive line, forming ranks running south to north and perpendicular to the wall. In this way, Taqī al-Dīn established a defensible corridor that connected with the gate of St Michael. The blockade had been broken.[35]

The repercussions of the day's fighting soon became apparent: a caravan full of laden camels was seized by the garrison, Muslims entered and exited the city as they liked, and one of Saladin's sons was escorted out of the city, while Emir Ḥusām al-Dīn Abū'l-Hayjā "the Fat," a Kurd from Irbil, entered.[36] Ibn al-Athīr writes of a steady stream of soldiers, money, and supplies being sent into Acre. It must have been maddening for the crusaders to watch, for their blockade of the city had been broken only days after having first been established. Symbolically, what happened next must have been devastating to their morale: Saladin himself entered Acre. Ascending to the top of its walls, the sultan grandly surveyed the enemy camp beneath him, looking down upon the encamped Christians. No wonder "the Muslims rejoiced at their God-given victory."[37]

The speed and success of the Muslim soldiers evidently also impressed the western authors, who saw fit to compliment them. Although they "did not believe in God," "they were truly the most preeminent men," because "virtue is praiseworthy even in an enemy."[38] Matters might have been worse. Ibn al-Athīr speculates that, had Taqī al-Dīn pressed home his advantage, he may have routed the crusaders entirely. As it was, the assault was soon called off. None of the Arabic sources reveal who gave the order, although another witness, 'Imād al-Dīn ('Imād al-Dīn al-Iṣfahānī), offers an image of a watchful Saladin gazing over his army as night fell that could be read as suggestive. 'Imād al-Dīn was a well-situated witness and Saladin's secretary (kātib). His original text is no longer extant, but comes to us via the compiler Shihāb al-Dīn Abū'l Qasim Abu Shāma (d. 1267), who copied portions of it into his later thirteenth-century Book of the Two Gardens. 'Imād al-Dīn was Abu Shāma's chief source for the reigns of Nūr al-Dīn and Saladin, likely because of the affinity between both writers' views on life and history.[39] Our other Muslim witness, Ibn Shaddād, thought the soldiers were negligent: it was after noonday dhuhr prayer, the horses needed water, and the men needed rest, but the plan had been to resume combat after a short break.[40]

In any event, even one night turned out to be a costly delay. On Sunday morning, 17 September, the Muslims drew up their ranks once more, but in a different fashion. Most of them dismounted – even the emirs – and they advanced on the crusader camp on foot. The crusaders maddeningly refused to engage but remained close to their tents; even when prodded with some light skirmishing (not described but likely missile fire) they refused to take the bait. As a result, some of Saladin's emirs effected a postponement of the attack. Some of the soldiers were sent inside Acre instead, from where they were told to sally forth alongside the garrison on the next Tuesday, 19 September; the rest of Saladin's forces, the emirs argued, should charge from the outward side at the same time. "They carried out the plan but the enemy resisted strongly, protecting themselves amongst their tents"; the plan therefore failed, despite Saladin personally leading the men from Acre, and the Muslims settled down for skirmishing during the rest of the week.[41]

The fighting on 16-17 September is interesting and has not been properly studied. After a great cavalry victory, the Muslims deliberately advanced on foot, rather than astride. Why? The tradition of Muslim infantry tactics is not incredibly rich in the period overall.[42] The crusader camp was not ringed with any physical defenses beyond the height of the Toron (the digging of protective ditches would not begin until October); they had only their tents for protection. The Muslims also outnumbered the westerners in the general Montmusard area.[43] There is no mention of the Christians utilizing buildings in Montmusard for protection, although if they did that could explain the use of foot soldiers, who are better suited for house-to-house fighting. The traditional eastern methods of horseback archery, mobile harassment, and feigned retreats would not have worked so well had the Christians been protected by roofs.[44] Alternatively, the answer may be that Taqī al-Dīn and his men were simply overconfident. R.C. Smail noted that the final defeat of an enemy was usually at close quarters, after Muslim archers and light cavalry had severely reduced their ranks.[45] Perhaps, then, they believed the besiegers to be on their last legs and that they would crumble quickly.

The situation was quite the opposite: having survived two direct assaults on their flank, the crusaders now began to increase their activities in the area. On Friday, 22 September, they were organized enough to march out in force against the Muslims surrounding them: "The battlefield remained a lively market where lives were sold for precious gain and the storms of war rained down on the heads of captains young and old."[46]

No western source describes this particular battle in any detail – or indeed provides any operational details at all from the remainder of the month, perhaps because it was filled with disaster. From Ibn Shaddād's telling, a huge wall of foot soldiers marched in front, protecting the crusader horses walking behind it. As one, they moved forward towards the Muslim advance guard. Saladin cried out "Huzzah for Islam!" and this advance guard immediately mounted and charged, engaging and scattering the infantry at close quarters. The crusaders fled en masse, trampling each other in a panicked attempt to return to their camp. Periodic skirmishing continued for three days; Ibn Shaddād claims that he himself entered Acre, climbed atop its walls, and hurled missiles at the besiegers below.[47]

The repulse of the crusader march must have left an impression on Saladin. As opposed to the previous week, when his men had marched towards the western camp to little effect, the benefits of drawing the enemy out into the open field were blindingly obvious. He therefore instigated a new strategy: he would lure the crusaders out of their camp by giving quarter. The Muslim lines were pulled back a distance, and the baggage train was sent to Tel al-'Ayyāḍiyya, a nearby hill to the east of Acre.[48] This gave the crusaders some room to venture out and forage, and the Muslim baggage might provide a tantalizing target. In the short term, the idea worked: on either the next Friday or Saturday (29/30 September), some crusaders on Saladin's left flank emerged from camp and walked to the River Belus, gathering wood for fires, and also plants and grasses for horse fodder. Some mounted Bedouin soldiers, whom Saladin had placed at the river as a guard, attacked them, killing some and taking others prisoner. The Bedouins then exchanged the severed heads of their victims with Saladin in return for robes and gifts.[49] Greater victories were yet to come.

## The October battle

October's dawn saw the fulfillment of Saladin's plan: the crusade leaders decided to attack the sultan head on and in full strength. There were legitimate and sensible reasons behind the advance. King

Guy and his allied barons met in council to discuss the plan, and their reasoning was logical enough. The Christians could not devote their full attention to the siege with such a large army behind them, waiting to intervene as soon as the catapults began firing. Food stores were also running low. Although some supplies had arrived on ships two weeks before, these were evidently not enough to keep filling the stomachs of both Guy's army and the reinforcements. The Old French *Continuations* of the chronicle of William, archbishop of Tyre, also speak of the clear and present dangers of the Muslim encirclement. The *Continuations* were finished by the 1220s at the earliest, and so provide a later recounting of events from the preceding generation. The four main versions have a complicated array of similarities and differences; but for the siege of Acre, the most useful is the fullest for the period 1184–97, the so-called Lyon *Eracles*, which was probably completed by 1250.[50]

Moreover, Guy had numbers on his side. New soldiers were arriving every day, led by some of the more notable magnates present at Acre: Erard II, count of Brienne, and his brother Andrew; the seneschal of Flanders and a host of Flemings; Henry I, count of Bar-le-Duc; Count Robert of Dreux and his brother Bishop Philip of Beauvais, and five archbishops (of Arles-le-Blanc, Besançon, Montreal, Nazareth, and Pisa). The crusaders now had enough soldiers for a general action, and so they undertook one.[51] Ibn al-Athīr offers a modification of this same notion. Far away in Mosul, and obviously not present for Guy's council, he surmised that the leaders were aware that large portions of the armies under Saladin's titular control had not yet arrived at Acre. Their best chance, then, was to attack before these reinforcements did arrive.[52] Unstated, but also likely, was a general frustration over the constant harassment of their camp and a corresponding inability to break into the city. As a result, Guy and his allies decided to engage Saladin's lines on the morning of Wednesday, 4 October, with the intent of reaching and destroying the Muslim camp at Tel al-ʿAyyāḍiyya.

Every western account gives a different arrangement for the crusading forces, and so some sorting out is necessary (Map 2). The attacking force was arranged in three lines, with archers and cross-bowmen in the first rank, followed by infantry in the second, and cavalry in the third. The lines were then split into three sections: left, center, and right.[53] The left wing, springing from the path Taqī al-Dīn had opened alongside the Mediterranean Sea, was led by Conrad of Montferrat and Gerardo, bishop of Ravenna.[54] The infantry and missile ranks were primarily Italians. The right wing extended to the River Belus and was directed by Guy himself, but it is unclear whether he remained on the Toron or advanced with the others.[55] The cavalry on the right wing consisted of Knights Hospitaller, and the infantry and missile troops were Italian and French.[56] The center, which would see the most fighting, was near the mosque of ʿAin-Baqar, outside the city walls, and was commanded by Andrew of Brienne and Ludwig III, who sat in the rearguard with their knights.[57] Gerard of Ridefort, the master of the Templars, led the vanguard of this center division, riding alongside the other Templars; in front of them, in the infantry rank, were Catalan and German foot soldiers and missile troops. Remaining in the camp as a check against sorties from the Acre garrison was Guy's brother, Geoffrey of Lusignan, accompanied by James of Avesnes and the respective men under their command.[58]

Opposing the crusaders were the divisions of Saladin's army, which are well described in the Arabic sources. Once again, the sultan had ordered the men to camp in position the night before. On his extreme right wing (opposing Conrad on the crusader left) was the sultan's nephew, Taqī al-Dīn, who at that point had been the most accomplished general during the conflict. He and his men took position on the end of the line, by the sea. On the near right, closer to the center division, were Saladin's sons al-Afḍal and al-Ẓāhir, as well as Ḥusām al-Dīn ibn Lājīn (lord of Nablus) and the *tawashi* Qaymāz al-Najmī.[59] The rest of the right consisted of soldiers from Mosul,

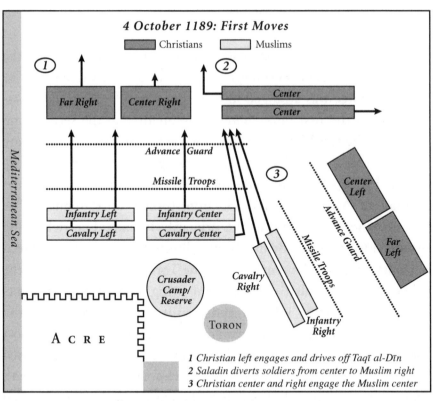

# 4 October 1189: First Moves

■ Christians    □ Muslims

① Far Right    Center Right    ②    Center
Center

Advance Guard

Missile Troops    ③

Center Left

Advance Guard

Infantry Left    Infantry Center

Cavalry Left    Cavalry Center

Missile Troops

Far Left

Crusader Camp/ Reserve

Cavalry Right

Mediterranean Sea

ACRE    TORON    Infantry Right

1 *Christian left engages and drives off Taqī al-Dīn*
2 *Saladin diverts soldiers from center to Muslim right*
3 *Christian center and right engage the Muslim center*

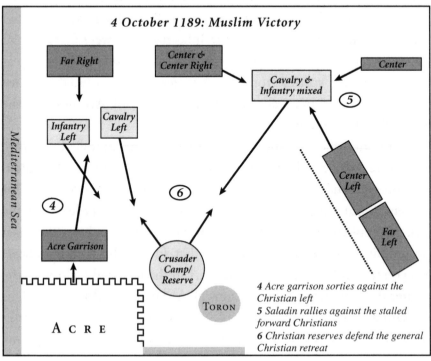

# 4 October 1189: Muslim Victory

Far Right    Center & Center Right    Center

Cavalry & Infantry mixed    ⑤

Infantry Left    Cavalry Left

Center Left

④    Far Left

Mediterranean Sea

⑥

Acre Garrison

Crusader Camp/ Reserve

ACRE    TORON

4 *Acre garrison sorties against the Christian left*
5 *Saladin rallies against the stalled forward Christians*
6 *Christian reserves defend the general Christian retreat*

2. 4 October 1189 battle.

led by Ẓāhir al-Dīn Ibn al-Balankārī, and soldiers from Diyār Bakr, led by Quṭb al-Dīn ibn Nūr al-Dīn (lord of Ḥiṣn Kayfā).

The Muslim left wing, opposing Guy and the Hospitallers on the crusader right, was more diverse. On the far left, by the River Belus, were a company from Asadiyya and the mamluks of Asad al-Dīn Shīrkūh (Saladin's deceased uncle); two mamluk champions, Sayf al-Dīn Yāzkūj and Ruslān Bughā, are mentioned specifically. On the near left, positioned towards the center division, were soldiers from Sinjār, led by Mujāhid al-Dīn Yarunqush, another group of mamluks, and soldiers commanded by Muẓaffar al-Dīn (the aforementioned lord of Edessa and Harran). There were other groups of Kurds, too: Emir Mujallī led the Mihrani and Hakkārī Kurds, while others were commanded by their chief Sayf al-Dīn 'Alī ibn Aḥmad al-Masht ūb.[60] In the center rode Saladin himself, presumably accompanied by his regular troops ('askar) and personal guard of military slaves, the *halqa*. Each wing was protected by an advance guard of skirmishers; leading them in front of the center was the lawyer 'Īsā, the holder of the former Templar revenues in Acre.[61]

The battle began at nine o'clock.[62] The crusaders moved forward and, "like a plague of locusts," came into contact with the Muslim advance guard and began to disperse it, with the Templars and Hospitallers evidently riding forward through the infantry and missile ranks in order to chase those who fled.[63] But the fighting quickly became bogged down along the lines, and Ibn Shaddād claims that four hours passed in this initial combat.[64] In the afternoon matters shifted: the Italians on the crusaders' left wing had managed to push forward deep into the Muslim right, and Taqī al-Dīn ordered his soldiers to pull back. He might have been trying to lure the crusader wing away from the main army so that it could be destroyed in a feigned retreat; alternatively, he may simply have been losing. Theobald and Peter's letter provides most of the information on the fighting against Taqī al-Dīn, for they themselves were on the crusader left wing. Their letter claims that the Muslims were overwhelmed, with 500 enemy cavalry killed, as well as one of Saladin's sons.[65] However, when Saladin saw his nephew retire east, he assumed the worst and sent reinforcements from his own center to assist him.[66]

This was a critical error: when the crusader center and right wing saw the thinning ranks ahead of them, they moved straight towards the sultan's position, hitting the Muslim line in the gap between the center and the near right wing. Richard of Templo describes the tactic:

> The Turks stood as if in one mind to defend their camp. As our people came nearer, the unit of infantry which marched in front divided in two, allowing the cavalry to charge boldly between them into the enemy. The Gentiles turned in flight, deserting their camp.[67]

This eruption of the heavy cavalry was irresistible; but so, too, was the crusader infantry. The foot soldiers kept pace with the horses: three separate units abreast (infantry–cavalry–infantry) all charging together as one. The second Muslim rank crumbled, as the advance guard had done previously; Ibn Shaddād places the blame on inexperienced soldiers from Diyār Bakr. A general rout began: the right wing fled towards Tel al-'Ayyāḍiyya with crusaders hot in pursuit, while those from the center made for either al-Qaḥwāna, across the bridge to Tiberias, or even Damascus. Those Muslims that remained in place met their deaths, and others were caught by the Muslim tents and killed there.[68]

R.C. Smail included this battle in his well-known chapter on "The Latin Field Army in Action," but he missed the significance of the morning and afternoon of 4 October.[69] The crusaders engaged in sync and rhythm, methodically using their advantage of mixed troop types to frustrate the Muslim cavalry. The leadership was steady and control was sound: the army leaders, despite hailing from different regions and commanding diverse contingents of soldiers, were able to communicate and work together. This is especially impressive when one considers that the bulk of the army had been encamped for less than three weeks. In a tactical sense, it suggests a certain uniformity of military preparation across western lands. Had the crusader army maintained discipline, the battle could have been the moment of victory. Ibn al-Athīr suggests that the Muslims would have been completely routed, had the crusaders only thrown down Saladin's tents: upon seeing this, the fleeing Muslims on the right wing and even those on the left (which had so far not seriously engaged in the battle) might have presumed Saladin dead or captured and abandoned the field.

But at this moment the crusaders halted and, instead of destroying the Muslim camp, chose to loot the tents.[70] They were driven by greed, certainly, but also by hunger, and many stopped to eat lunch! They "greedily plundered the booty. Pavilion ropes were cut, and the courageous count of Bar seized the tent of the sultan himself ... Elsewhere ... the Germans were greedily pillaging the enemy's camp."[71] They were not the only ones. The Muslim servants, having seen the camp guards driven off, had hurriedly grabbed spoils of their own before deserting the tents: "People lost vast sums. This was more disastrous than the rout itself."[72] Many of these servants were caught by the crusaders, who cut them down and in turn stole the (stolen) goods. But the looting had brought a halt to the crusader charge and all momentum was lost.

Saladin, meanwhile, accompanied by only a few personal retainers, was busy trying to save his army. He rode to the mamluks and Kurds on the left wing, urging them to turn and join in the fight. He also tried to rally the fleeing remnants of the center ranks, encouraging them specifically with a call to *jihad* and promising eternal rewards: "On, on for Islam!"[73] Saladin and other Muslim soldiers frequently called upon God in such a manner before launching an attack.[74] Calls of "Allahu akbar!" are peppered throughout the Arabic sources, as are shouted declarations of monotheistic affirmation.

While feasting and looting, meanwhile, the crusaders were startled back into action by several developments. First, the Acre garrison had finally joined in the fight. It was unclear in the thick of battle whether it sought to attack the crusader camp or the rear of the distant army: if the former, then Geoffrey of Lusignan and his men might be positioned to counter; but the latter meant that the advanced Christians could be cut off from their base.[75] Ibn al-Athīr makes a similar point, but instead claims that it was the Muslim right wing that posed the threat, not the garrison. This seems highly unlikely, since every other source has that right wing being routed. Rather, Theobald and Peter's letter claims that the garrison – some 5,000 strong – hit the crusader left wing from behind, trapping the Christians between it and Taqī al-Dīn's dispersed soldiers.[76] Second, there was an incident with a horse. During the looting, a horse bolted and began galloping back towards Acre, so its owner and a few companions ran to catch it. But other crusaders thought these men were fleeing the battlefield, so they began to flee as well. Soon hundreds of men began running in disorganized fashion and the crusader ranks (which – amazingly after several hours of fighting – had remained in rough formation) began to jumble together. Ibn Shaddād, accompanying Saladin on the eastern downslope from the looted camp, could not see the horse, but rather assumed that the crusaders had fled on seeing the advance of the mamluks on the Muslim left wing.[77]

All day the course of battle had favored the crusaders, but this constellation of events signaled their doom. Their left wing was now fully sandwiched between the Acre garrison troops and Taqī al-Dīn's men, and their center was either looting the Muslim tents or running away in panic. Saladin seized the opportunity and sent his men towards the disorganized enemy ranks. His left wing engaged, as did those remnants of his center that he had managed to rally back. The looters were caught in the tents and killed, while those running away were caught from behind. As Saladin's left wing rolled up the center, the remaining crusaders there broke and hurtled back towards Acre, with Muslim riders hot on their heels. To make matters worse, the crusader left wing eventually succumbed to pressure and retired to camp, which allowed the Muslim right wing under Taqī al-Dīn – which, up to this point, had had a terrible day – to turn and hit the center as the second claw of a pincer movement.[78]

It was a massacre: "The Saracens killed so many that the river ran with blood."[79] The battle had turned and the remaining crusaders fled back towards Acre in a chaotic mass, with their enemies in close pursuit. "On and on went the killing," and it seems that the Muslim counterattack soon reached the outskirts of the crusader camp and nearly pushed through to its tents. Instead, the Muslims withdrew and eventually retired from the field, perhaps for afternoon prayer. A too-convenient excuse?[80] Indeed, the western accounts indicate that they were repulsed. King Guy went to help the marquis, and once the Muslims reached the camp the crusader reserve, under the command of Geoffrey of Lusignan, joined the fight:

> Despite previous injuries and the rivalry between them, he showed humanity to that undeserving man and rescued him when he was about to perish. The king's brother, Geoffrey of Lusignan, had taken on responsibility for defending the camp. When he saw that the army was thrown into confusion and that everyone was struggling to get away he hastily left his post and, anxious for his brother's safety, ran forward to stem the rout. O! Wretched reversal of fortune![81]

This was to be one of Geoffrey's finest moments. As he drove forward to rescue the stragglers, another portion of the Acre garrison sortied from the city and attacked the now undefended camp. He nonetheless prevailed, simultaneously holding his camp while rescuing many of his defeated comrades, and "that day he had the praise of everyone in camp, for he had done more by his own hand than all the others put together."[82]

Yet many crusaders still perished, and two of their notable commanders were among them. Andrew of Brienne tried to rally his men by urging them to halt their retreat and stand firm, but in the process he was wounded and fell off his horse. His own brother, Count Erard II, passed him and heard his cries, but rode on, leaving him to die. Richard of Templo praised Andrew, whose "valour had raised him so far above all the French that he was regarded as first among knights, while all the rest contended for second place"; for Ambroise, "never did another such knight die, nor any who came to the rescue of so many." Erard, on the other hand, was dubbed a coward.[83] James of Avesnes, who had guarded the camp beside Geoffrey and evidently charged forward with him, nearly perished when he, too, was unhorsed; luckily, another knight chivalrously gave James his mount and he escaped.[84] Perhaps the most notable casualty was Gerard of Ridefort, the Templar master who had commanded in the center ranks alongside Andrew. The Templars had fought well but had pushed too far forward of the other ranks, and they were subsequently caught up in the Muslim counterattack. Gerard's fellows pleaded with him to retreat, only to be rebuffed: "Never! It would be my shame and scandal for the Templars. I would be said to have saved my life by running away and leaving my fellow-knights to be slaughtered."[85] Gerard was captured and then put to death on the orders of Saladin for duplicity: he had actually been captured at the Battle of Hattin two years previously but had been released after making a vow to abandon the war. His recidivism now cost him his life.[86]

Several casualty figures are provided in the narrative sources, and although they differ the picture is one of disaster for the Christians. Roger, the parson of Howden, relates that, besides Gerard, there fell eighteen Templar knights, along with forty other knights and a hundred Turcopoles; 'Imād al-Dīn claims rather more, some 5,000.[87] Ibn al-Athīr claims that 10,000 crusaders died in total, and maintains that most of them were knights, not infantry. This was certainly not the case at all.[88] Ibn Shaddād's figures, at least for the crusader casualties, should be considered the most accurate. He claims Muslim clerks spent the next day counting the dead on both sides, and he himself watched the bodies being carried away. One clerk, he wrote, estimated that 7,000 crusaders had fallen, although he himself doubted that number and considered the total somewhat smaller. His story is rather detailed:

> The sultan ordered a cart to go from Acre to carry the Frankish dead to the bank of the river and throw them in. One of the persons who looked after this business of the cart told me that he took a thread and every time he loaded a corpse he made a knot. The number of dead from the left wing reached 4,100 and a few extra. There remained the dead from the right wing and the centre, whom he did not count, for others dealt with those.[89]

His figures for the Muslim casualties, however, are dramatically lower and not to be believed: only 150 dead, including the jurist 'Īsā's brother, Ẓāhir al-Dīn, and Emir Mujallī ibn Marwan. 'Īsā himself had been unhorsed but was recovered by several relatives, who also died. The letter from Theobald and Peter claims that, along with Saladin's son and brother, 500 Muslims were killed on the crusader left flank alone.[90] Another Latin source, Roger of Howden, includes 100 of the best Muslim warriors (presumably the heavily armed and armored *tawashi*), but he also claims that Saladin lost his eldest son, a seneschal, and (incorrectly) his nephew Taqī al-Dīn, who actually died in 1191, and not even at Acre.[91] Roger was not present for the battle, but arrived later: he joined Richard the Lionheart and the English and Norman crusaders in Sicily in August 1190. After Acre was taken, he returned to England in August 1191, this time in the company of Philip Augustus.[92]

One would like better figures for the Muslim dead, especially given the near total success of the crusaders for most of the battle's duration. But in any event, if the Arabic numbers of 7,000 to 10,000 crusaders killed in action are anywhere close to accurate, this battle was a massive setback for the besiegers. The losses would have equated to between a quarter and a third of the total army strength. It was not, as Paul Cobb has offered, a stalemate: the crusaders had been crushed.[93]

In the aftermath of the fighting, Saladin proceeded to clean up the mess and excesses of the event. The stench from the dead was intolerable and was making his men sick. He therefore ordered all the crusader corpses to be thrown into the River Belus. As they floated down the river, both their smell and their hacked, dismembered appearance reached and revolted the crusaders, whose drinking water had now been polluted. The southern edge of the camp was pulled back from the river until the bodies could be buried.[94]

The Muslims likewise shifted their arrangement. Saladin himself was struck with a recurring colic, for which the smell was blamed, and he was unable to leave his tent. A council was therefore called on 13 October to discuss the next steps. Some argued that an immediate follow-up assault on the enemy camp was necessary. The crusaders had been whittled down, they reasoned, but would receive reinforcements in time, perhaps even before the winter season, but most assuredly in the spring. With few Muslim reserves on the way, the battle had to be now. Other advisers were more reluctant. They fretted that news of the sultan's illness might reach the crusaders and inspire them to start new assaults. More than that, however, was the general condition of the army. The soldiers had been enrolled for over fifty days and were mentally and physically tired, as were their horses. Since the crusaders were essentially trapped in place, between Acre and Saladin's men, there was no harm in resting and attacking only when at better strength.[95] It was a similar situation to late August, when Saladin had decided to allow the crusaders to encamp at Acre, instead of destroying them on the march; and once again, he elected to delay his attack. His decision on this occasion is perhaps more understandable, given his serious illness; but once again, the Muslims had deliberately prolonged the siege by not seeking a decisive victory.

In the meantime, the sultan sent the *qāḍī* Ibn Shaddād on a recruiting mission. Word had come that Emperor Frederick Barbarossa had begun his great march towards Syria, bringing with him between 200,000 and 260,000 men. These numbers were greatly inflated, but the specter of another army descending on Acre convinced Saladin that he needed more men. To raise them, he decided to employ the call of *jihad*. Ibn Shaddād traveled around Saladin's domains (excluding Egypt) and even visited the Abbasid caliph in Baghdad, Nāṣir al-Dīn (Nāṣir al-Dīn Allāh Abū'l-'Abbās Aḥmad). The *qāḍī* left Acre on 24 October and did not return until 12 April 1190. His mission was a stunning success: the *jihad* persuaded several Muslim lords to bring their armies to Acre in the spring, and they responded by telling Ibn Shaddād, "to hear is to obey." These included the armies of Sinjār and Jazīrat, led by 'Imād al-Dīn Zankī ('Imād al-Dīn Zankī ibn Quṭb al-Dīn Mawdūd ibn Zankī) and his nephew Sanjar Shāh (Mu'izz al-Dīn Sanjar Shāh ibn Sayf al-Dīn Ghazī ibn Mawdūd bin Zankī, lord of al-Jazīra), respectively. The army of Mosul came too, led not by their lord 'Izz al-Dīn ('Izz al-Dīn Mas'ūd ibn Quṭb al-Dīn Mawdūd), but rather by his son, 'Alā' al-Dīn Khurramshāh ('Alā' al-Dīn Khurramshāh ibn 'Izz al-Dīn Mas'ūd ibn Mawdūd); and so did the army of Irbil.[96]

Four days after the council, Saladin accompanied his baggage train south to the hills of al-Kharrūba, taking a goodly number of his regular soldiers with him. The advance guard, however, was left in encirclement around the crusader camp, and the Acre garrison was ordered to shut the gates and hold the city firm. There he waited for his brother, al-'Ādil, who arrived with reserves on 23 October.[97]

The relationship between Saladin and the *jihad* has been much discussed.[98] Peter Partner has pointed to *jihad*'s primary role in the period as serving the Ayyubid themselves, bolstering them as political leaders and legitimizing their dynasty. When Saladin rode among his men, "urging them to perform their Jihad duty" and calling out "On, on for Islam!" he was replicating and expanding upon Nūr al-Dīn's example from the 1160s.[99] Islamic writers such as Ibn al-Athīr and the Hanbali jurist Ibn Qudāma al-Maqdisī believed that the holy war had been continuing for some time, indeed since the First Crusade, if not earlier.[100] And the topic of *jihad*, particularly in relationship to the importance of the city of Jerusalem, was a popular constant in Arabic poetry of the period.[101] These are all reasonable points.

Still, it is clear that Saladin's declarations of *jihad* at Acre were concerned with the immediacy of the military situation before him and that he firmly believed he was waging a holy war. Saladin's behavior at Acre matches the explanation of *jihad* in the period as offered by Cobb: that it was not militarism per se, but rather "war with a pious intent."[102] In fact, Saladin called for *jihad* throughout the siege of Acre, not just in optimistic or desperate moments, leading one to believe his sincerity in waging it.[103]

One overlooked aspect of holy war at Acre is the role it played among the soldiers. The Muslims in Saladin's army are cast as the *jihadi* warriors, champions of Islam, and "heroes of the true unitarians." Such soldiers might be referred to by different terms, such as *mujāhidūn* (volunteers) or *ghuzāh* (simply, fighters).[104] Two such warriors are identified in particular: Mujāhid al-Dīn Yarunqush from Sinjār and an unnamed man from Mazandaran; the former "loved to fight for the faith" and the latter asked Saladin for permission to join the *jihad*. Collectively, the soldiers were said to have fought fiercely and they "gave Jihad its due."[105] For Ibn Shaddād, who could expect Saladin himself to read his writings, the soldiers bought into the notion of fighting for God and heeded the sultan's call to holy war. In his eyes, Allah would save those who endured in the face of trials; accordingly, "those on either side gave their lives to purchase the next world's peace."[106] His words ring credibly, for one reads in the *Eracles* that Philip Augustus declared the crusaders had "come for the sake of God and for the salvation of our souls."[107] Numerous Christians are singled out for their pious combat, such as a marksman who shot a Muslim defender atop the wall when he attempted to urinate on a crucifix: the "lethal wound transfixed the Turk in the groin."[108] In another instance, a small vessel transporting the knight Ivo of Vipont to Tyre was caught by a Muslim galley off the Levantine coastline. When his companions despaired at being captured and killed, Ivo chastised them for their lack of faith: he leapt aboard the enemy vessel and began decapitating Muslim sailors with an axe. His men followed his lead and soon the galley was taken, for "those who placed their hope in God were given a triumph."[109] God's rewards awaited faithful soldiers on both sides of the lines.[110]

## Ditches and ramparts

In what was surely the understatement of the year, the crusade leaders decided it was "best to refrain from open battle for a while."[111] With their numbers severely depleted, there was little chance of breaking through either Saladin's lines or Acre's walls. The campaign had suffered a major setback, and much hand-wringing and rethinking needed to take place. However, the sultan's withdrawal to al-Kharrūba and the resulting expansion of the Muslim encirclement gave them some encouragement and room to breathe, although they continued to face daily attacks from the advance guard. While Saladin convalesced in the south, the first pieces of his eventual defeat in the north could be put in place.

The break was a godsend in two respects. First, reinforcements arrived by sea toward the end of October, fulfilling the fears of Saladin's advisers. Because the crusader ships still held Acre's natural harbor (outside the mole), the ingress and egress of western vessels would be possible until the winter winds set in. The newly arrived magnates and prelates included the count of Ferrers, Guy of Dampierre, and Adelardo, bishop of Verona, along with numerous other barons and 400 Danish warriors accompanying a nephew of the Danish king Canute VI.[112] Roger of Howden claims that 500 knights and 10,000 men arrived at Acre. No other source offers such large numbers, and events subsequent to these landings do not suggest an infusion of so many new troops. Howden, then, was probably conflating the landings of October with those back in September. He does provide an interesting anecdote about the ships, however: while some vessels returned to Italy (Apulia), those carrying Danes and Germans remained at Acre, where they were disassembled and used as firewood and building materials by the crusaders, who had been cut off from the wooded areas east of the Toron.[113]

Second, the pause in major action allowed the crusaders to properly fortify their camp. They began to dig protective ditches on both sides of their tents: one to protect them from Saladin's men and the other to forestall sorties from the Acre garrison.[114] The ditches were filled with sharp pieces of wood and metal, some from broken shields, and they ran from the bay all the way to the Mediterranean. These trenches were then fronted by earthen ramparts and, in some places, wooden palisades. The former slowed Muslim cavalry attacks by forcing them to ride up, and the latter offered protection for western crossbowmen shooting at them. An interesting detail is offered in the *Chronica* of Otto, abbot of St Blasien in the Black Forest. Although his account of affairs in the East continues to 1197, he was not a participant on the crusade and he was evidently uninterested in events at Acre, to which he devotes only four paragraphs. Here, however, he claims that gates were installed in the palisades on either side of the camp, which allowed crusader sorties against both the city and Saladin, when desired.[115] All of the crusaders dedicated themselves to the huge task, taking shifts in which one group would dig while the other guarded the laborers from Muslim attacks. The frustration of the Muslims was palpable: despite showers of arrows and multiple charges at the crusader lines, they were unable to break through, much less lure the workers away from their task. Once the defenses were complete, the crusader artillery was brought fully behind the perimeter, where it could lob projectiles at Acre at will.[116]

These camp fortifications had three major effects. First, the ditch in front of Acre encircled the city and cut it off, once again, from Saladin's forces. At those times when crusader ships were actually able to control the harbor, the garrison had no way of getting supplies in or out. Compounding this problem was the issue of water: the Lyon *Eracles* reports that the crusaders diverted the flow of the River Belus away from the city, denying fresh water to the people there.[117] Second, the Acre ditch prevented easy sorties from the garrison and allowed the crusaders to prepare, coordinate, and launch new attacks against the city walls. This included not only projectiles shot from the artillery, but scaling attempts by Conrad of Montferrat's men and the Hospitallers.[118] Third, the outward ditch and rampart prevented penetration by Saladin's cavalry. Although his advance guard continued to harry the defenders with daily attacks and periodic skirmishing, large-scale attempts to gain entry into the camp were now stymied by the defenses and the men guarding them. There would be no repeat of Taqī al-Dīn's success in September. As a result, the sultan had no practical way to actively disengage the crusaders from their siege. He would have to settle for a continued encirclement of their position, attempts to cut off their supplies by seizing the harbor, or perhaps drawing their armies outside of the fortifications with harassment tactics or feigned retreats.

The Muslims watched these construction efforts with great concern. Messengers brought the news to Saladin, and some of his emirs urged an immediate attack upon the crusaders before they could finish the project. It appears that Saladin wished to take this advice (Ibn Shaddād actually makes it sound like his idea) but demurred because of his illness. When the prospect was raised of sending the army but under another command, the sultan refused, figuring that the soldiers would not perform well without him. Other advisers suggested that he wait until all his forces and reinforcements were assembled before attacking, no matter what the state of the enemy fortifications. The operation was therefore delayed, which allowed the defenses to be finished without serious issue.[119] Once again, Saladin had hesitated when direct action might well have served him better. He had superior numbers and a recent triumph over the Christian army, but his pride was his downfall. And although no one knew it at the time, his decision not to engage was the beginning of the end: as John Pryor has written, "once they completed their fosse and rampart protecting the camps, it was over."[120]

## Winter arrives

As the end of 1189 approached, nature interceded to bring the Muslims some relief. The winter weather in the Acre region is brusque and windy, although not necessarily snowy. The wind atop the Toron in particular can be strong enough to knock over posts and even inattentive tourists. Ships could not remain in the harbor outside the city port for the duration of the season because of the rough conditions. Most of the crusader vessels either left in late October or became fuel for the camp fires. New ships were not likely to arrive either, due to numerous issues with winter travel across the sea.[121] There was thus a slender window in which to access the city via the Mediterranean Sea. Such logistical issues boded ill for the Muslims in the city as well. As it waited, hoping for relief, the starving and desperate Acre garrison actually began negotiations with the crusaders to surrender the city. Their terms were simple: they would surrender the city in exchange for their lives. The deal was foolishly refused by the crusade leaders, who desired either to gloriously take the city by storm or to receive it with no conditions at all.[122] The offer of capitulation is astounding, given the Muslim successes of the fall, and so the lack of food inside Acre must have been severe indeed.

Fortunately, Ayyubid reinforcements from Egypt arrived in two waves before the end of the year. The dating of these events is tricky because, while the Arabic accounts put them in November and December, the western accounts place them around 31 October.[123] In any event, first an Egyptian army arrived at al-Kharrūba, led by Saladin's brother al-ʿĀdil, who brought infantry and a large quantity of supplies, weapons, and food. Syrian cavalry arrived at about the same time.[124] Second, the much-anticipated fleet from Alexandria, whose assembly and provisioning had been ordered by Saladin himself, approached the Acre harbor on 26 December, commanded by Emir Ḥusām al-Dīn Luʾlu. Luʾlu was "energetic, brave, bold, knowledgeable of the sea and naval warfare and blessed with good fortune."[125] With fifty heavily laden galleys (shīnīs) he steadily approached the harbor. This constituted a major fraction of the Egyptian fleet. The number of ships available in 1189 is unknown, but as a baseline guide we know that a few years earlier, in 1179, Saladin had had at his disposal sixty galleys and twenty transports (ṭarīda).[126] On a clear day, one can see ships from as far away as Haifa; but now the distance was such that the crusaders could not tell whether the vessels were friend or foe. They soon found out when the galleys attacked a crusader vessel outside the harbor, one of the few remaining in the area.[127] The boat was taken (some of the sailors managed to jump overboard and swim to safety) and pulled through the port entrance along with the Muslim fleet. Its cargo was seized, its remaining sailors were executed, and their bodies were hung from the city walls by the garrison. The remaining crusader ships in the area moved into the Mediterranean and north to Tyre, where they would spend the rest of the winter. Thousands of Muslim sailors and infantry (rajjāla) then disembarked from Luʾlu's ships.[128]

In the wake of the reinforcements and the opening of the port, Acre's residents could now look forward to being resupplied by sea and, possibly, being succored from the land side by Saladin's new armies. The garrison subsequently broke off surrender negotiations. Due to the cold and muddy conditions in the plain of Acre, both sides took a break from major fighting, and Saladin allowed many of his veterans to take seasonal leave.[129] Saladin had made several strategic errors in the first few months of fighting, squandering some good opportunities to dispense with the besiegers. Looking back at the sequence of events in late 1189, however, the crusaders had committed an even bigger error: despite their taking horrendous losses in battle, they had nonetheless refused an opportunity to receive Acre without further bloodshed. The pride of the crusade's leaders would be costly indeed.

# III

# SPRING AND SUMMER
## *1190*

*"Two parts of the world attacked the third, Europe, which alone –
and not entirely – acknowledged the name of Christ."*[1]

As 1189 ended and the days marched towards spring in 1190,
Saladin's mistake in not attacking the beleaguered crusaders
was not immediately apparent. No one could have foreseen the ultimate effectiveness of the ditches and ramparts, which would succeed
in holding off a series of attacks from the massive Islamic host.
Ensconced within their camp, the Christians were able to turn their
attention to the actual siege of Acre and finally make some serious
and concerted attacks. But issues of supply loomed large. Blockaded
themselves from the land beyond their camp, they struggled to maintain sufficient stores of food. The garrison and residents within Acre
faced a similar conundrum and, like their opponents, had to be resupplied principally by sea. The year 1190 thus featured a series of naval
engagements, as ships from both sides tried to run deliveries through
to their comrades. It was a year of ebbs and flows, in which hope
soared for the Christians with the arrival of ships and a renewed

assault on Acre, but was then tempered by operational setbacks and the death of thousands of crusaders in battle.

Little fighting took place over the winter, and even in the early spring the only action was a skirmish outside the ramparts. The sultan, having recovered from his illness, went on a hunting expedition, and the Christian leaders somehow learned of his absence. They took the opportunity to attack the Muslim advance guard outside their camp. Saladin's brother, al-'Ādil, assembled his men and eventually drove them off after some intense fighting. Ibn al-Athīr plays up the severity of this action, claiming that the Muslims fought desperately and that large numbers fell on both sides. Two mamluk champions engaged in the fighting: one, Arghush, was cut down, while the other, Sarāsunqur, managed to escape after a host of crusaders ambushed him and dragged him by the hair.[2] The location of the fighting is not mentioned, and the western sources failed even to notice it.

The Muslims had little time to despair about the small defeat, because more severe problems were on the horizon. Sometime around Easter 1190 (25 March), a new crusader fleet of fifty vessels, coming from Tyre and led by its marquis, Conrad of Montferrat, appeared off the Mediterranean coast, tacking south towards Acre. Guy of Lusignan and Conrad had reconciled: the king had agreed to allow Conrad to retain possession of Tyre and also Beirut and Sidon, once they were back in Christian hands.[3] As a result, after wintering in Tyre, the marquis returned to the siege. Saladin's advisers had fretted about the eventual springtime resupply of the Christians since the previous October, and now it had begun in earnest.

### A crescent by the cross

Conrad's fleet was intercepted by Muslim ships before it could navigate past Acre's port and to the shoreline of the bay next to the Christian camp. What resulted was the second of ten naval

# EMMA PAISEY

## DAISY PARK
28 BROAD STREET
SOUTH MOLTON
NORTH DEVON
EX36 3AQ

01769 579077
EMMA@DAISYPARK.CO.UK
WWW.DAISYPARK.CO.UK

daisy
PARK

encounters during the siege of Acre. The battle is narrated in a fair amount of tactical and technological detail by Richard of Templo, who fused together elements from *Itinerarium1* and Ambroise.[4] Some of his description makes little sense: he depicts the Muslim fleet as leaving port to initiate some sort of grand duel, at which sailors from the crusader camp then boarded their ships and responded. If this was the case, then presumably crusader vessels had already run past the harbor and re-blockaded Acre; but preceding accounts relate that all their ships had either left for the winter or been used as firewood. Ambroise's account makes more sense: as Conrad's fleet arrived, the Muslim fleet simply sortied to meet it.[5] Thousands of the city's defenders piled out of the streets and boarded the Muslim ships in the port like "the scrambling of ants coming out of an anthill in all directions."[6]

The ships rowed past the Tower of Flies, into the bay, and finally out into the Mediterranean Sea, moving in a column of ships paired two-by-two. Conrad's fleet tacked west and permitted the Muslims to form up. Both fleets seem to have maneuvered into horizontal lines before engaging, but then the crusaders bent theirs into crescents, with the concave facing away from the approaching ships. The purpose was to create a pincer that could trap the Muslims if they tried to puncture the line. This reflected contemporary tactics and was a time-honored Byzantine formation mentioned in Leo VI's late ninth-century military manual, the *Taktika*.[7] In a preceding passage, however, Richard of Templo, copying from the *Itinerarium1*, also discusses the ship-types used at the Battle of Actium in 31 BC, Agrippa's great victory over the fleet of Mark Antony. At Actium, Agrippa bent his line in a similar crescent, so it is plausible that our author was actually borrowing this detail from an ancient source. Such copying of classical military operations was a feature of some medieval writing; moreover, because there is no further reference to the formation or how well it functioned, we can rightly be skeptical.[8]

The alignment of the fleet aside, Conrad positioned the strongest, best-equipped galleys in the first line, and every galley arranged shields on its upper decks: rowers were sent down to the lower deck, while soldiers manned the tops. The Muslim fleet was a mixture of double-decked galleys and lighter, single-decked *galliots*. The former were known in Arabic as *shīnī*, which carried 100–200 oarsmen and up to 150 marines; they also had forecastles from which arrows could be shot. By the twelfth century, these ships were no longer equipped with rams. Given the mention of Greek Fire, the latter ships were probably *ḥarrāqa*, equipped with catapults for lobbing ceramic jars of naphtha.[9] A petroleum-based incendiary, its flames could resist being quenched by water and were therefore perfect for destroying wooden structures such as ships and siege engines. Arabic varieties were lobbed in small jars, as opposed to the Greek method of propulsion through mounted metal tubes; moreover, they were not true "Greek Fire" in that the jars were full of crude oil or naphtha, whereas Greek varieties were distillations of crude oil.[10]

The sea was calm and quiet as the fleets drew nearer to each other. As the ships closed to within missile range, trumpets were sounded on both sides, and the battle began. First came volleys of arrows and bolts, with the Muslims shooting first and the crusaders responding. The Genoese and Pisan arrows fell on Muslims protected by long shields. Once at close quarters, the crusader galleys turned inward: their ships were equipped with iron "spurs" (*ferratis*), and these were directed against the sides of Muslim vessels. As the ships interlocked, men on both sides threw grappling hooks and rushed the other's decks. The Muslim *ḥarrāqa* lobbed jars of naphtha at the galleys, igniting the wood and incinerating some Christian sailors. One galley was nearly taken in such a fashion: its rowers abandoned ship as the fires took hold, but it was saved by armored knights who, not knowing how to swim, remained and fought off the Muslims who had jumped onboard.[11]

The fighting lasted the better part of the day, with the entangled ships drifting back to the harbor. As the battle came to a close, the vessels gradually disengaged and the surviving Muslims were able to make port. One crusader galley was the scene of a wild display of grit on both sides. Muslims had taken the top deck and, seizing the oars, tried to row the ship away; meanwhile, on the lower deck, the Christian oarsmen rowed in another direction, so the ship spun around in a circular contest of sheer strength. Eventually, some crusaders reached the top deck and slew enough Muslims so that the oarsmen could steer the vessel back to the shore east of Acre.[12] People from the camp ran to the water and boarded once it landed. In a bloody scene, Christian women grabbed the Muslims and, dragging them ashore by their hair, began to decapitate them:

> Our women pulled the Turks by the hair, treating them dishon-ourably, humiliatingly cutting their throats; and finally beheaded them. The women's physical weakness prolonged the pain of death, because they cut their heads off with knives instead of swords.[13]

This is an odd passage. The writer is sympathizing with the victims, perhaps believing that soldiers deserved a better or less cruel death. It is also the first passage of several in the Acre accounts to note violent deeds committed by women.[14] Other than these two rescues of crusader vessels, there were other reasons to count the battle a victory. Two Muslim ships were sunk, a galley and a *galliot*, and more Muslims than Christians were killed in the action. In addition, the Muslim fleet was driven back into port ("beyond the chain"), allowing the crusade vessels once again to blockade it. Combined with the land-side fortifications, Acre was once again cut off from all material support from the outside. Most importantly, Conrad's fleet had survived and was able to deliver badly needed supplies and reinforcements to the camp.[15]

As it turned out, however, access to the port was only temporarily restricted. It was closed for less than three months, in fact, because with the dawn of summer, Muslim ships started running the blockade. On 14 or 15 June, a fleet of twenty-five ships from Egypt appeared in Haifa Bay, carrying mostly supplies and food for the starving populace in the city.[16] The Christian ships in the harbor quickly set a course to intercept, and a third naval battle ensued. In the meantime, Saladin had once more ordered attacks along the eastern trench lines, in order to distract the crusaders' attention from the water. One or two crusader galleys were taken, and another may have been wrecked on the rocks east of the harbor. Of the Muslim vessels, two were wrecked after missing the narrow port entrance and sliding past the Tower of Flies; Ibn al-Athīr claims that one Muslim ship was captured, and this may have been one of those so wrecked. The rest of the Muslim fleet appears to have reached safety, bringing significant relief to the citizens and garrison in Acre.[17]

In addition to these naval engagements, the Arabic sources focus on the arrival of Saladin's other reinforcements, most of whom were returning after their winter rest. He and his army moved north, from his winter camp at al-Kharrūba back to Tel Kaysān, where it then reestablished the strong assault lines around the crusader periphery. He arrived on 25 April, a month after the naval encounter with Conrad, only then learning that the city had once more lost its connection to the sea. Saladin sat and waited for his allies to arrive. When they began pouring into the area and in such great numbers, the sultan might well have imagined that he had made the correct decision in giving the crusaders quarter the previous October.

The reinforcements arrived in two waves. The Arabic sources differ on who arrived first and last, but the first wave seems to have arrived at Acre between 4 and 29 May and the second between 13 June and 5 July. In the first wave were men under the command of Saladin's son, al-Ẓāhir Ghiyāth al-Dīn Ghāzī (lord of Aleppo); he was followed by Muẓaffar al-Dīn and his retinue, and then the army of 'Imād al-Dīn Zankī, lord of Sinjār. In the second wave came Sanjar Shāh, 'Alā' al-Dīn Khurramshāh, and finally Zayn al-Dīn.

In turn, each retinue and troop bedecked itself in fine armor and standards and paraded before the sultan, who reviewed them; afterward, he stationed the soldiers in various positions on the line and welcomed their leaders as honored guests, showering them with gifts and favors.[18] Other, smaller contingents came as well, including an envoy and his retinue from the court of the Abbasid caliph in Baghdad. This envoy, unnamed but called a descendant of Muhammad, brought along two wagons of Greek Fire and men expert in mixing and using it, as well as a loan authorization from the caliph for 20,000 dinars, which the sultan politely declined. It was an incredibly small and insulting sum, equal to only one day of his campaign expenses.[19]

From the Christian point of view, it was the nature, as well as the number, of these other armies that merited attention. Some they believed to be contingents of mercenaries; others religious pilgrims who fought without pay. The African contingents were noticed above all others due to their black skin and red hats:

> There was there in great number and full of evil intent a hideous black people, against God and against nature, with red head-dresses on their heads – never did God make more ugly creatures. There were great numbers of them, all turned towards evil. The waves of people in red caps were like cherry trees covered with ripe fruit … Those with the red caps had a standard to which they all rallied; this was the standard of Mohammed, whose image was there in chief and in whose name they came to fight, to defeat Christianity. These scum protected themselves with the great projectiles that they carried.[20]

Richard of Templo embellished his account further, speaking of these soldiers' huge size, deformity, and savagery, and of their massive clubs spiked with shards of metal.[21] He also speculates on their origins, calling them Nadabares (either Nobades or Nabataeans), Gaetuli

(Algerians), Numidians, and Mauritanians.[22] Such groups, called *'abīd* (slaves), had traditionally been components of the Fatimid armies that preceded the Ayyubid. However, black contingents were much smaller during the Ayyubid dynasty, for Saladin was not inclined to use them very much in his Egyptian army. This had been the case since 1169, when Saladin killed the black eunuch of the Fatimid caliph al-'Ādid, an act that sparked the "Battle of the Blacks": within a few years, the black Africans in the army were crushed and their units disbanded.[23] No wonder, then, that these particular men had been brought rather by Saladin's brother, al-'Ādil, and not by the sultan himself.[24]

The Christian sources speak of a combined Muslim army numbering in the hundreds of thousands, but this is far off the mark. At Saladin's greatest victory, the Battle of Hattin on 4 July 1187, his army numbered some 12,000 regular cavalry and, John France has speculated, perhaps up to 28,000 additional auxiliary troops.[25] This likely represents the upper end of what the Christians saw at Acre by the time most of the Muslims had arrived in the spring of 1190. In Egypt, the base of the sultan's power, Saladin had reorganized the army into a group of 8,640 men, which were maintained at an annual cost of over 3.6 million dinars. However, custom was to leave half of that force in Egypt for defense.[26] The other soldiers available to him were helpfully quantified in 1962 by Hamilton Gibb: Egypt: 4,000 (roughly half of the aforementioned force); Saladin's guard (*halqa*): 1,000; Damascus: 1,000; Aleppo and north Syria: 1,000; Mosul, Diyar Bākr, and the Jazīra: 5,000.[27] This represents a total of roughly 13,000 soldiers drawn from both Saladin's *halqa* and those of his lords entrusted with fiefs (*iqtaat*); the latter would have an obligation to provide soldiers in time of need. The size of the sultan's army was considerable and, unlike the crusader forces at Acre, was not substantially degraded in number by disease, starvation, or defeats in battle. After the end of the siege of Acre, Saladin met Richard the Lionheart at the Battle of Arsur with a force of 25,000 – still a mighty force indeed.[28]

Depending on the operation, the Ayyubid army would have been organized in different-sized units. The *tulb* (alternatively, *katiba*) was a unit of between 70 and 200 horsemen led by an emir and accompanied by both standard-bearer and trumpeter. In 1171, Saladin's Egyptian army consisted of 174 *tulbs*, amounting to some 14,000 men. Smaller groups were the *jarida* (seventy men) and *sariya* (twenty riders, often used for ambushes).[29] To these would then be added whatever auxiliary forces were available at the time.[30] For the auxiliaries, we are fortunate to possess a document that purports to list the major groups present at Acre. Discovered by Hans Eberhard Mayer in two manuscripts, it is an addition to the *Tractatus de locis statu sancte terre Jerosolimitane*, a document describing the Kingdom of Jerusalem in the two decades before 1187. Benjamin Kedar published the text of the addition in 1997 and compared the groups to those identified by Gibb. In addition to Turks, Kurds, and Arabs, the *Tractatus* addition describes Idumeans, Ammonites, Nabataeans (which confirms Richard of Templo's identification), and Africans along with their weaponry and relative prowess, but it omits mamluks, who we know from other sources were present.[31]

### The three towers

The arrival of Saladin at Acre in late April, followed by his reinforcements, meant a return to regular engagements on both sides. The crusaders had been quite busy over the winter break. With their entrenchments complete, they had spent the remaining hours constructing siege engines for the next assault on the city. Several different devices are mentioned: cats and sows (*cattos* and *testudines*: covered huts that could be placed against the walls to protect the men inside), battering rams (*arietes*), *cercelia* (similar to cats, but with openings from which to return counterfire), siege towers (*turres* or *castella vehiculis*), and catapults and mangonels (*machinas*: tension- or torsion-powered artillery pieces). Mines (*vias subterraneas*) were also dug.[32] Along with Ambroise, the source for these details is the verse account of "Monachus," an unidentified witness, perhaps Italian, who arrived at Acre in 1189 and was the only Christian writer to have been present for the entire siege. The poem has limitations: it is relatively brief and was likely written down much later than the siege, in the early to mid-thirteenth century. Its passages are blunt but, while offering far less detail than the others, they avoid some of the drama that intrudes into the thoughts of Ambroise and Richard of Templo.[33] Both writers also describe the further garrisoning of Acre, made possible by the opening of the port by Muslim ships the year before. Into the city flowed artillery and engineers to man and fix it, a supply of Greek Fire, and enough food and supplies to maintain, if the numbers can be believed, a force of 30,000 men.[34]

The most prominent engines were the siege towers built by the crusaders. There were three of them, financed, respectively, by Guy of Lusignan, Ludwig III, and Conrad of Montferrat. Witnesses describe the size, design, and function of the towers. They were about 60 cubits tall, mobile (either mounted on wheels or rolled atop logs), and covered with fireproofing made of cloth and animal skins soaked in vinegar to protect from naphtha missiles.[35] In front of each tower was stretched a rope net, designed to catch or repel any projectiles shot from Acre's artillery. They were multi-story: Ibn al-Athīr, who was not an eyewitness, claims they had five stories apiece; 'Imād al-Dīn, who was, gives four. Richard of Templo speaks of archers and crossbowmen positioned on the top platform, and men equipped with staff weapons on the middle levels, so the historian from Mosul may actually have been close to the mark. Ibn Shaddād claims that each tower held 500 men. Finally, each structure was flanked by catapults, whose purpose was to return fire at Muslim artillery if needed; or if not, to pound Acre's walls.[36]

The Acre garrison was struck with fear by these towers, the sight of which even prompted it to enter into surrender negotiations for the second time. However, once again the crusaders refused, believing that their machines would help them win a complete victory instead. The early stages of the ensuing assault on the city are not well described: the walls were stormed and the crusaders began to fill in sections of the town's moat with stones, which would facilitate the movement of the towers against the walls. Ambroise makes an astounding claim: that Guy of Lusignan, Conrad of Montferrat, and Ludwig III were each positioned in a tower when the attack began. This would have been an extraordinary risk for these leaders, no matter how well the towers were protected; given the fate of each structure, it is extremely unlikely that Ambroise's information here is correct.[37]

Saladin was not watching the siege unfold in front of him because he was still at Tel Kaysān, but he heard news of the crusader mobilization. The sultan therefore moved farther to Tel al-'Ajūl on 2 May, where he could be nearer to the action and direct his men. There, a messenger from the city arrived to communicate the city's status and, most likely, the fact that the garrison was considering surrender; he had secretly swum across the harbor in order to elude the Christian blockade. Saladin moved his armies into position, with the men arranged into left, center, and right contingents; this time, his son al-Afḍāl took command on the right instead of Taqī al-Dīn. The Muslims then attacked the crusader defenses, hoping to draw their attention away from the siege works. Despite heavy fighting, there was no breakthrough, and each night the Christians and Muslims retired to their respective camps. Inexorably, the siege towers continued their slow roll forward towards Acre's walls. They finally arrived on either 5 or 6 May 1190, the latter being the Sunday after the Feast of the Ascension. Bridges were dropped between their platforms and the city parapet and "they overtopped the wall."[38]

The towers had taken a heavy barrage of fire on their trek to the walls. The garrison was, after all, equipped with artillery and had the stores of naphtha given to it by the Abbasid caliph. Unfortunately, the jars thrown by Acre's defenders simply had no effect on the towers, protected as they were by the vinegar-soaked skins. One day, however, a specialist in combustibles and erstwhile metal worker from Damascus, named Ali, came forward to speak with Saladin about the issue.[39] Ali was apparently an enthusiast who had tinkered with incendiary recipes in his youth, and he claimed to know a variety of naphtha that would do the trick. After gathering various ingredients, he was smuggled into Acre, where he met with the city's governor, Emir Qāraqūsh, and asked him to arrange for his concoction to be launched from the city's catapults.[40] Qāraqūsh initially refused, balking at Ali's temerity; but he was eventually persuaded when someone opined that this might be a gift from Allah. Without this appeal to the divine, the city may well have fallen to the crusader assault.

Ali mixed together his recipes and brought the finished product to the artillery crews. Several pots of liquid were shot from the catapults, breaking and splashing their contents over the protective shielding of one of the siege towers. The exact contents are not clear, but they seem to have had no effect. Then Ali lit the fuse on another pot and had it shot against the now-soaked tower; when this pot hit the inundated surface it burst into flame. Two more lit pots had the same effect, so the entire front of the tower caught fire; the fire spread to engulf the entire structure and kill nearly everyone within it. The other two towers were struck similarly, so in a brief time all three of the crusader towers were destroyed.[41]

The reaction to this spectacle was naturally mixed. The Christian accounts lack substantive detail and are rather morose, as is to be expected. Richard of Templo laments that certain victory had been lost. William of Newburgh, writing later and back in England, seems more intrigued by the notion of Greek Fire itself than by the loss of the towers. In his *Ymagines historiarum*, Ralph of Diss, the dean of St Paul's in London, notes the great expense that had been poured into the towers (*sumptibus magnis construxerunt*), which had now been wasted.[42] The normally lucid Ambroise offered no interpretation at all, speaking only of the towers' destruction and the escape of a few lucky souls from within them. Monachus lamented the personal anguish among the soldiers.[43] The Muslims, on the other hand, were quite naturally ecstatic with the results of Ali's labors: "Our people were seized with such joy and delight that staid and stern men were as excited as flighty girls."[44]

Other types of siege machinery, such as the catapults flanking each tower, may have been destroyed as well – the sources are vague on everything except for the towers – and the rest of the assault seems to have completely fizzled out once the fires died down. It was a comprehensive defeat.

In a broader context, however, the crusaders had now forced Acre to the brink of surrender twice: first with their blockade and then with their machines. Saladin was a pragmatic leader, and he likely knew that unless he could drive off or destroy the western armies the city would eventually be lost. Soon after the incineration of the towers, he ordered a series of general assaults on the trenches. From a strategic perspective, this was more or less common sense, given the material and moral condition of his entrapped enemies. The attacks occurred around Pentecost (13 May), and the fighting lasted several days.[45] There were no formal battles during this stretch, but rather a continual push near the crusade camp perimeter, both from the east and from the city garrison.

The danger along the ramparts and in the camp was real. Crusader watchmen sat within range of Acre's garrison and vice versa, and there was always the danger of being hit by a chance bolt or arrow. One crusader was said to have been struck in the neck by a bolt fired from a Muslim crossbowman atop Acre's wall. The missile pierced his mail and quilted doublet, but was purportedly stopped by a piece of parchment on which the man had written the name of God and hung on a cord around his neck.[46]

There were other dangers in unexpected places. A Christian was attacked by a Turkish rider while relieving himself in one of the ditches: running awkwardly with his lower garments down, he none-theless called upon God, scooped up a rock, and – while falling – threw it, hitting the rider on his temple. The Muslim fell off his horse and broke his neck.[47] Within the Christian camp, traps were set around the camp's interior as precautionary measures, in the event that any Muslims were able to penetrate the outer defenses. In some cases, these actually worked: one rider tangled his horse up in some fishing nets from a partially set trap and had to abandon it; another lost his horse when its hooves got stuck in a trap set by Count Robert of Dreux.[48]

Barring such deliberate acts of provocation, however, the spaces between the ramparts and the Muslims were not necessarily a zone of death. Despite the religious antagonisms between Christians and Muslims at Acre, the shared experience of combat and the sheer length of the siege elicited noticeable expressions of respect, and even an adversarial camaraderie. The participants regularly conversed with each other across the divide, as soldiers at war often do. Occasionally, humanizing anecdotes pop up in crusade narratives and throughout the crusading period. At Acre, there is a story, for example, of a crusader who simply walked up to the wall and shouted questions to the defenders, asking them how many reinforcements had arrived the previous day.[49] We catch glimpses of young crusaders practicing their marksmanship outside camp, and even of contests of skill. In one instance, a Muslim archer called Grair challenged a Welshman named Mardoc to a duel, in which each would take turns in loosing arrows at the other. This duel – which the Welshman won – took place after a whole host of archers and slingers had been lobbing missiles at each other "for amusement and practice."[50] In another case, a wrestling match was arranged between two young Muslims from Acre and two young Christians. One of the Christians was pinned and became a prisoner, but another crusader ransomed him for two dinars. He was lucky: a white falcon belonging to Philip Augustus was caught while perched on Acre's wall, and his men were unable to ransom it even for

1,000 dinars. The relative veracity of these tales can be debated, and it has been pointed out that they can serve to illuminate or even justify different perspectives within a narrative. In this case, they also demonstrate the humanity of a shared hostile experience. Despite the elevated religious tensions and copious violence of the siege at Acre, respectful and even friendly interactions with the enemy were not beyond the realms of possibility.[51]

However, in the wake of the siege towers' destruction, strict discipline was enforced along the camp defenses. Standing orders went out to the Christians to defend the trenches at all costs: travel outside the perimeter was forbidden, and soldiers were stationed up and down the line. The Muslims approached in large numbers, indeed so many that "arrows fired at random found a target, and no one bothered to aim a blow when the dense crowd provided so many potential targets."[52]

But there seems to have been an overall lack of coordination between the Muslims, which made them easier to repel. Some of their infantry tried to fill the ditches in order to effect a crossing; others actually jumped into the ditches and tried scrambling up the opposite slope.[53] Both ideas only made the Muslims easier, more stationary targets. Moreover, the city soldiers and Saladin's men attacked not in tandem, but in alternating waves. Although the crusaders kept a guard on the entire camp perimeter and had no idea which group of Muslims would attack first or next, they were able to drive off the Muslims on one side before pivoting to deal with the other side.[54] After more than a week of fighting, there was a respite and both sides took some rest; but because they had saved their camp, the crusaders had won an important victory.

## The German crusade

The clock continued to tick for Saladin: while he dithered in regards to the Christian army at Acre, steady news reports arrived pertaining to the advance of yet another crusader army, that of Emperor Frederick Barbarossa. The reports came from one of Saladin's former Muslim opponents, Qilij Arslān, the Seljuk sultan of Rūm in Asia Minor. He, the lords of Mosul, and Saladin had concluded a peace treaty together in 1180, and now, ten years later, Qilij was tasked with preventing the Germans from marching through his territory.[55] Unfortunately, he simply lacked the troops to do so.[56] As the Germans moved through Anatolia, heading for the southern roads towards Antioch, Saladin faced the very real possibility that he would either be driven off from Acre or, worse, trapped between two hostile Christian armies.

Saladin now faced a dilemma: march north to cut off Barbarossa, or stay in Acre and wait for the Germans to arrive? He chose a third, less painful, option: he sent large contingents of his gathered armies north on intercept, while he remained at the siege.[57] Leading their troops away were Nāṣir al-Dīn ibn Taqī al-Dīn (lord of Manbij), ʿIzz al-Dīn ibn al-Muqaddam (lord of Kafarṭāb and Baʾrīn), Majd al-Dīn (Majd al-Dīn ibn ʿIzz al-Dīn Farrūkhshāh ibn Shāhinshāh, the lord of Baalbek), and Sābiq al-Dīn (lord of Shayzar); accompanying them were soldiers from Aleppo and Hama, as well as some Turks. Saladin's son al-Ẓāhir was sent to Aleppo to coordinate these forces and to gather new reports. Worse, Saladin then lost his son al-Afḍāl and the prefect of Damascus, Badr al-Dīn, both of whom retired due to illness, and finally his nephew Taqī al-Dīn, who was sent north on a mission similar to that of al-Ẓāhir. All of these departures occurred by 14 July, and when combined they constituted most of the strength of the Muslim right flank. To compensate, the sultan put his brother al-ʿĀdil in charge of the extreme right side, where Taqī al-Dīn had formerly commanded.[58]

Saladin was right to be worried about Barbarossa's approach. The emperor was leading an army that was impressive in terms of size, speed, and organizational capability. By the time it departed Regensburg on 11 May 1189, it had grown to around 15,000 soldiers and included hundreds of imperial knights and nobles.[59] It moved with deliberation and strict discipline over thousands of miles, averaging 18 miles per day on level roads, while encumbered with not only the normal supplies and armaments of a crusading army but also an increasing number of ingots and coins of precious metal.[60] A second group came by sea, taking the roundabout Atlantic route to the Mediterranean Sea. It had been delayed by the siege of the Almohad stronghold of Silves in Portugal: the crusaders had arrived at Silves in July 1189, and by September that same year the city had surrendered. From there, their cogs overwintered in Marseille or Sicily and then proceeded to Acre by way of Brindisi, Antioch, or perhaps Tyre, finally arriving between April and June 1190.[61]

As the army marched through the Balkans, Barbarossa busily maintained communications with his own lands and also with Byzantium and allies in Anatolia, and he fought several minor and major engagements against Bulgarian bandits and forward detachments of Turks. On 18 May, his army captured the city of Iconium (modern-day Konya), but less than a month later fortune smiled on the Muslims (or, as Ibn al-Athīr put it, "God saved us from his evil"), when on 10 June the emperor drowned in the River Saleph (modern-day Göksu).[62]

The death of Frederick Barbarossa is mentioned in nearly every narrative source for the Third Crusade. The exact circumstances are actually a little obscure: his body was taken out of the river, but he is variously reported to have drowned in his armor after either falling off his horse or trying to swim across; or perhaps a heart attack was the culprit.[63] Whatever the reason, news of his demise simultaneously cheered the Acre garrison and aggrieved the crusaders:

Inside Acre there was such rejoicing when they heard the news that there was dancing and playing of drums, and they worked at nothing else. They climbed into the turrets to tell the news to our people for Saladin knew of it and had told them of it. They shouted in a loud voice, many times, from the turrets, and had it shouted by the renegades: "Your emperor has drowned." There was in the army such sadness, such despair and such distress . . ."[64]

Barbarossa's death was a serious blow, but it was not the end of all hope. The French crusaders, in particular, knew that their king Philip Augustus would eventually arrive, as well as King Richard with knights and soldiers from England and Normandy. And in the short term, Barbarossa's army did not just melt away with the death of its leader. His son Frederick, the duke of Swabia, assumed command of the Germans and they continued to move south, engaging local Islamic forces along the way.[65] This explains why Saladin had continued to send soldiers north until July, a month after the emperor's death. Had the army retained its cohesiveness and made it through the Principality of Antioch intact, it would still have been a dangerous foe.

As it was, however, Duke Frederick's march south was a near-total disaster. The army that had so effectively cut its way through Anatolia began to stumble before reaching Antioch. The principal imperial (or German) source, the *Historia de expeditione Friderici imperatoris* of the so-called Ansbert (who may represent more than one author and a mishmash of sources), reports that the army divided, with some heading for Tripoli and others for Antioch. Those marching to Antioch were struck with disease and famine along the way, and the deaths may have numbered in the thousands. He writes, "whatever age or condition, for both noble and poor, young and old, were all struck down indiscriminately."[66] Muslim riders from Aleppo followed their progress and kidnapped or killed any foragers who strayed from the main body. Of particular interest to the Muslims were reports of the great mortality of the German horses: Ibn Shaddād twice claims to have heard of this, and also reports that the bones of some sixty mounts were discovered in a pile outside Latakia.[67] The remains of the army finally reached Antioch on 21 June.

Frederick seems then to have assumed control of the city, although whether by invitation of its prince, Bohemond III, or not is obscure. He stayed for two months, allowing his army to recuperate and "toyed with the idea of establishing himself as a power in northern Syria."[68] But the *Itinerarium* posits Conrad of Montferrat as persuading him to continue south to Acre. Why? The author suggests that Saladin had bribed the marquis with 60,000 bezants, for which he was to get Frederick out of Antioch as a way of reducing the threat to the sultan's northern flank. Conrad then sent messages to Frederick, insinuating that the leaders at Acre were jealous of the duke's prowess and preferred for him to remain in the north. Ibn Shaddād likewise suggests that Guy of Lusignan feared a loss of prestige should the duke arrive.[69]

Whether or not these stories are true, in August Frederick indeed decided to abandon his plans for a Syrian expedition and continue south instead. He and his army left on 29 August and marched to Tripoli. There, they rejoined their German comrades and also linked up with Conrad of Montferrat.[70] From thence Frederick moved to Tyre, and finally arrived at Acre on 7 October, bringing an army of only 700 knights with him. Over the winter, he caught a severe illness and died on 20 January 1191.[71] Although many of his men survived and remained active in the siege, Duke Frederick's death made for a miserable end to the grand imperial expedition.

## The St James offensive

The spring of 1190 was difficult for all parties involved in the siege. In addition to all the fighting, illness had struck in Saladin's ranks, and severe food shortages afflicted both the people of Acre and the crusaders camped outside. The plight in the city had been lessened somewhat when the Muslim supply fleet ran the Christian blockade in mid-June, but no such relief had come to the besiegers. No western ships had arrived at Acre since Conrad of Montferrat's reappearance at Easter, and food shortages had become pronounced.[72] Monachus, the Lyon *Eracles*, and Roger of Howden relate the supply-and-demand issues within the camp and point to increased prices that kept the best foods out of reach for the common soldier.

| | Acre price | in bezants | 1939 value[73] | 2016 value[74] |
|---|---|---|---|---|
| One egg: | 12 deniers | 0.17 | £0.51 | £30.91 |
| One gallon of milk: | 10 soldi | 1.7 | £5.10 | £309.06 |
| One chicken: | 60 sous | 10 | £30 | £1,818 |
| Four bushels of corn: | 15 shillings | 30 | £90 | £5,454 |
| A loaf of bread: | 60 shillings | 120 | £360 | £21,816 |
| A horseload of corn: | 64 marks | 427 | £1,281 | £77,628.60 |

The conversion to bezants and then modern values in pounds sterling gives a rough indication of just how expensive food had purportedly become during the siege.[75] Beef and mutton were not available, so the only meat to be had (besides chicken) was horse, donkey, or mule.[76] Most meals consisted of beans and biscuits. If we can believe Ibn al-Athīr on the matter, the crusaders were forced to purchase food at inflated prices from local Muslim merchants operating in the Acre plain.[77]

The volume of food required by armies such as that at Acre was considerable. A horse required 35 liters of water and between 5 and 6 kilograms of feed per day (or more – perhaps 8–9 kilograms – if grazing only on green grass). For the men, something in the region of 8 liters of water and 800 grams of food per day was needed. Historians have worked out a variety of calculations that indicate possible gross amounts: for example, it has been estimated that an army of 15,000 soldiers would need over 288 metric tons of provisions to sustain it for less than a month.[78] The situation at Acre was compounded by the army's entrapment before its walls: lacking access to additional markets, the soldiers were forced to pay the high prices, steal from Christian merchants and each other, or buy from Muslim merchants who used the scarcity to their advantage.

As shortages continued to mount, many of the crusaders grew frustrated, not only on account of the lack of food, but also the lack of progress against any of the Muslim forces arrayed against them. On 25 July, their impatience brought about the second massacre of Christian soldiers at the hands of Saladin's army. With their stomachs empty, some of the Christians began to direct their anger and frustration at a new opponent: their own leaders. They repeatedly asked for, and were denied, permission to attack Saladin's army; excommunication was actually threatened for anyone who disobeyed.[79]

The leaders may have believed that such an over-the-top threat would frighten the soldiers into compliance. Or perhaps its intent was to remind the soldiers of the pious reasons for their presence at Acre – that the goal was winning the Holy Land back for Christ, and not simply winning battles here or there. Alternatively, the leaders may have been desperate: knowing the fragile state of the camp, they made a last-ditch attempt to restrain the men and save the army. No doubt the nobles recalled the disaster of the previous October. These would have been sensible objections, but the reluctance of the knights and princes was instead interpreted as cowardice and roundly mocked by the men.

Eventually, the crusade leaders relented, but only to the extent that they gave permission for others to engage Saladin's advance guard if they wished – the leaders themselves refused to accompany them. As a result, on 25 July, these soldiers decided to form ranks and advance against the Muslims on their own.[80]

The agitators were *gregarii milites*, who were not "common knights" but rather sergeants or constables, the unit leaders of the commoners, the foot soldiers and missile troops.[81] None of them had commanded large divisions of men in battle, and Richard of Templo lamented their eagerness and lack of wisdom:

> Madness overcame good advice, impulse overcame reason, and the multitude took command. Whenever an impulse seizes the common people, they think that rashness is a virtue, judge that what they want is best, do not stop to think about the outcome, flee correction and despise direction.[82]

These *gregarii milites* led a mass of Christian infantry (*pedites*) – 'Imād al-Dīn puts their number at 10,000 – towards the Muslim lines.[83] Unhappily for the soldiers, the result was the ill-fated offensive on 25 July 1190 – the feast of St James.

The initial attack actually seems to have taken the Muslims by surprise. As the soldiers hurriedly grabbed for their arms and rushed to the lines, the heralds cried "On for Islam!" and the cavalry mounted. Saladin himself struck a drum, signaling his emirs to gear up for battle. The crusaders had lined up in rough formation of left, right, and center divisions, but the line of advance seems to have drifted left, towards the west. Ibn Shaddād claims that this was because the crusaders knew that the Muslim right flank had been weakened by the departure of the many soldiers sent north to intercept the approaching imperial army.[84] The fiercest fighting was therefore on the seaward side, where the Egyptian cavalry commanded by Saladin's brother al-'Ādil was driven away after a short clash. Hurrying to rise for battle, the riders had not been fully prepared for fighting and quickly fell back, surrendering their camp in the process. The Christians entered and began looting, with some men even taking spoils from al-'Ādil's own tent.[85]

There is another dimension to these events. Three of the western sources claim that Saladin executed a feigned retreat, ordering his men to pull back eastward of their camps to allow the crusader foot soldiers free ingress. The Lyon *Eracles* even claims that Saladin knew no knights had accompanied them, so he did not have to worry about a cavalry charge and would be able to counterattack at his leisure. Roger of Howden incorrectly claims that Saladin himself retreated and that it was his tents that were looted.[86] Rather, it was al-'Ādil who led a feigned retreat on the right wing only. Ibn Shaddād claims that it had all been a ruse. But reading between the lines, the situation was more complex: the Muslims had mounted and fought, were quickly driven back, and al-'Ādil called a retreat on the fly, improvising in a moment of near-catastrophe.[87] Luckily for him, the tactic worked: as his men backed off, the hungry crusaders stopped to loot and seem to have forgotten about their enemies in the course of filling their empty stomachs. Once the crusaders on the flank had become preoccupied with their pillaging, al-'Ādil ordered a counterattack.[88]

The Muslim charge did not erupt all at once, but rather rippled down the ranks from right (west) to left (east). Al-'Ādil and his son, Shams al-Dīn, charged, and the *tawashi* Qaymāz al-Najmī, who was farther left, joined them. Thereafter, men nearer the Muslim center gathered themselves and joined in until the tumult finally reached the troops from Mosul, led by 'Alā' al-Dīn Khurramshāh, who were on the leftmost edge of the flank. Saladin kept feeding troops into his right flank to exploit the advantage. He sent in men from his own *halqa*, as well as some Egyptians led by Sunqur al-Ḥalabī, but he himself remained in the center in case the crusaders tried to shift away from the heavy fighting. In a progressive, staggered line, then, the Muslims smashed into the crusader left wing:

> They charged the enemy like lions upon their prey. God gave them the upper hand and a rout followed. The Franks recoiled on their heels in precipitous flight back toward their tents, while the sword of God was gleaning spirits from persons, detaching heads from bodies and separating souls from their human frames.[89]

Ibn Shaddād's account is contradicted slightly by Ibn al-Athīr. The latter claims that Saladin's *halqa* did not engage, but remained in the center ranks. He does corroborate the participation of the Egyptians, however, and he adds that none of Saladin's left flank, commanded by 'Imād al-Dīn Zankī, joined in the fight.[90] But in any case, the St James offensive featured yet more fighting on the Mediterranean side of the Acre zone by Montmusard, which had been the principal place of battle ever since the first engagement between the Christians and Muslims on 14 September 1189.

As repeated waves of attackers swarmed around them, the crusaders fell back in disarray and madly fled back towards their camp. They had little chance of outrunning the Muslim riders, and many were cut down from behind.[91] As the survivors ran, they were spotted by their comrades in camp. But rather than charge to assist their fellow crusaders, they elected to remain within the trenches:

> Our princes heard the roar and saw the carnage, but pretended not to notice. Hard, inhuman and pitiless! – they saw their brothers being cut to pieces in front of them yet made no attempt to rescue them from death ... Some held back out of cowardice ...[92]

It seems that only a few Christians rushed out to rescue the stragglers. Most prominent among these was not a knight, but rather Ralph of Alta Ripa, the archdeacon of Colchester, who was famous "both for his learning and the feats of arms." He fell dead while fighting to rescue the men.[93] No prisoners were taken, so apart from those lucky enough to reach camp all the crusaders on the offensive were killed.[94]

The final death toll was certainly in the thousands, but just how many is an issue of debate. The Lyon *Eracles* claims 16,000 dead, with 100 sergeants escaping; Ambroise says 7,000 dead; Richard of Templo, adjusting Ambroise's numbers, maintains it was only 5,500; Monachus claims 5,000; Archbishop Baldwin of Canterbury's chaplain goes lower to only 4,000; Ibn al-Athīr, who was not present, suggests 10,000; and Ibn Shaddād, who was present, says it was anywhere between 5,000 and 8,000.[95] If we discount the largest numbers from Ibn al-Athīr and the *Eracles*, which are not eyewitness accounts, the number of dead ranges from 4,000 to 8,000 foot soldiers. The Muslims dumped these bodies into the River Belus.

Who was to blame for such carnage? Certainly, the offensive itself was ill-advised and the sergeants and constables leading the infantry should bear the brunt of the blame. But there is also the question of their fellows in camp who refused to come to their aid once the battle had been lost. The reluctance of these Christians receives some condemnation in the sources; but in others, most notably the *Eracles*, their inaction was justified. The *Eracles* author saw a sort of social justice in the battle results, wherein the arrogant sergeants had disobeyed their superiors (the princes and knights) and now reaped their proper reward, along with the foot soldiers who had foolishly followed their lead; and yet he also critiqued the knights' cowardice.[96]

Richard of Templo was likewise torn: he admitted the rashness of the offensive, but also wondered if it might have been successful had the princes and knights elected to join in – "if only they had a chief."[97] The chaplain of Archbishop Baldwin was very critical of the elites: "our knights lurk in their tents ... as if defeated, they let the insults of the enemy go unpunished."[98] On the other hand, one could argue that there was reason to remain in camp because Acre's garrison had, once again, sortied out against the crusader camp in support of Saladin's men on the other side. In that case, the knights might have remained behind the trenches because they were repelling an assault.[99]

Ambroise's explanation for the St James affair was initially more morose – that the devil was involved in the disaster; but he then rethought the matter and concluded that it was God who not only permitted it, but even *desired* it, so that he could gather more martyrs unto Himself.[100]

Between the St James offensive of July 1190, the disaster of early October 1189, and the various other setbacks suffered by the crusaders, it is clear that the besieging army had sustained significant casualties. Ascertaining exact numbers is difficult, but even using the lowest numbers offered by Ibn Shaddād – who walked the battle-fields, saw the full carnage, and spoke to those men who counted the dead – we can figure that the crusaders lost something over 10,000 men in the first full year of the siege of Acre. Given that their total manpower did not exceed 30,000 – a figure reached only by relying on Ibn Shaddād's own numbers – this constituted a third of the entire crusader army.[101] Were it not for their defensive perimeter of trenches and ramparts and periodic reinforcements from the sea, there is little chance that the siege could have continued past 1190.

Fortunately, reinforcements steadily arrived. In October 1190, Duke Frederick of Swabia finally arrived with his 700 knights in tow. More immediately, in the week after the St James debacle, one of the more prominent figures of the Third Crusade arrived: Henry of Champagne, count of Troyes and nephew of Philip Augustus. He arrived by sea and brought with him "hordes of new arrivals [that] not only restored the army to its previous strength, but actually increased it."[102] None of the Christian sources describe exactly how many ships or soldiers arrived under Henry's command. Ibn Shaddād, who had acquired some information from sources within Acre, puts the number at 10,000; if true, then the besiegers may well have regained their lost strength.[103]

This can only be regarded as a major setback for Saladin who, despite the great victories achieved so far, now faced not only a resurrected army but also one that was ensconced within a fortified position and buttressed with an array of formidable secular and ecclesiastical leaders. A number of notable figures had landed alongside Henry of Champagne. These included an impressive number of magnates and prelates and an assortment of other named men: six counts, twelve bishops, two abbots, and several Norman and French knights, as well as an unnamed priest with a crossbow! These leaders and soldiers were accompanied by money, supplies, and the wooden and mechanical components for siege engines – most notably several catapults that belonged to the king of France. Before long, Henry would put these weapons to good use against Acre's walls. There was one notable departure, however: Ludwig III of Thuringia decided at this point to return home.[104]

Saladin and his emirs seem to have been uncertain as to their next moves. Ibn al-Athīr tells an interesting story, in which reports were coming in at the time of the death of Frederick Barbarossa and the poor state of the German army residing around Antioch. According to him, the Muslims were too consumed with this news to bother dealing with the Franks in front of them, figuring that the German plight would demoralize them at any rate. And then Henry of Champagne's ships landed, surprising everyone. It was Ibn al-Athīr's habit to critique Saladin, so this small dig at the naiveté of the sultan's inaction might be written off as bias. However, Ibn Shaddād adds details that similarly, though perhaps unintentionally, question the wisdom of the Muslim leadership. After hearing not only reports of the new crusader arrivals, but also rumors (purportedly from Christian deserters) of potential night attacks against the Muslim advance guards, Saladin gathered an advisory council. The emirs recommended that he move his guard back from its close proximity to the camp trenches and thereby expand the encirclement, in the hopes of goading any sorties of Christians out into less secure confines.[105]

Increasingly, modern scholars have been revising the strategic reputation of Saladin downward, and his decision to take his emirs' advice on this occasion is enlightening in this regard.[106] The sultan agreed and decided to expand the encirclement of the crusader camp. He also took the bulk of his soldiers from the army center and withdrew south, once again, to al-Kharrūba, leaving only a thousand soldiers in the advance guard. His left and right wings stayed in place, although the right was still greatly reduced after the departure of so many units to the north.[107] In other words, history had repeated itself: this was essentially the same move that Saladin had made in mid-October 1189. On that occasion, his departure allowed the crusaders enough breathing room to fully fortify their camp; now, ten months later, it gave Henry of Champagne free rein to renew the assault on Acre, which he would do to significant effect.

Why did Saladin repeat his mistake? Certainly, the psychological impact of seeing his battered enemy almost instantaneously regain full strength must have been considerable. And logically, with so many Muslims attending to the German problem farther north, it made little sense to fully address the crusader camp. The pollution from the strewn corpses (and presumably any illness accompanying it) may also have been a factor, as it had been the October before.[108] But whatever the reasons, it is undeniable that Saladin was deliberately offering his enemy space to operate. There was no conceivable way that the move could enhance his advantages.

One might ask why Saladin did not withdraw from Acre completely at this juncture. The crusaders were back to full strength, and even if all of those Muslim units sent north were to return, he would still be back to square one. Moreover, the sultan knew that more enemies were on the way, for the armies of King Richard and King Philip had not yet arrived in the Levant. Staying at Acre was a costly endeavor in both money and manpower, and every extra week of service added burdens on his allies, many of whom had pressing issues at homes to which they longed to attend. And given the blockade of the city, time was not on his side, because there was always the risk that the Christians might actually penetrate the city's gates or walls.

The prospect, then, was for a long, grinding affair, in which one side would eventually run out of troops through sickness, starvation, desertion, and continual fighting. Such a war of exhaustion was not in keeping with Saladin's strategic inclinations: over the course of his military career, he tended to prefer quick seizures of weakly defended targets – a strategy that allowed him to maintain a momentum of success that drew allies to his side and filled his coffers.[109] But in the summer of 1190, despite a clear trajectory of developments in favor of the Christian army, the sultan resigned himself to the slog.

# IV

## AUTUMN AND WINTER
### *1190*

*"The initiatives on which they had wasted their money came to a halt and their cunning plans were baffled."*[1]

Count Henry of Champagne usually takes a back seat to the more famous crusaders at the siege of Acre, such as Richard the Lionheart, Philip Augustus, or even Guy of Lusignan; but his efforts there deserve to be better known.[2] He assumed command of the entire army and brought some semblance of order to the crusade, redirecting the focus of operations away from Saladin's army and back to the city itself. For the previous year, the Christians had alternately addressed the city walls and fought battles, but there was no overall strategy guiding engagement decisions. Only the fortification of the crusader camp could be considered a strategic move: the two offensives against Saladin and the periodic assaults on the city were reactions to immediate conditions and ad hoc in nature. Under Henry's leadership, however, all that changed and the crusaders dedicated themselves to the plan of taking Acre first, and dealing with the Muslim field armies second.

This shift in strategy is most clearly observed in the Arabic sources. They note Count Henry's dedication to siege warfare and, in particular, his focus on the use of artillery against Acre's stone walls. Trebuchets were arranged around the perimeter of the city and projectiles were launched in a regular bombardment as the weapons were shot both day and night. In time, the walls began to crack from the constant pounding.[3] Henry may also have ordered his sappers into action. Ibn al-Athīr relates a curious story about a moving pile of earth: the crusaders built up a huge mound of dirt that slowly advanced towards the city, and shielded behind the mound were two of Henry's trebuchets. This was probably dirt excavated by men tunneling towards the walls.[4]

In the face of such coordinated attacks, the Acre garrison resorted to what can best be described as counter-battery fire. First, they returned the trebuchet shots with projectiles of their own. Two types of artillery are described. One was a stone thrower that tossed large rocks (presumably salvaged from structures within the city) at the Christian engines, severely damaging several of them and at long range. Ambroise claims that two men were required to load the weapon's sling (*funde*); the word probably indicates that it was a rope-pulled trebuchet.[5] The garrison also had at least one *balista* at its disposal. On one occasion, the tips of two bolts were set on fire, and the missiles were shot successively into the side of a crusader trebuchet, burning not only it, but supposedly another engine sitting astride it.[6]

The second countermeasure followed the same principle of destroying the crusader artillery with fire, but with naphtha rather than lit sharps. Although artillery of the period could launch jars of Arabic Greek Fire at a short distance (the technique had been used to destroy the three crusader siege towers in April), naphtha was too expensive to potentially waste on long-distance shots. Indeed, due to the blockade, those quantities available to the Muslims had to be sneaked in by way of swimmers, whose arrival would then be signaled to Saladin via carrier pigeons.[7]

Instead, these jars needed to be delivered to their targets by hand. The two leaders of the garrison, emirs Qāraqūsh and Ḥusām al-Dīn Abū'l-Hayjā, decided to use cavalry sorties to do the job. Acre's gates opened simultaneously, and Muslim riders bolted straight for the siege engines. When they got within close range, they threw the jars of naphtha and rode away. Several of the devices were consumed by fire, and Ibn Shaddād claims that seventy crusaders were killed in the melee and others were taken prisoner.

Given the protective ditches carved in front of the Christian camp, these artillery pieces must have been positioned just inside the perimeter. The sorties must also have truly taken the crusaders by surprise, because one of the engines, for which Count Henry had supposedly paid 1,500 dinars, was farther away and had not yet been pulled within attacking range of the city. It, too, was destroyed.[8] Not all the riders returned safely, however: Emir Ḥusām, who personally took part in the charge, was apparently knocked off his horse by a knight and, in the process, immolated his testicles with his own Greek Fire. Depending upon which version of the story one reads, he either accidentally dropped a phial on himself or he was tortured by the knight.[9] The dating of these countermeasures is uncertain, but they seem to have occurred during August, and they were concluded by 3 September.

Over the same stretch of time, some provisions were smuggled into the city. In the week of 24 August to 2 September, a supply ship (*botsha*) from Beirut managed to reach Acre's inner harbor by disguising itself as a Christian vessel, flying flags adorned with crosses and its sailors dressed in western garb. Although the *botsha* was met and queried by crusader ships, the ploy worked and they allowed it to pass through to the harbor area. The chain was quickly lowered and it entered the port, delivering 400 *ghiaras* of wheat, cheese, corn, onions, and some sheep to the hungry defenders.[10] The ineffectiveness of the Christian blockade was exposed again only two weeks later. Lu'lu, who had so effectively run the crusader blockade the previous December, sent word from Acre that provisions were about to run out. Saladin arranged for three Egyptian *botshas* to resupply the city, and on 16 September these subsequently managed to slip through the blockade of crusader vessels, again by disguising themselves as Christians.[11]

## The Tower of Flies

Clearly, the Christian harbor defense was poor, and so Count Henry now took a different angle on the problem of Acre's seaside resupply: he aimed to capture the Tower of Flies, the tower posted at the end of the mole on the southeast side of Acre's port. Between it and another tower, a giant chain was stretched across the port entrance to protect the Muslim ships within. Control of the chain would finally close the entrance for good. And so commenced the second, naval phase of Count Henry's siege operations in late September.

Henry was not involved in the attack personally, and the *Itinerarium* makes clear that he had delegated the task to the Pisans. It was to be a two-pronged assault. First, the Pisans had fitted one of their galleys with a siege tower, whose height rivaled that of Acre's own walls. It was three stories high and housed missile troops who could thus fire at the Tower of Flies from a comparable elevation. The tower was also covered in leather to ward off missile attacks; in this way, it resembled the three land towers built the previous year on the land side of Acre, but with an important difference: there is no mention of these hides having been soaked in vinegar. Two siege ladders were also built. The plan was to busy the tower's defenders with missile fire, in order to safely land troops, who would then scale the tower with the ladders. Other ships were assigned to escort the tricked-out galley and defend it from any Muslims sorties from the port.

The initial phases of the fighting went well for the crusaders. As the siege galley approached the Tower of Flies, the latter's defenders put up a strong fight that was evenly matched, as missiles flew back and forth. Eventually, the crusaders threw anchors and lashed the galley to the end of the mole upon which the tower stood. This allowed soldiers to disembark with the siege ladders and scale the tower. Meanwhile, the other galleys successfully held off the Muslim ships sallying from the port and killed many of their sailors.[12]

But then matters turned: the Muslim defenders in the tower dropped large pieces of wood and rocks onto the scaling ladders, knocking some of the soldiers off and crushing others. More problematically, the close proximity of the galley enabled the Muslims to lob jars of Greek Fire at it, and its siege tower – unprotected by soaked skins – was immolated. The fire spread to the galley itself and its sailors abandoned ship; those Pisans around the Tower of Flies likewise had to withdraw, and so the attack failed.[13] Ibn Shaddād's account is very different from that in the western sources, likely because he was not in the immediate vicinity of the harbor and had to rely on later reports acquired from the city garrison. He portrays the attack as consisting of three galleys: one with the siege tower, a second "fire ship" that was set alight and thrust into the middle of the Acre fleet, and a third landing ship on which crusaders used a "Welsh cat" to protect them when they landed on the mole. The attack then failed, because the winds shifted and the fire ship drifted into the other crusader ships, burning them and precipitating their retreat.[14] Ibn Shaddād also claims that the Germans attacked the same tower a month later, on 17 October, this time not only placing a siege tower on a galley, but also equipping it with a drawbridge. They did no better than the Pisans and could only watch as their ship, too, was consumed by Greek Fire.[15]

After the failed attack, the volume of Muslim ships trying to succor the city only increased. On a dark and stormy night in late October, fifteen vessels from Egypt moved towards the harbor, three large dromonds preceded by thirteen smaller *shīnīs*. The storm was so bad that the crusader ships refused to engage, but the Muslims had difficulty navigating the open, yet churning waters. Some ships collided but were still able to reach port, and two others were smashed on the rocky breakwater. A third, a galley, drifted to the shore and was taken by the crusaders, who seized its supplies and killed its sailors.[16] At around the same time, contrary winds had also forced two crusader ships ashore, where they were seized by Muslims in a similar manner.[17]

The assault on the Tower of Flies had failed, but it and the other siege works demonstrate important facets of the shifting strategy under Henry of Champagne. The crusaders had established focal points for their attack, zoning in on portions of Acre's walls, instead of simply launching direct rushes at the city. The various trebuchets and the siege galley were mechanical contrivances that depended more on engineering and creativity than had the general offensives into Saladin's ranks. The focus on the port is also intelligent: given the mutual dependence on seaborne resupply, the crusaders sought to halt Muslim resupply while simultaneously facilitating their own on the harbor shore. As Ibn Shaddād notes, he who controls the tower controls the harbor.[18] These were sensible, albeit unsuccessful, operations.

The Tower of Flies operations may also have inspired later crusaders to attempt similar feats of naval engineering. During the Fourth Crusade, the doge of Venice, Enrico Dandolo, ordered "flying bridges" attached to the masts of his ships, and the ships were protected from Greek Fire with animal skins. On 16 July 1204, those vessels crossed the Golden Horn to the harbor wall of Constantinople, returning artillery fire from the defending Byzantines with catapults of their own. When the ships reached the walls, the bridges were lowered and the crusaders soon captured a quarter of the towers on that side of the city.[19]

Although these were, arguably, "in effect, siege towers,"[20] a closer comparison with Acre would really be Damietta during the Fifth Crusade. Two galleys were lashed together to support a massive siege tower designed by the *scholasticus* Oliver of Paderborn; like the one at Acre, it was protected with animal hides to ward off naphtha attacks. On 24 August 1218, the ship was anchored to the chain tower (*Burj as-Silsilah*) at Damietta that guarded passage on the Nile, and the crusaders managed to cross the lowered gangplank, take the tower, and cut its chains.[21]

Returning to Acre, Henry of Champagne had more tricks up his sleeve. The autumn assault on the city continued after the destruction of his trebuchets and the failure to take the Tower of Flies. On 15 October, the crusaders pushed forward two enormous battering rams and began striking the stone walls. The first ram belonged to Thierry, archbishop of Besançon. It was a ship's mast tipped with iron on both ends, and it swung from ropes strung inside a moveable cat whose sides were covered with sheets (most likely strips) of iron to protect it from Muslim artillery. The front of the ram was capped with a blunt metal head. The second ram belonged to Henry himself: according to Ibn Shaddād, who would later inspect the ram personally, its head was tipped with a metal rod, better for penetrating than smashing. This ram was housed in similar fashion to Thierry's, although no mention is made of iron on the cat housing. Curiously, both rams were said to have been employed against Acre's walls, not its gates; one imagines that the tipped ram, in particular, would have been better suited for driving through wooden doors than mortared stones. Large numbers of other Christians joined in the assault: some were stationed down in Acre's moat with crossbows; others moved towards the wall, protected within cats and sows or by wooden shields; while still others carried siege ladders forward.[22]

Despite the high expense and sophisticated construction of the battering rams, the attack was unsuccessful. Although the crusaders managed to strike the walls several times, their engines were destroyed. The neutralizing of Thierry's ram, which was visually more splendid, is described well. The city defenders waited until the ram was flush with the wall – and therefore directly beneath them – and then began to bombard it. Heavy objects such as pieces of stone columns and wooden beams were dropped on top in an effort to crush the housing. Crossbow bolts flew at the cat, as the Muslims looked for vulnerable gaps. Then came the fire. First, they dropped some kindling in the form of dried-up bushes on top of the cat, and then sulfur, tar, animal fat, and pitch – basically everything combustible in their possession. These were all followed by jars of naphtha, which ignited the cat's roof and beams and eventually snaked its way to the ram itself.

When the fire spread, the ram's operators fled; on seeing this, the Muslims opened the city gates and sallied forth against the other besiegers, dashing towards their wooden coverings and also jumping into the moat to kill the missile troops. In the process, they managed to set Count Henry's battering ram on fire, although they lost eighty men in the process.[23] This second ram was not as badly damaged as Thierry's, and the weapon was captured by the Acre garrison. It was pulled into the city, where the people put out the fire, removed the metal cap from the ram, and sent it to Saladin as a souvenir.[24]

Overall, Henry of Champagne's strategy had mixed results in the short term. On the one hand, he had redirected crusader energies against Acre's defenses, which were, after all, the primary target of the army at that time. Although the continual missile strikes had not broken the wall, they had softened it in many places, and these were weak spots that could be exploited in future attacks. On the other hand, he was interested in assaulting only the walls, not the Muslim ranks outside the camp. This meant a long, static attack plan that did not involve much of the army. That is not to say that the Christian soldiers had nothing to do: defense of the ditches and ramparts remained a high priority. For example, on 2 October, Roger of Howden reported that about 4,000 Muslims streamed out of the city and used Greek Fire to burn portions of the wooden rampart. A month later, the Muslims tried again, but were repelled: held at the perimeter by soldiers led by Baldwin of Carun, Walter of Oyri, and Baldwin of Dargus, they were sent running when Count Henry and Geoffrey of Lusignan led the Knights Templar in a cavalry charge.[25]

But the lull in the offensive engagement by the bulk of the soldiers and knights is still noticeable. The issue was addressed directly by Archbishop Baldwin's chaplain in his letter to the monks at Canterbury. After reporting Baldwin's safe arrival on 16 September, the chaplain laments the moral and spiritual deficiencies of the soldiers within. Indeed, upon arriving, Baldwin himself "heard that the army had lost all discipline, concentrating on taverns, prostitutes and games of dice." But his chaplain's complaints also highlight a lack of activity on the part of the soldiers:

> The Turks besiege us; daily they incite us; continually they attack us. Our knights lurk in their tents, and those who promised a speedy victory are cowardly and slothful. As if defeated, they let the insults of the enemy go unpunished. Saladin's strength grows daily; every day our army gets smaller and fails.[26]

The letter is dated 21 October, and therefore usefully reports the state of affairs in the aftermath of the destruction of the crusader engines, which itself must be read in the context of the entire summer of 1190. The death of Frederick Barbarossa, the disaster of the St James offensive, the repeated sorties from Acre, and the (so far) failure of the siege engines had combined to reduce morale, as the army sat behind its defenses waiting for more reinforcements to arrive – particularly the tardy kings of England and France.[27] While Henry's strategy of investment was sound, the results were lackluster, and enthusiasm had waned.

In fact, the only sally taken in the early fall seems to have been a German thrust against Saladin's advance guard, which followed on the heels of Duke Frederick's arrival on 7 October. It is recorded by Ibn Shaddād, who was, of course, not in the crusader camp but claimed to have acquired information from spies and deserters. Nonetheless, he certainly captured the spirit of the camp. He relates that Frederick "reproved his fellow Christians for the length of the siege ... they warned him about venturing on this course." The Germans marched east towards Tel al-'Ayyāḍiyya and encountered Saladin's guard; news of the fighting reached the sultan, who hurriedly assembled the riders nearest him and headed for the battle. Frederick did not last long: his men were cut down after an indeterminable length of combat, and he only escaped with the coming of nightfall.[28]

### Losing the initiative

Adding to the crusader woes was the return to Acre of those Muslim allies whom Saladin had sent north the preceding June and July. Four notable magnates returned: his son, al-Ẓāhir, lord of Aleppo; Sābiq al-Dīn (Sābiq al-Dīn 'Uthmān ibn al-Dāya, lord of Shayzar); 'Izz al-Dīn of Kafarṭāb and Ba'rīn; and Majd al-Dīn of Baalbek, along with all their soldiers. Since Duke Frederick and his surviving Germans were in Acre, there was no more need for Muslim advance units to be operating in Lebanon or Asia Minor. All of them returned by 15 October, the very day of the crusaders' failed attack with their battering rams. Thus, just as the siege operations were fizzling out, the Muslim field armies were growing – it was a bad portent for the Christian army.

As it was, however, Saladin had serious problems of his own. Although he and his lords had periodically left the immediate vicinity for various reasons (such as moving north to block the Germans or retiring south on account of illness), Muslim forces had essentially been on campaign for over a year without decisive result. They had yet to break the crusader siege. Now, as winter approached yet again, the sultan was finding it difficult to hold his army together. John France has pointed to the core problem of Ayyubid military organization at the time:

Essentially [Saladin] depended upon numerous governors and warlords who, by one title or another, actually controlled the machinery of state in their areas. Their allegiance to him was always conditional and dependent upon him recognizing their interests ... Everything depended upon the interplay between local circumstances and Saladin's personal prestige at any given moment ... Great as his resources were, Saladin could not support a large standing army for long periods of time.[29]

France's analysis is self-evident at the siege of Acre. On 21 October, Saladin once again fell ill and soon elected to retire to Shafar'am, 17 kilometers south. Muslim field operations ground to a halt. In fact, he would end up losing an entire month (mid-October to mid-November) to manpower issues that had little to do with the efforts of the crusaders.

At the core of the sultan's difficulty was the bickering of his lords and a steady stream of requests for permission to leave Acre and return home. Some of these requests were due to illness, others to impatience, financial considerations, and/or frustration with the fighting at the trenches.[30] First came Zayn al-Dīn (Zayn al-Dīn Yūsuf ibn Zayn al-Dīn 'Alī ibn Baktakīn, lord of Irbil), who asked leave to depart on account of a severe fever. His request was denied, although Saladin did allow him to recuperate southeast in Nazareth, where he thereafter died.[31] Zayn al-Dīn's brother, Muẓaffar al-Dīn, had fought well at Acre, and so subsequently received control of Irbil from the sultan; but then apparently left to establish his position there. The soldiers of Irbil had occupied the center-left wing of Saladin's army, and their departure opened a gap in the line, so Saladin summoned his nephew Taqī al-Dīn back from Hama and shifted his men into it.[32] Next was 'Imād al-Dīn Zankī, lord of Sinjār. Zankī complained that he had insufficient cold-weather gear and would not be able to remain for the approaching winter, and he therefore asked for permission to return home. Saladin called his bluff by instead offering to procure winter tents, as well as extra money for his hardship. Zankī refused. A steady stream of his messengers pressed the case within the sultan's tent; Ibn Shaddād claims that he himself was forced to play the diplomat as the argument grew more heated. The matter was only settled when Saladin personally scribbled a note to Zankī: "Whoever loses such as me, would that I knew what gain he has!" The unstated message – that disobedience would have a lethal price – had the desired effect, and Zankī ceased his protestations.[33] But while the men of Sinjār remained, those of Irbil left, reducing the overall Muslim contingent from the Jazīra.

The most difficult case was that of Mu'izz al-Dīn Sanjar Shāh, the lord of al-Jazīra. He had apparently been lured to Acre by the promise of *jihad*, not any particular monetary gain; but the lack of total victory over the Christians had left him frustrated. Throughout the Ramadan fast he sought permission to leave, via messengers, but his requests were all denied. On Eid al-Fitr (31 October), he appeared in front of Saladin's tent in person and demanded entrance, but he was rebuffed when the sultan once again ordered him to remain in camp. Sanjar Shāh left camp and left for home anyway, contrary to Saladin's wishes. He took his soldiers with him: the accounts differ as to whether he had ordered them to begin packing before or after he met with the sultan.[34] This would have been a difficult loss for the Muslim armies. The men from al-Jazīra, including various territories ruled by Sanjar Shāh, probably totaled around 4,000; since those from Irbil had already left, this new departure was another important reduction in manpower. Moreover, Sanjar Shah's temerity was conspicuous and, given the previous departures of other lords, might have inspired further defections.

As it was, however, he was corralled back into obedience. Saladin first tried to bring him back with a threat, sending a letter after him that contained the warning, "guard yourself against whoever may attack you. I have no longer any concern for your welfare." Sanjar Shāh received and read these words but was apparently unmoved and trekked on. Near the town of Fīq, which lies a few miles east of Lake Tiberias, he crossed paths with Taqī al-Dīn.[35] The latter was returning to Acre from Hama and, after hearing the story, urged him to return to the sultan. Sanjar Shāh, however, repeated his complaint, until Taqī al-Dīn condescendingly dressed him down. Telling Sanjar Shāh, "you are a child and you do not know the disaster that can come from this," he forced him to return to Acre. Once there, Saladin issued a pardon, but the lord of al-Jazīra wisely asked to remain encamped near Taqī al-Dīn, whom he now saw as a benefactor – and probably a buffer against the sultan's anger and resentment as well.[36]

Although the matter seemed settled, such disobedience and disrespect did not bode well for Muslim unity. Even after Sanjar Shāh had received his pardon, Saladin took it upon himself to write a letter to 'Izz al-Dīn Mas'ūd ibn Mawdūd ibn Zankī, the Atabeg lord of Mosul and Sanjar Shāh's own uncle. Saladin commanded him to besiege his nephew's lands in Jazīrat in Mesopotamia. 'Izz al-Dīn obeyed: the siege commenced in late March 1191 and lasted four months, ending only with a peace conference between him and his nephew in which the territory was divided in half.[37] Thus did the impatience of Saladin's magnates cause ancillary disputes and conflicts elsewhere. Moreover, the root problem of extended service duties halted any progress he might have made against the crusader camp.

## The St Martin offensive

The Muslims had lost the initiative, but could the Christians capitalize? Their own numbers remained limited because the kings of France and England had not yet arrived. The fleets of both Richard (departing from Marseille) and Philip (from Genoa) had arrived in Sicily in September 1190, but once there Richard swiftly became embroiled in two disputes over marriage issues. The first was the dower to his sister Joan from her recently deceased husband King

William II of Sicily, which his successor, Tancred of Lecce, inherited but refused to turn over.[38] The second was Richard's own betrothal to Alice, the half-sister of Philip Augustus. The king sought a release from the engagement, in order to be married instead to Berengaria, the daughter of King Sancho VI of Navarre.[39] These disputes led to violence, including Richard's seizure of two monasteries and a riot in the streets of Messina by citizens who believed the king was trying to take Sicily entirely. Richard personally fought the rioters and found ways to settle the other affairs to his advantage. All these matters took time to sort out, and both kings ended up wintering in Sicily.[40] The major infusions of men and supplies offered by the French and English fleets were thus delayed and would not arrive in the Holy Land until spring and summer 1191, respectively.

Nonetheless, some of the Christians at Acre were ready to press ahead with campaigning. In mid-November, a portion of the crusaders departed camp and marched toward Saladin's lines. The result was a four-day, looping march south towards Haifa and then back north to Acre, dubbed by John Pryor as "one of the most curious incidents of the entire siege" that "seems to have had no point" (Map 3).[41] The march began on Monday, 12 November, the day after the feast of St Martin of Tours, and seems to have had multiple causes, including boredom and/or exasperation with the siege's lack of progress, a desire to engage the Muslims in combat, or a general frustration over the shortage of food and/or money. Ibn Shaddād also claims that the crusaders had caught wind of Saladin's illness and subsequent withdrawal to Shafar'am.[42] None of these causes were mutually exclusive.

Unlike the disaster on the feast of St James, this army was commanded by several Christian elites. Count Henry of Champagne led the march, and he was accompanied by Conrad of Montferrat, Geoffrey of Lusignan, and Bishop Hubert Walter of Salisbury. Others remained to protect the camp: Duke Frederick of Swabia, Count Theobald of Blois, Patriarch Heraclius of Jerusalem, and

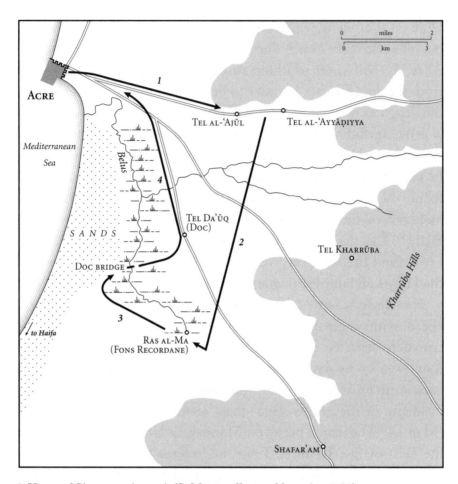

3. Henry of Champagne's march (St Martin offensive, November 1190).

Archbishop Baldwin of Canterbury.[43] In the army were contingents of Knights Templar and Hospitaller and 200 knights and 300 men-at-arms provided by Baldwin; Roger of Howden also mentions the presence of the Normans Baldwin of Carun, Walter of Oyri, and Baldwin of Dargus, but the complete size of the assembled men is unknown. Four days' worth of provisions was brought along. The status of its leaders and the presence of the military orders suggest that this was no mere foraging expedition: the crusaders expected, even sought, hostile contact along the way. The St Martin march was an offensive that sought not only to capture much-needed supplies, but also to hand a defeat to the Muslims encircling the Acre plain. A general blessing and absolution was given over the crusaders before their departure, led by Baldwin and the other bishops present.[44]

Given the course of the River Belus, the army could not simply march south to Haifa. They had two choices: either head immediately south toward the river crossing at the Bridge of Doc (*Da'ūq*) or march first east and then south. The first option posed significant danger: after crossing the bridge, the crusaders would have been trapped against Haifa Bay. Moreover, there were fewer enemy combatants there: the closest enemies were in fact the Muslim advance force stationed due east of Acre at Tel al-'Ayyāḍiyya. Looking for a fight, the crusaders therefore marched east.[45] South in Shafar'am, Saladin received news of the muster within the crusader camp and ordered two adjustments: he ordered the advance guard to withdraw farther east to Tel Kaysān and he also sent his own heavy baggage farther south to al-Qaymūn.[46] The Acre garrison also reacted: no sooner had the crusaders departed than the city gates opened and the Muslims attacked the camp defenses. Periodic fighting along the trenches continued for most of the week, only ceasing when Count Henry returned four days later.[47]

The marching crusaders arrived at the wells at Tel al-'Ajūl just as the Muslim advance guard was in the process of repositioning, and the western sources naturally interpreted the move as weakness, "the action of a beaten and despairing mind."[48] More likely, the Muslims were once again widening the operating zone of their enemies in an attempt to goad them farther into hostile territory, where they could then be surrounded and destroyed. There seems to have been only a small skirmish at Tel al-'Ajūl and the Muslims lobbed some flaming arrows in the Christians' direction.[49] The Christians then pitched tents for the night. On the morning of Tuesday, 13 November, they broke camp and turned south. Ambroise explains why: "When they did not get a battle they turned towards Caiphas [Haifa] where there was said to be food, of which there was a shortage among the besiegers."[50]

In other words, the army's first goal was contact with the enemy, not foraging. Once a quick battle was denied, Count Henry shifted the mission to a journey for supplies and food south in Haifa. The crusaders marched with the Belus near their right (west) flank and encountered the bulk of Saladin's army at Recordane (Tel Kurdani). The point of contact was near the head of the river, where the Muslims had blocked the passage south.[51]

The Muslims were stationed in their typical left, center, and right divisions. On the right were Saladin himself, commanding from behind, his brother al-ʿĀdil and the cavalry from Egypt, along with Ḥusām al-Dīn ibn Lājīn (lord of Nablus), the *tawashi* Qaymāz, ʿIzz al-Dīn, Ḥusām al-Dīn Bishāra (lord of Banyas), Badr al-Dīn Dildirim al-Yārūqī (lord of Tel Bāshir), and other unnamed emirs. On the left wing, by the river, was Taqī al-Dīn, along with the men of Sinjār, and with him the aforementioned deserter Sanjar Shāh; they were accompanied by tribal members of the Mihrānī and Hakkārī Kurdish emirs, including al-Mashṭūb. The center was split between Saladin's royal guard, at left-center, and his sons al-Afḍāl, al-Ẓāhir, and al-Ẓāfir Khiḍr at right-center. Reserves occupied the Kharrūba Hills and skirmishers fronted the main ranks.[52]

The details of the ensuing battle are not well reported, and there is no information on the disposition of the Christian army. The crusaders were apparently undaunted by the size of Saladin's force, which suggests that they had enough men to somewhat match it. Certainly, had the odds been overwhelming, Count Henry could simply have wheeled around and marched back north towards Acre, knowing that only the Muslim advance guard at Tel Kaysān might prevent his progress. Instead, he chose to engage, and no doubt the severe lack of food back at camp influenced his decision. Saladin's skirmishers and advanced guard assailed the crusaders with missiles as they pushed forward, moving towards the river head.[53] Essentially,

Henry was trying to outflank the Muslim left, not to win a victory, but rather to clear the river and access another route to Haifa. He pushed through the enemy ranks in a classic crusading "fighting march" and kept his soldiers from engaging fully:

> Having seen this, they crossed to the west of the river, while the advance guard kept up a close quarters battle. The Franks had gathered together, holding close to one another. The aim of the advance guard was that the Franks should charge them, so that the Muslims could meet them, the battle be fully engaged and lead to a decision, allowing the men to rest.[54]

'Imād al-Dīn quips that the Muslims "introduced them to the laws and customs of holy war," but the crusaders nonetheless held formation, rounded the river head, and encamped there for the night.[55] Saladin countered by shrewdly shifting his lines. He placed his left wing next to Haifa Bay and his center in front of the crusader position, which cut off the southern route Henry was trying to reach. The sultan then bent his right wing perpendicular to his center, creating a roughly ninety-degree angle of soldiers to prevent the Christians from retreating back from where they had marched.[56]

The crusaders awoke on Wednesday morning to find themselves trapped. Equally disappointing must have been the intelligence Henry had received that the Muslims had carried off the purported food supply at Haifa, which suddenly rendered his entire expedition meaningless.[57] The only road now open to him was to the north, passing between Haifa Bay and the Belus. Thus began a fighting retreat to the north: "The pilgrims turned to return to the place whence they had come, but they would have many attacks before they got back to their tents."[58]

As morning broke, Saladin began arranging his soldiers for renewed combat, with skirmishers again in front and the main cavalry bodies behind them. Likewise, the crusaders had prepared, and no doubt Henry of Champagne expected an immediate return to the fighting. Henry actually seized the initiative and attacked first, driving south into the Muslim lines, probably in an effort to create some buffer space between the armies, so that the crusaders could conduct a safer retreat. The tactic worked: the Muslims refused to commit fully, and as the fighting ebbed, the Christians began their withdrawal.[59] Moving north, they marched with the swollen river and its outlying marshes on their right; across the Belus they were tracked by Saladin's pivoted right wing, and the rest of the Muslims pursued them from behind.[60]

Taking fire from both south and east, the Christian retreat again took the form of the classic fighting march, with one important adjustment. The best soldiers were placed in the rearguard; in this case, this meant English infantry and dismounted Knights Templar. These men formed a protective wall on foot, while their horses were walked in the center of the army; they were accompanied by groups of missile troops as well. Marching backwards, they fended off showers of bolts and arrows: "for God never created storm of snow or hail, nor shower in the dews of May, which fell more heavily than the storm of bolts that fell on the army."[61] The enemy fire was severe and the many crusaders who were killed were buried along the way, with their fellows in the front ranks quickly digging holes to be filled as the army moved north.[62]

The burials are emblematic of a coordinated, competent, and efficient march. The retrieval of the dead and wounded took time and slowed the retreat, but such seems to have been the goal all along. The Christians deliberately reduced their pace to ensure good order, knowing that units left stranded ran the risk of being cut off and destroyed. Given the close-quarters action (Ibn al-Athīr notes both missile and melee combat) and the size of the pursuit (Ibn Shaddād claims that Saladin kept feeding soldiers into the pursuit, even to the detriment of his own personal guard), their ability to stave off panic was impressive.[63] To achieve a steady pace, the army rallied around a standard, most likely a Templar banner, mounted atop a tall pole and pulled on a mule-cart. The standard was key to preventing a rout because it not only served as a physical rallying point but also inspired the soldiers to keep fighting.[64] 'Imād al-Dīn indicates that the army moved slowly and steadily, covering only about 3 kilometers, but it held together under what has been called "the fiercest field action since Ḥaṭṭīn."[65] The crusaders refused to leave their ranks to charge, but remained disciplined, fighting and dying, "impassive and silent," until they finally reached the bridge and encamped for the night. Saladin did not order a night attack, probably thinking that the chance of stranding his men between the Christians and the river was an unnecessary risk.[66]

The next morning, Thursday, 15 November, the crusaders struck camp and, making their way to the Doc bridge, found the crossing blocked. After unsuccessfully trying to destroy the structure the night before, Muslim soldiers had stationed themselves upon it.[67] The Christians attacked and eventually broke through when Geoffrey of Lusignan and five fellow knights charged and scattered the front ranks of defenders, knocking thirty of them into the Belus. The other crusaders moved forward and in time the entire army reached the east bank. After everyone had crossed, they destroyed the bridge and thereby stranded some two-thirds of Saladin's army (the former left wing and center) across the river.[68] From there, the army made its way back to the camp outside Acre with little further incident.[69]

The Arabic sources refrain from criticizing Saladin's failure to crush the St Martin offensive, choosing instead to attribute it to his illness. Neither do they applaud the pluck of his adversaries. But credit must be given to Count Henry's leadership, tactics, and the professionalism of the men under his command. Certainly, the march towards Haifa can be read as foolhardy: even accepting the dire food shortage in the crusader camp, one can readily question why the logistical phase of the march was directed south – straight at Saladin's main body – and not north or east. Leaving that strategic question aside, however, there is no doubt that Henry led a brilliant, disciplined retreat over the course of two days and while under heavy assault.[70] He saved his army and, by virtue of doing so, saved the crusade. Without the thousands of soldiers under his command, the remainder of the crusading army outside Acre would not have lasted long. Even during the retreat itself, Saladin was ordering more garrison attacks on the camp, and still more followed into the winter of 1190.[71] By year's end, the full complement of crusaders remained strong and confident enough to launch an assault against Acre on New Year's Eve.[72] Once again, Saladin had caught the beast, only to watch it slip through his trap to fight another day.

In the wake of the Christians' escape, the Muslims returned to smaller-scale provocations. More attempts were made to goad the crusaders out of their fortifications. On 23 November, the technique seems to have worked. Saladin sent a detachment of riders to the hilly landscape north of Montmusard, where they lay in wait as other skirmishers rode at the crusader perimeter and showered the soldiers there with arrows into the evening. The next morning, a group of cavalry numbering perhaps between 200 and 400 rode out to locate the archers and promptly fell into the trap. The Arabic sources differ on just how many knights died; while Ibn al-Athīr claims that all of them were killed, Ibn Shaddād spills significant ink on describing those who were taken prisoner. Two prisoners are identified as both the treasurer and commander of Philip Augustus' men. If true, this may refer to French Templar knights: in 1190, Philip moved his treasury to the Paris Temple, and in 1202 his treasurer was a Templar, Brother Haimar. He claims they were taken south to meet with Saladin himself and then sent on to Damascus, where they were permitted to correspond by letter with their fellows back at Acre.[73]

But were the Arabic authors telling the truth? The violence of 24 November is also reported in the western sources, but their version is radically different from that of their counterparts, none of whom were witnesses (Ibn al-Athīr was in Mosul and both Ibn Shaddād and 'Imād al-Dīn were in attendance with Saladin south in al-Kharrūba). The story, in fact, revolves around a wedding. Queen Sibylla, Guy of Lusignan's wife and queen of Jerusalem, had died inside the crusader camp in either September or October.[74] Given that his claim to the throne came through her, Guy's political position instantly became precarious. Conrad of Montferrat, who had already schemed to secure the kingdom for himself, took advantage. On 24 November, he married the new heiress, Sibylla's half-sister, Isabella.[75] The union was controversial because it was wholly polygamous: Conrad was already married (probably to two women, one in Italy and the other in Constantinople) and so was Isabella, to Humphrey III of Toron. Archbishop Baldwin of Canterbury had fought against the proposed union and was supported in this by other ecclesiastics, such as Patriarch Heraclius. Unfortunately, Baldwin died on 19 November and the patriarch soon followed.[76] Conrad's allies moved to support him. Philip, bishop of Beauvais, and Archbishop Ubaldo of Pisa, the papal legate, both got involved: Isabella's marriage to Humphrey was annulled, Bishop Philip married her to Conrad, and Conrad's other marriages were simply ignored.[77] The fighting described by Ibn Shaddād thus took place within this political context.

The wedding reception lasted long into the night of 24 November. Some of the intoxicated knights decided to hold a mock tournament beyond the camp ramparts. During the fun and games, or perhaps as the guests staggered home afterward, these knights were ambushed by Muslim riders and many were killed. Ambroise claims that twenty men were either captured or killed, including Guy III, the butler of Senlis.[78] This is a very different story from the Arabic version. The marriage of Conrad and Isabella is an historical fact and was reported beyond the Levant, as were the political repercussions of it.[79] It thus seems more likely that the Muslim writers had heard about an ambush – which did, in fact, occur – but amplified the story with erroneous details. The religious rhetoric in the accounts is heavy, and one might reasonably wonder if they were glorifying a trite event in order to distract from the disappointment over the crusaders' escape from the Doc bridge.

## A desperate winter

Newly married, Conrad and Isabella set off for Tyre, with the marquis promising that he would immediately send ships full of supplies to the hungry crusaders. He never followed through, and despite the Christian authors' attempts to be charitable (suggesting that, perhaps, he had only forgotten), it is clear that most in the camp believed him guilty of outright duplicity.[80] The resulting famine would become profound in the new year, and all blame would fall upon the marquis. Conrad's poor historical reputation is thus based not only on his cynical politicking but also on his abandonment of his fellows before Acre. Compounding the issue were the winter winds and cold. By December, the western ships were once again forced to seek safer confines due to the rough Mediterranean waves; they departed for Tyre, Tripoli, or safe harbors farther west.

Saladin once again granted the bulk of his soldiers and their commanders a winter rest. The crusaders would be marked for the season principally by the royal guard and the men of a few emirs. Several lords immediately departed for their own lands: 'Imād al-Dīn, lord of Sinjār, and his nephew Sanjar Shāh, who had caused such a stir in the fall, both departed laden with gifts from the sultan; 'Alā' al-Dīn Khurramshāh left for Mosul before the new year. Taqī al-Dīn, Muẓaffar al-Dīn, and Saladin's son al-Ẓāhir waited a little longer, leaving between late January and early March.[81]

After the crusader ships departed, Acre's port was once again opened to the Muslims, and its garrison and citizens finally received some material relief. Saladin recognized that the garrison in Acre had been under arms for too long. However, he could not simply give

it a break, because the crusaders would undoubtedly attack an undefended town. Instead, at the request of Acre's commander Emir
Ḥusām (the same man whose testicles had purportedly been immolated by naphtha), he chose to swap out the soldiers there. Saladin
sent his brother al-ʿĀdil to the Haifa shore, where seven ships were
filled with a year's worth of food, money, and supplies, as well as fresh
reinforcements; these were then shipped to Acre and, once unloaded,
refilled with garrison soldiers and returned to Haifa. This occurred
on 31 December. Only six of the seven ships completed the journey,
for one was wrecked near Acre, killing sixty men.[82]

The material assistance to Acre was obvious and necessary, but
whether or not the garrison needed to be relieved is an open question. In his account of the seaborne activity, Ibn al-Athīr gives an
overt critique of this aspect of Saladin's strategy. We must keep in
mind that he was writing with the benefit of hindsight, and of course
his anti-Saladin inclinations have already been noted. Still, his criti-
cisms are worth pondering. First, he points to a steep drop-off in
leadership. He claims that sixty emirs left Acre, but were replaced by
only twenty, implying that the garrison would be less effectively led
in 1191. Further, he criticizes two of these newly arrived emirs (the
Kurd al-Mashṭūb and ʿIzz al-Dīn Arsul, commander of the Asadiyya,
the mamluks of Shirkuh), complaining that they were negligent in
carrying out sallies against the Christians. Second, Ibn al-Athīr
believed that Saladin should have left the original garrison in place,
for it was more experienced at repelling the Christian attacks. Fresh
supplies were all that was required to bolster their efforts. The author
claims that Saladin had actually received such advice, but refused it,
wrongly believing that the men were too tired to continue.[83]
Determining the truth of the matter is difficult. As will be seen,
Acre's garrison would indeed operate less effectively in 1191 than it
had in 1190; but attributing this to a lack of leadership and experience requires us to ignore a whole host of other causes that will be
examined in depth in the next chapter.

The Christian leaders observed the approach of the Muslim ships and the great movement of Acre's defenders down to the port to receive them. Moving rapidly, the crusaders launched a general assault on Acre's walls. Ibn Shaddād pins the fighting between New Year's Eve and 5 January 1191. On 31 December, the crusaders employed siege ladders: these were first brought down into the trenches and then, at the moment of attack, carried forward and placed against the city walls. The garrison responded by sallying out of the gates and rushing the trenches, where several of the ladders were tied to ropes and dragged away before they could be moved into place. Another ladder collapsed. As one particular ladder was being pulled away, four knights (Ralph of Tilly, Humphrey of Veilly, Robert of Lalande, and Roger of Glanville) jumped on top of it and so weighed it down that the Muslims could not drag it any farther. Their fellows atop the walls, therefore, responded by dropping jars of Greek Fire. Howden claims that the knights extinguished the fire four times before Ralph was finally able to slash the ropes and save the ladder.[84]

Suffice to say, this latest crusader attack on Acre – and the last attack of 1190 – initially seemed to have achieved little. But just five days later matters changed abruptly when a section of the city wall collapsed right in front of the Christians' eyes, in the process taking down one of the barbicans overhanging a gate. The location of the collapse is not identified, and nor is it known why it fell, but a reasonable guess is that it was a section that had been weakened by the artillery assaults of earlier in the year.[85] The crusaders, hardly believing their good fortune, immediately took advantage. Rushing forward, they poured towards the gap and tried to enter the city. The Muslim garrison, which had only been in residence for a few days at that point, responded admirably and managed to defend the breach with missile weapons, while masons worked hurriedly to repair and rebuild it.[86]

The writing was on the wall, so to speak: Saladin's apparent comfort with the status quo was becoming risky. Ibn al-Athīr's aforementioned criticism forces us to consider, once again, that Saladin's strategic choices at Acre do not accord with his modern reputation. The sultan had wasted multiple opportunities in 1190 to dispense with the Christian threat, and the artillery barrage on the city walls was beginning to have some real impact. He would pay dearly for his mistakes, and would lose Acre entirely, in the next year.

V

# THE SIEGE CONCLUDES
*1191*

*"This was the first sign that the city was going to be taken and overcome."*[1]

The siege of Acre had now lasted a year and a half, and as 1191 dawned the city sat in a precarious state. Its garrison was new and less familiar with the routine procedures of defense, a portion of the city wall had collapsed, and the enemy remained camped outside, despite Saladin's best efforts to dislodge them. Had those Christians been well supplied, they might have pressed the advantage and taken Acre, even during the cold months. But in fact the opposite was the case: severe shortages of food had brought famine, disease, and a corresponding halt to military operations. Christian efforts against the city ceased completely, and there are no recorded initiatives at all until 31 March, after the start of spring. In the meantime, they withered away in front of the city that had so far frustrated their ambitions and, they believed, the very desires of God.

The suffering in the crusader camp was evident to both sides. The Christian authors place most of the blame for the famine on a single person: Conrad of Montferrat. Although the marquis had fought well at Acre, his personal and political maneuvering soon earned him opprobrium among the rank and file. Specifically, he had returned north to Tyre after his controversial wedding, but never shipped back the food and supplies he had promised. Ambroise assails him by inserting a repeating refrain into his anecdotes of the crusaders' suffering: "Then they cursed the marquis who had brought them to this sorry pass."[2] Richard of Templo, imitating him, went further by adding dramatic poetic flourishes for each particular sin:

Then they curse and damn the marquis, / Who stole their consolation / He cheated of their food those / In danger of starvation.

Then hear the voice of the people cursing / The marquis' perfidy, / For he's indifferent to their suffering / And all their misery.

Then they curse and damn the marquis, / Transgressor of his word, / And call evil down upon him, / And deadly woe.

So what do they wish for the marquis, / All these complaining voices? / Certainly all would pronounce him guilty / Of causing so many dangers![3]

For all the outrage, however, both authors tell of other factors that caused such appalling suffering. These include not only lack of food but also illness, injury, mud and muck, and the cold. The constant exposure to the elements was taking its toll, as was the weariness of being encamped in one place for so long. Disease, which Malcolm Barber has identified as either scurvy or severe gingivitis, caused people's faces and legs to swell and their teeth to fall out.[4] Beyond this specific condition, the soldiers would have been susceptible to any number of other maladies, given the length of their exposure to the elements: dysentery, fevers, malaria, or trachoma (an eye infection spread by flies).[5]

At this point, the authors again take a moment to run through the prices of food. Already expensive, the cost of basic items had gone up again. This was due to the usual dearth of ships sailing to Acre in the winter months as well as the particularly bad weather and the loss of those Christians ships that had been seized. Still, it is interesting that in 1191 some prices were comparable to (or lower than) those during the shortages of 1190 – for example, eggs (which in 1191 were 0.085–1 bezant apiece, compared to 0.17 bezants in 1190) or chickens (which could be had for 2–24 bezants in 1191, as against 10 bezants in 1190).

Given that thousands more crusaders were now encamped before Acre, this is an odd problem. Contributing factors may have included the aforementioned shipments sold by Muslims, which kept the food supply higher, or perhaps the crusaders had been planting enough herbs and root vegetables the previous year. Some of the scarcity driving the price increases was due to hoarding, as those with extra food concealed it from others instead of selling it.[6] Merchants were also artificially raising prices, although Ambroise claims that divine justice was visited on one such seller from Pisa, whose grain storage caught fire and burned down, consuming all the food within. Once again, horse meat and horse entrails were eaten, with chunks costing ten sous apiece.[7] These foods were supplemented with grass (when it could be found, as the ground was stamped down in most of the camp), mashed-together herbs, carob beans (*ceratonia siliqua*, which grow on trees in edible pods), nuts, and large amounts of wine, which unlike food, seems to have been in ample supply. Some men tried to sustain themselves on wine alone and "died in threes and fours." Soldiers gnawed on old bones that had even been rejected by the dogs, while others searched for the carcasses of dead animals "like vultures to a corpse."[8]

Food was expensive enough for people to resort to desperate measures to appropriate it. Some of the more elite crusaders were said to have been reduced to begging and even stealing on occasion, although it is an open question whether such was reality or rather moralizing on the part of the sources.[9] Bread, in particular, was highly prized, and two stories are related about it. In one, a crowd pestered a baker to sell a fresh loaf and the scene became an auction, with pieces selling to the highest bidders. Only the rich could afford the exorbitant prices, leaving the poorer soldiers with nothing, and the scene descended into violence.[10] In the other, an anonymous nobleman tried to steal some bread but was apprehended by the baker, who tied him to a chair and then left to call the guards. The man managed to wriggle out of his restraints, there and then ate some of the bread in the baker's house, and then escaped, although not before grabbing another loaf.[11] Even carob beans were costly. In another story, two friends walked across 7 acres of the camp to buy thirteen beans with their last remaining coin. After trekking home, they discovered that one of the beans had spoiled, so they returned to the seller to demand an exchange.[12]

Other crusaders simply walked away, either deserting to the Muslims or wandering off into the Acre plain. Sometime in early 1191, Hubert Walter wrote a letter to Richard, bishop of London, describing the conditions in the camp that year, and we are fortunate that Ralph of Diss copied it into his chronicle *Ymagines historiarum*. In the letter, Hubert explains that many crusaders simply could not be compelled to stay: they do not seem to have lost faith in the cause, but rather had run out of money, were tired of the constant work and fighting, or were suffering from illness. The magnates and prelates implored them to stay by offering bribes, special pleas, and even threats, but nothing worked. So off they walked to parts unknown. Desertions earned the ire of crusade authors in general, for such men were not simply leaving a campaign but rather a holy quest and, as such, were denounced in harsh and even violent language.[13]

More troublesome were those men who defected to the Muslims. Ibn Shaddād claims that one group of deserters actually offered to fight for Saladin and split with him half of whatever booty they could capture. On 11 January, Saladin lent them a ship: they attacked what Christian vessels they could find and brought him back booty of silver coins and a silver table. Saladin was apparently so pleased that he allowed the traitors to keep everything. Added to this was the apparent capture by Muslim sailors of three ships that may have been trying to sail into Acre despite the contrary weather on 22–23 January. Some 250 and their cargo were seized, which only added to the frustration of the starving Christians.[14]

Ambroise claims that some of the deserting crusaders not only joined the enemy but also rejected the Christian faith, denying the Incarnation, the Crucifixion, and the efficacy of baptism.[15] This would have been the worst lot of all, for they abandoned the siege, their fellows, and their religion in a desperate attempt to stay alive. Other accusations of treason had periodically been leveled at Christians; for example, that Saladin had tried to bribe some of the crusaders defending the ditches into allowing Muslim penetration of the lines, and that some had accepted gifts of money, as well as hawks, leopards, and camels.[16]

At one point, Hubert Walter, Archbishop Ubaldo of Pisa, and Bishop Monaldus of Fano organized a collection on behalf of the poorest crusaders. They gave sermons and persuaded those who were better off to donate money to a common pot, from which it was dispersed to those who could not afford food. This mainly benefitted the common soldiers, but lesser knights gained, too, as the monies were distributed according to need. Roger of Howden claims that the collection was sufficient to tide the army over until seaborne shipments of food began arriving again in the spring. Ambroise names Henry of Champagne, Count Ralph of Clermont, and the knights Walchelin of Ferrieres-St Hilary, Robert Trussebot, and Joscelin of Montoire as the most charitable givers.[17]

The famine lasted through the end of Lent (in 1191, Easter was on 14 April) and the death toll among the crusaders was high. The Germans seem to have been hit particularly hard. Ansbert reports that many fell to disease, including Frederick of Swabia himself, that "most ardent athlete of God and terror of the Saracens": surely an overly kind posthumous compliment, given how little success he had seen in battle.[18] Both Theobald of Blois and Henry of Champagne became dangerously ill as well, and Theobald eventually died from his sickness.[19] The mortality rate must have been high, although the numbers in the sources seem exorbitant. Ibn Shaddād claims to have read reports stating that 100–200 Christians were dying every day, which, if correct, would amount to over 9,000 dead by the end of Lent. Given that by springtime the crusaders were able to operate in significant military capacities, this number seems overly (but not impossibly) high. Richard of Templo's figures are even more fantastic: a thousand dead every single day! Such a death rate would have eradicated the army entirely within a month and cannot be believed. More reasonable is William of Newburgh's generalization that the army was diminished daily, but its numbers were speedily replaced by the coming springtime reinforcements from Europe.[20]

Most of the fatalities of the winter of 1191 were due to starvation and illness, and there had been little in the way of fighting since a portion of Acre's walls had collapsed on 5 January. A stray western vessel was driven ashore on 2 March and its crew of fifteen captured. On 31 March, the royal guard skirmished with some crusaders, losing a man named Qāraqūsh in the process (not the emir, Bahā' al-Dīn al-Asadī Qāraqūsh). On 6 April, Saladin tried to lure some crusaders into an ambush behind Tel al-'Ayyāḍiyya. The sultan himself may have been there, along with his son al-Afḍāl and three of his grandsons; also present was the writer and *qāḍī* Ibn Shaddād himself. On the scene as a witness, the latter reports that the Muslims were unable to lure any crusaders out of camp.[21] No other conflict is reported between the Muslims and Christians between January and March.

After Easter, ships finally began to arrive from the west, bringing relief to the suffering Christians. The first was a single boatload of grain, which made port on a Saturday afternoon: its cargo instantly brought down prices from a hundred bezants to just four (for an unspecified amount).[22] Other ships brought fresh reinforcements.

The most notable was a group of Germans, who had been waiting at Zara on the Adriatic for the weather to turn favorable. This group included Duke Leopold of Austria and Count Siegfried of Moerl, as well as several of the duke's *ministeriales*, all of whom ended their lives at Acre.[23]

Of course, the better weather was a boon to the Muslims as well. Reinforcements started arriving even before Easter, on 7 April, and included both Majd al-Dīn of Baalbek, who had left for the winter rest, and 'Alam al-Dīn Sulaymān ibn Jandar, an emir from Aleppo who was loyal to Saladin's son al-Ẓāhir. 'Alam al-Dīn was a particular asset, for Ibn Shaddād credits him with having significant military experience. Unfortunately, Saladin also lost one of his most steadfast allies at about the same time. His nephew Taqī al-Dīn had returned to Syria in March to check in on his lands in Hama and Edessa and also to recruit soldiers for Acre's relief. After gathering nearly 4,000 cavalry (not all new recruits – many were likely on their winter rest), he marched west but was stricken with illness after crossing the River Euphrates and died before making it back to Acre. The cavalry dispersed and Saladin therefore lost not only a sizable contingent of soldiers, but also one of his closest confidants.[24]

## Philip Augustus

On 20 April 1191, King Philip II Augustus of France arrived in Acre. His highly anticipated arrival, which had been delayed by both the season and the numerous political issues in Sicily, is reported in every major source of the Third Crusade and brought instant relief to the beleaguered Christian army. He came with six ships laden with his own personal retinue, food and supplies, and soldiers and horses. Accompanying him were several French elites: Philip d'Alsace, count of Flanders; Hugh, duke of Burgundy; Hugh IV, count of St Pol; Rotrou III, count of Perche; and several knights, as well as Conrad of Montferrat, his ally. Perhaps we should not be surprised that the account of Rigord celebrates his arrival the most: Philip was received like "an angel of the Lord" with weeping and songs. Rigord, a physician and monk at St Denis, discusses the siege in his *Gesta Philippi Augusti* but primarily during the period of Philip's involvement, between April and July 1191.[25] The Lyon *Eracles* speaks of a magnificent reception for the exalted king. Ambroise, a Norman, was more muted, but still valorized the king and his companions. The other western authors are less verbose, simply recording his arrival and in a tone that one could read as "what took you so long?" The Arabic accounts are mixed: Ibn Shaddād calls Philip a "great man and respected leader"; Ibn al-Athīr writes of his impressive ships, but also points out that there were only six and that "his kingdom was not a great one." Philip of Flanders, in fact, was accorded respect equal to that of the king because he was a known quantity: he had been in Syria during the action at Mont Gisart on 25 November 1177, in which Baldwin IV "the Leper King" of Jerusalem defeated Saladin in open battle.[26] Nonetheless, all sources agreed that Philip Augustus' arrival greatly bolstered the morale of the camp.

Just as importantly, Philip was a man of action. His behavior upon arriving at Acre was all business: he rode through the camp and circled around the city, examining the arrangement and state of the walls. He then situated his own tents precariously close to the walls and, Rigord claims, within range of the garrison.[27] He was impatient; the *Eracles* author puts a poignant and obvious complaint in his mouth: "Considering how many nobleman have been at this siege, it is extraordinary how slow they have been to take it [the city]."[28]

Such an assessment was obvious. There had been only a few extended phases of concerted attacks upon the city walls, with the rest of the time at Acre having been spent on fruitless and/or disastrous offensives, combined with a lot of off-season downtime filled with supply issues and mass illness and starvation. On the other hand, as a new arrival, Philip did not yet appreciate the difficulty of besieging a city such as Acre, while simultaneously fending off attacks from Saladin's army. He would learn soon enough.

Philip ordered a reopening of the siege. Construction of siege works began, and on 30 May seven new trebuchets began to shoot projectiles at the Ox Spring Tower over one of Acre's eastern gates. Rigord refers to them as "*petrariis et mangonellis et aliis ingeniis*": *petrariae* and *mangonelli* are both terms that refer to hand-pulled lever engines, or "traction-trebuchets," depending on their period of use, but Rigord's use of both terms together may suggest two different types of engine.[29] The *aliis ingeniis* ("other engines") to which he refers included iron-covered screens used to protect the archers, whom the king had ordered to maintain ready fire at any person seen moving atop the walls, and a Welsh cat. The cat was placed against the wall adjacent to the Cursed Tower, where Acre's northern and eastern walls met, and under it sappers began to dig a tunnel towards the wall.[30] In addition, efforts to fill in the moat were renewed (so that rams and towers could be moved again towards the walls), and Ibn Shaddād claims the crusaders used the bodies of their dead horses, as well as their own deceased and mortally wounded comrades, to speed this task.

There is an anecdote demonstrating this macabre notion. A Christian woman was hit with a bolt while helping to fill Acre's moat with stones. She begged her husband to bury her by placing her in the moat so that it might be filled more quickly. Her devotion was highly inspirational to the authors:

> O admirable faith of the weaker sex! O zeal of woman worthy of imitation! Even after death she did not cease to work with the workers, for even when dying she wished to continue her work.[31]

The story is also indicative of the renewed morale in the camp. Philip's arrival and swift action evidently inspired the crusaders and gave them the first serious hope of victory since winter.

The Muslim garrison responded ably. It concentrated its missile fire at the trebuchets, attempted to set the cat on fire, and sent teams of men into the moat to chop up and remove the bodies filling it.[32] But their efforts were in vain because the Pisan sappers managed to tunnel underneath the wall, prop it up with timbers from below, and, setting fire to the wood, collapse the stones themselves. The crusaders immediately charged at the breach: led by Philip's marshal Aubery Clement, a host of Frenchmen fought through the wall and actually entered the city for a time until they were driven back out by the Muslims, who then hastily rebuilt the wall from within.[33]

Given Philip's arrival and the renewal of the siege, as well as the arrival of even more French forces in early summer, Saladin decided to move north and closer to Acre.[34] He left Shafar'am on 4 June and arrived at al-Kharrūba, still south of the action but close enough for his army to resume its customary raiding of the crusader camp while remaining in close contact with him. Over the course of two days, Saladin ordered attacks against their ramparts, even sending some of his own guard to join in the fighting. But the Muslims were unable to lure any crusaders out of their confines; instead, the Christians seem to have intensified the assault on the city as more of Saladin's men arrived. The sultan therefore moved even closer, relocating his tent to Tel al-'Ayyāḍiyya but keeping most of his baggage safe at al-Kharrūba. He ordered all his units to attack the camp and also to pass their nights in armor, ready to fight at a moment's notice. By the end of 5 June, the constant Muslim pressure finally paid off: Philip was forced to deploy soldiers to the camp defense and the siege attacks slowly abated. In the aftermath, certain Muslims hid themselves in the ditches, where they could spy on developments in the camp.[35]

For the time being, Acre had been saved. The Christian authors claim that Philip Augustus could have fought on and taken the city outright, despite the pressure from Saladin's attacks, but that he deliberately paused. The reason given is that Philip was unwilling to take Acre without King Richard present – according to the agreements reached between them in Messina, they would both share in the glory of conquest.[36] This seems quite convenient: Frenchmen had only recently charged through the wall collapsed by Philip's sappers, and their failure to exploit the breach fully had perhaps encouraged some excuse-making in the aftermath. The Englishman Roger of Howden offers the exact opposite sentiment: that Philip's engines had achieved practically nothing.[37] Ibn Shaddād suggests, somewhat dubiously, that a crusader requested an audience with Saladin in order to parley but was rebuffed.[38]

In any case, the sultan could enjoy at least a temporary success, and it was one buttressed with some other lesser victories that spring. On 1 June, the crusaders lost one of their more prominent nobles, Count Philip of Flanders, to illness. And on that exact same day, one of the emirs from Mosul, Ẓāhir al-Dīn Ibn al-Balankārī, arrived at Acre with soldiers to bolster Saladin's ranks. He was the second notable lord to arrive, for the prefect of Damascus, Badr al-Dīn, had returned with his soldiers on 14 May. Also on 14 May, the Muslims had raided the crusader camp and were able to fight off those Christians who managed to give chase, and then to escape.[39]

To the north, the ships of Saladin's ally Emir Usāma, the governor of Beirut, encountered either five or six English ships on 26 May that had broken away from their fleet. In the ensuing battle, all the ships were captured, along with their supplies and forty horses.[40] The sultan could take some small comfort, then, in knowing that while Philip Augustus' forces were making headway against Acre, he was at least holding his own on the fringes of the siege.

### Richard the Lionheart

The arrival of Philip Augustus had rejuvenated the crusaders to some extent, and the king's renewal of the siege works had taken a serious toll on Acre. Had the status quo been maintained, it is highly likely

1. The Toron, viewed from the north, the site of the most ancient settlement in the area, dating back to Canaanite and then Phoenician times. On its southern side are the remains of the ancient harbor, wherein water from Haifa Bay once flowed. At the hill's left (eastern) edge can be spotted the modern statue of Napoleon astride his horse, Marengo.

2. Remains of the Tower of Flies in Akko Harbor. The tower was rebuilt several times, and its base can be easily seen from Akko's southern areas. It sat at the end of a mole running north to the shoreline. The tower once served as the proper entrance to the port: a chain was stretched from it to another tower on the west–east quay, which, when strung, prevented seaborne access to the city.

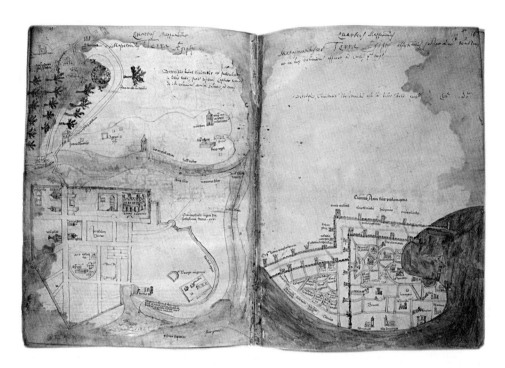

3. Pietro Vesconte's map of Acre, from Marino Sanudo's *Liber secretorum fidelium crucis super Terrae Sanctae recuperatione et conservatione*. Vesconte's map provides the most detailed contemporary illustration of medieval Acre. The double wall arrangement dates to the thirteenth century. It and the plethora of gates and towers have confounded historians of the Third Crusade siege, during which the city looked far different. Note the tower in the harbor. On the verso is a less detailed map of medieval Jerusalem.

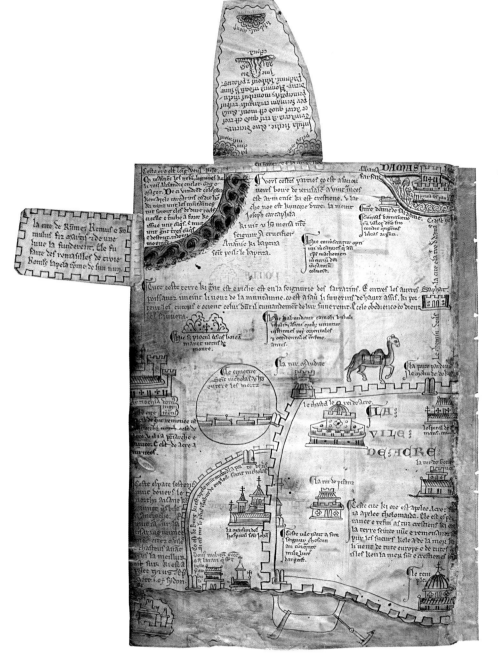

4. Matthew Paris' map of Acre, from *Chronica maiora*. A portion of Paris' map of the route to the Holy Land, the only drawing depicting a single circuit of walls around Acre. It is, however, less detailed than others, in that it does not illustrate the different quarters of the city. It does show a wall around the suburb of Montmusard, which was erected after Acre's recapture in 1191.

5. Evidence of northern crusade-era walls in Akko. Because most of Acre's walls were rebuilt by the Ottomans there are few visible sections of the crusader-era fortifications. In certain places, though, one can spy elements of the crusader walls that were reinforced in later centuries. The section here existed during Napoleon's siege in 1799 – it was bombarded with cannon fire but never collapsed.

6. Old Akko, viewed from atop the Toron. The height of the Toron (today, Tel Akko) provides a superb 360-degree view of the city and its surroundings. The distance between the hill and the city in the twelfth century was much shorter, perhaps half the distance, because Acre's defensive wall lay farther east. The walls were later pulled back in the Ottoman period.

pres en lan de grace enfuuat
m̄. CC iiij. ix au temps de cel
lui roy de france en lan de son

7. The siege of Acre, from *Chroniques de France ou de St Denis*. This is one of a few miniatures of the siege, but it is not contemporary, dating from between 1270 and 1380. It is likely of Parisian origin. The crusaders are assaulting Acre's walls with missile weapons: note the bow, crossbows, and spear about to be hurled. There are foot soldiers and knights, the latter of whom have evidently dismounted to fight. Note the wooden shield behind which a crossbowman hides; such portable defenses were commonly used to protect both attackers and the operators of siege engines from counterfire.

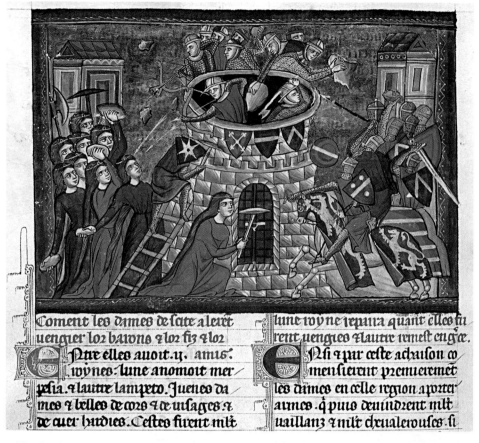

8. The Scythian women attacking a castle, from *Histoire ancienne jusqu'à César*. The combat roles of women are periodically featured in both Christian and Muslim sources for the siege of Acre. Women can be found fighting in armor and riding on horses, filling the city moat with stones in order to effect the crossing of crusader siege engines, and they are even said to have executed Muslim soldiers shipwrecked upon Acre's shoreline.

9. A crusade-era western sword, Oakeshott Type XIa, one of the sword types popular in the late twelfth century, with a longer blade and straight hilt. This one has a "brazil nut"-shaped pommel, while other examples have a pommel in the shape of a disc.

10. One of a pair of tiles illustrating the legendary joust between Richard the Lionheart and Saladin. In that encounter, Richard was said to have unhorsed the sultan and killed him; afterward, Saladin's Muslim guards rushed the king but Richard decapitated thousands of them with his battle axe. Note the crown and "three lions" crest on his shield.

11. Coin, Ṣalāḥ al-Dīn. The Ayyubid sultan Saladin enthroned and holding what appears to be an orb. This coin was contemporary to his rule, probably minted in 1190 in southeastern Asia Minor (Mayafarikin). Saladin had money problems for nearly his entire reign, as he tended to distribute or spend the sums he acquired rather quickly, rather than hoarding them.

12. Saladin captures the Holy Cross, from Matthew Paris' *Chronica maiora*. Saladin captured the purported piece of the True Cross at the Battle of Hattin on 4 July 1187. It had been acquired by crusaders after the conclusion of the First Crusade, and it accompanied Guy of Lusignan during the disaster at the Horns. The return of the cross to Christian hands was negotiated following the fall of Acre in 1191, but Saladin eventually balked at the surrender terms and decided to retain it.

that, under his leadership, the Christians would have eventually broken through the city walls again and finally fought their way inside. The continued inability of Saladin's cavalry to break through the fortifications of the crusader camp meant that he could never destroy the enemy army but only delay them from their efforts. Moreover, having already survived two winters of extreme hardship, it was increasingly unlikely that the crusaders could be brought to terms with a continuing blockade of their camp. Conrad of Montferrat had returned to the siege, and between his lands in the north and Philip's own resources, the army's relative comfort would be secure for at least the remainder of 1191. The rough equilibrium between the Christian and Muslim armies remained.

On 8 June, however, everything changed with the arrival of Richard the Lionheart. His coming constituted a decisive break with the narrative of the nearly two-year-long siege; as Ibn al-Athīr could only lament, "In him the Muslims were tried by an unparalleled disaster."[41]

After sailing from Messina on 10 April, the king had been delayed by matters on the island of Cyprus. Over a score of ships had been blown off course by a storm, one of them carrying his sister Joan and fiancée Berengaria. They survived, but ended up in the hands of the island's titular ruler, Isaac Ducas Comnenus, along with plundered wares from other vessels that had been wrecked along the shoreline. Richard himself arrived at the southern Cypriot city of Limassol on 5 May. In a rapid series of violated peace agreements and engagements, he pursued Isaac around the island and eventually conquered all of Cyprus in the process. More than one historian has suggested that such had been his plan all along, from his departure from Sicily.[42]

Richard's fleet of twenty-five ships cast off from Cyprus during the week of Pentecost and was en route to the siege on 7 June when, somewhere off the coast of Lebanon, it spied a large ship. This was, in fact, a Muslim vessel from Beirut on its way to deliver reinforcements, weapons, and supplies to the beleaguered garrison inside Acre.[43] What followed was a fascinating naval battle between it and Richard's fleet that is recorded in every narrative source for the siege of Acre.

The Muslim ship is described in different ways. The *Eracles* calls it a dromond, Ibn al-Athīr and others a *butsa* (buss), and still others just a *navem* (generic ship), but all comment on its unusually large size and bearing. It was captained by Ya'qūb al-Ḥalabī of Aleppo, commander of the *jandarīyaa* soldiers.[44] It was a three-master, but was also powered by oarsmen, covered with green and gold felt (or perhaps tarpaulin, a tarred canvas) to conceal the cargo on the top deck, and its freeboard was of impressive height. William of Newburgh likened the ship to a tall keep. The writer Richard of Devizes, a monk at St Swithin in Winchester, thought it had towers atop its deck.[45] Richard of Templo claimed that it was so tall Christian archers were unable to loft their arrows up high enough to hit the Muslims on board. Ambroise (and Richard of Templo, following him) claims that the contents of its cargo were later reported by a witness who was in Beirut when it was loaded: bows, spears, crossbows and bolts, phials of Greek Fire, and 100 camels – along with seven emirs, and 800 soldiers (Ibn Shaddād counts only 650, Howden 1,400). Also aboard were 200 snakes, presumably kept in barrels, which the Muslims planned to let loose in the crusader camp.[46] Rigord adds even more cargo – fifty *balista*! – a number that is certainly high, although Ibn Shaddād also believed that artillery was on board.[47]

As Richard approached, the identity of the ship and her crew was unclear. Roger of Howden claims it flew the French flag, but this is explicitly denied in the *Itinerarium*. King Richard ordered Peter des Barres to take a galley forward and make contact: the crew claimed to be French, but one of Richard's sailors insisted that it was a lie, telling the king, "I will allow you to cut off my head or hang me on a gallows if I don't prove before your very eyes that this is a Saracen ship."[48] Richard was still not sure, so he sent another detachment forward, which was attacked; and so the truth was revealed. The Muslims assailed the crusader vessels with missile fire from composite Damascus bows, and the rest of the king's fleet moved to engage, led by one Raymond of Bone Done. Richard of Devizes claims that the king himself took part in the action, but a later legend putting Richard on board the Muslim vessel has no basis in fact.[49]

The battle seems to have unfolded in four phases. In the beginning, the crusader galleys sailed around the dromond in circles, shooting arrows and bolts at it, but failing to accomplish much due to its height. Richard reportedly blasted his men's efforts, incredulous at their inability to damage the enemy. Trying again, the English galleys pulled right next to the dromond and some soldiers managed to board the ship itself, either by leaping onto it from their own galleys, grabbing hold of the dromond's rigging and climbing aboard, or by throwing and then clambering up ropes attached to grappling hooks. The Muslim sailors met the boarders in hand-to-hand combat and a fair bloodbath ensued as both sides dismembered each other with swords. The English had the better of the fight until the Muslim oarsmen appeared from below deck and either drove the crusaders back onto their own ships or pushed them off the rail and into the water. Some jars of Greek Fire also seem to have struck one of the crusader vessels, setting it on fire.[50] A third tactic worked better: those Englishmen who could swim dived into the water and, working together, bound one of the ship's steering oars to one side of the aft hull, which caused the large vessel to sail around in circles.[51]

Once the dromond had been incapacitated in this fashion, the fourth phase began, when Richard ordered his galleys into a ramming attack, using their iron spurs to damage the ship's hull. This was effective: water began to pour in and the dromond started to list. Many of the Muslim sailors abandoned ship: some were killed by crusader bolts as they tried to swim to safety, while others drowned; only a few dozen survived and were taken prisoner.[52] However, the

English were unable to capture the valuable supplies on board the dromond before it ultimately sank. Richard of Templo and others claim that, besides the prisoners, everything on board was lost to the sea, including the snakes.

How exactly the dromond sank was a matter of opinion. Ralph of Diss, writing of the ramming, compared it to the biblical story of Eleazar Maccabee, who stabbed from below a war elephant but was crushed when the beast died on top of him.[53] Other Christian sources also credit the rams. The Arabic authors claim that the captain, Ya'qūb, and a few other men scuttled the ship by boring a hole in its hull with pickaxes. At first glance, one might prefer the Christian version, because the victorious English would have reported the news when they arrived in camp. On the other hand, Ibn Shaddād claims that one of the prisoners, having been mutilated by the crusaders, was eventually released and, entering Acre, reported the real story. Most likely, the ship sank from holes inflicted both internally and externally. Whatever the reason, the loss was taken badly by both Saladin and the Acre garrison, with some Muslims ripping their cloaks and tearing their beards.[54]

After dropping anchor for the night near Tyre, Richard's fleet continued south towards Acre the next day, 8 June. Passing the same landmarks as had Guy of Lusignan two years before – the Scandalion Pass, Castle Imbert – Richard eventually spied Acre, the massive crusader camp arrayed before it, and the even larger Muslim armies of Saladin arrayed beyond it. Like his counterpart, the king was all business, studying the landscape and making plans as his fleet approached the shore.[55] Upon landing, he was greeted by Philip and all the nobles present in the camp. The English sources are effusive in their praise for their king, none more so than Richard of Devizes:

> Pursuing his course thence, the king came to the blockade of Acre, and was received by the blockaders with as much joy as if it had been Christ who had returned to the land to restore

the kingdom of Israel. The king of the French had arrived before him at Acre, and was highly esteemed by the inhabitants of the country; but when Richard arrived after him, he became completely forgotten and nameless, just as the moon loses its light on the rising of the sun.[56]

Hyperbole aside, the exuberance of the crusaders was real. Ambroise writes of the great joy in the camp, the playing of music from trumpets and bells, the pouring of libations, and the lighting of candles and great campfires everywhere. The pomp and those campfires are confirmed in the account of Ibn Shaddād.[57] Excepting Richard of Devizes, those authors who were not present at the siege offer much calmer accounts. Ralph of Diss simply records the king's arrival and moves on, while William of Newburgh cleverly remarks that the army's great joy was proportional to their great anxiety.[58] The Lyon *Eracles* notes the general enthusiasm and praises Richard's courtesy, but also that of King Philip, who welcomed his counterpart and even helped his new wife Berengaria to land, while holding his tongue about Richard's reneging on his prior betrothal to his sister Alice.[59]

Amidst the celebration, Richard moved swiftly to wrest control of the siege away from Philip, not through an outright declaration of his rights but rather through a sneaking set of appeals to the crusaders themselves. First, he entertained fealty offers from the Italians in camp. Both the Pisans and the Genoese offered to fight under his command, instead of Philip's: the Pisans' offer he accepted, but not the appeal from Genoa, on the grounds that they had already sworn to both Philip and Conrad of Montferrat. The Pisans supposedly swooned at the sight of Richard's power and majesty, but Roger of Howden points to the true reason: the king confirmed their prior liberties in the Levant after landing.[60] Second, Richard moved to trump Philip's generosity. The French king had offered largesse of three gold bezants to each knight at Acre on a monthly basis, and

Richard, not to be outdone, declared that he would pay four. Knights therefore flocked to his side and he was acclaimed throughout the camp.[61] Third, he won to his side Henry of Champagne with another monetary arrangement. Henry, out of money and supplies, came to the English king for assistance: Richard purportedly gave him thousands of silver coins, fattened pigs, and bushels of wheat, on the condition that the count shift his loyalties to him and away from Philip. The division of spoils within Acre he entrusted to the Templars and Hospitallers.[62] On the basis of these moves and the generosity and trust they implied, Richard was able to exercise control over major portions of the army and, thereby, some of the siege operations.

Then there was the issue of Conrad of Montferrat, which would come to a head before the end of June. While on Cyprus the preceding spring, Richard had received some visitors from Acre: none other than Guy of Lusignan and his brother Geoffrey. The titular king's position was precarious, due to events dating from the fall of 1190, when his wife Sibylla had died and her half-sister and heir to Jerusalem had married Guy's great rival Conrad on 24 November. Conrad's claim to be the new king of Jerusalem was unsettling, but by spring 1191 had resulted in little. As we have seen, Conrad himself was reviled by most of the crusaders at Acre because of his failure to send relief during the harsh famine of the preceding winter. The political balance had shifted, however, with the arrival of Philip Augustus, who backed Conrad as king.[63] Guy had therefore sailed to Cyprus to acquire Richard's support against Conrad. Once Philip took over the siege works at Acre, he had been able to slip away, taking perhaps 160 soldiers along for the trip. Since the Lusignan family was under the general rule of Richard back in Poitou, and because Sibylla had been Richard's cousin, the English king ultimately decided to back Guy over Conrad.[64]

In June, Richard's dominant position at the siege provided Guy with the opportunity he had been waiting for, and he formally complained about Conrad's attempts to claim the throne of Jerusalem. Roger of Howden lists the charges as oath-breaking, perjury, and treason; but it seems that Conrad was not about to wait around to hear his fate. On 24 June, he slipped out of the camp with some men and returned to his fortified city of Tyre. His departure was conspicuous and was even noticed by the Muslim authors. In his absence, it was left to Philip Augustus to defend his ally, and a month later the kings settled on an agreement, by which Conrad would keep Tyre, Beirut, and Sidon, but would not gain the throne of Jerusalem unless Guy preceded him in death.[65]

Returning to the military matters of early June, Philip called for a renewal of the assault on the ninth, the day after Richard's arrival. The English king turned him down and prevented any of his men from engaging, including his new Pisan allies. In practical terms, Richard's delay made sense: he had not yet assembled his own siege weapons and, having only arrived, was not yet prepared to address Acre's walls. However, this was clearly a power play and assertion of his own magnificence over that of Philip, his former friend and confidant, but now a distinct rival. Rigord claims that mediation was attempted between the two kings, with judges actually calling for Richard to cooperate. He refused, and the anecdote illustrates his general attitude towards his peer.[66] In the meantime, the crusaders spent 9 June repelling a light sally from the Acre garrison. Two days later, Philip appealed again for a renewal of the assault, and once again Richard refused. His engines were still not ready, he argued, and there were English ships en route that had yet to arrive in Acre. More decisive, however, was the sudden onset of illness – "Arnaldia," a form of scurvy or trench mouth that had incapacitated the English king.[67]

Philip was now out of patience and attacked anyway. The French divided into two contingents, one to attack Acre and the other to defend the trenches behind them from a Saladin reprisal. Philip was in command of the siege operations, while Geoffrey of Lusignan led the camp defense. Both infantry and knights on horseback were assembled, although it is unclear what purpose the horses may have served in the siege effort – perhaps the knights held crossbows or trotted the line to coordinate attacks. The Muslim garrison issued a smoke signal to Saladin, as per normal, who once again directed his horse-archers to attack the crusader ditches and ramparts. Preceding the riders were men carrying material with which to fill in the ditch, so that the horses could cross; but they were all driven off by Geoffrey's men. He himself reportedly killed ten Muslims with an axe and captured some others.[68]

The Muslims' lack of success at the trenches was mirrored by the crusaders' attack on Acre, for which Ambroise offers the judgment, "Good Lord, what a feeble effort!" Such a reckoning was not far off. The assault seems to have been relatively orderly, with crusaders dashing forward with arms and ladders, archers firing from behind them, and the cavalry stationed behind the missile troops. Philip himself fired a crossbow from his *cercelia*, and his trebuchets swung into action. A battering ram was also available, but its use was stymied when the crusaders failed to fill in Acre's moat enough to facilitate its passage to the walls. It was soon apparent that Philip commanded too few men to make any real progress against the city's defenses. Worse, riders sallying from the gates used Greek Fire to set aflame both the battering ram and some of the catapults: the latter had been left unguarded when Philip had ordered their caretakers to join the general assault.[69] In the end, the French were forced to withdraw, defeated. In the wake of the failed assault, Philip himself fell victim to the same malady from which Richard was suffering, and now both kings lay seriously ill.[70]

### The summer barrage

While the kings convalesced, the allies for whom Richard had been waiting began to arrive by sea. They were Englishmen and Normans from the king's own household, coming from Cyprus. Most notable among them were Bishop John of Evreux and Earl Robert IV of Leicester; the rest were knights who brought a wealth of military experience.[71] Still, even the infusion of these men was not enough to prompt the English king into action. Instead, it was Philip who continued to attack the city. He recovered from his illness first: it was supposedly on the same day his son Louis recovered from dysentery back in France, and Rigord pins both events to prayers and fasting at the convent of St Denis.[72] On 14 June, he ordered the artillery to be fired continually day and night.[73] The trebuchets employed in June 1191 are well described in the sources and have been objects of considerable fascination and study. One of them had a famous name, "Bad Neighbor" (*Malam vicinam*): it and another named weapon owned by the Knights Hospitaller, "God's Stonethrower" (*Petrariam Dei*), were aimed at the Cursed Tower at the northeast corner of Acre's walls.[74]

Other artillery struck elsewhere. One weapon owned by Duke Hugh of Burgundy was shot at the northern stretch of the wall by the Mediterranean shore, while another owned by the Knights Templar operated on the eastern side. In time, Richard joined in the effort and ordered his own artillery into action, although he was still confined to his sickbed. One of these was a catapult owned by the recently deceased Philip d'Alsace, which the king had acquired, along with a second, smaller type. Both were aimed at an unknown gate. He also added new weapons: he had ordered two new mangonels built, and one of them tossed some uniquely hard stones that the king had specifically brought from Messina for the purpose. At one point, Richard was moved to within view of the assault, although he himself could not join in it.[75] The catapults acquired by Richard demolished half of another, unnamed tower, and his new machines lobbed stones past the walls and into the city market.[76]

The constant artillery strikes caused significant damage to Acre's walls. Hits from the Hospitaller weapon eventually demolished a

30-square foot section of the wall adjacent to the Cursed Tower; in height, it was about five to six feet of stone from the top.[77] This took some time, however, because the catapult was constantly being damaged by Muslim counterfire. The garrison directed fire from one of its own trebuchets, dubbed "Bad Relation" (*Malam cognatam*), at the weapon and repeatedly put it out of commission. A certain priest preached next to it, periodically blessing the weapon and collecting money for its repair whenever a Muslim shot struck it.[78] In another story, a certain soldier was hit square in the back by a massive stone hurled from one of Acre's catapults, but it bounced harmlessly away. This was attributed to the compassion of God, "whose clemency always waits upon those who are fighting for him."[79]

There are also reports that Richard ordered the building of some sort of *berefredum* (siege tower or belfry) and for one of his new catapults to be assembled on top of it. It was covered with animal hides, wood, and rope netting in order to protect it from different missile types. This may be the four-story tower mentioned by Ibn Shaddād, which he claims was brought to within 5 cubits of the city before being destroyed by Greek Fire. If so, then this elevated catapult may also have been the one able to hit the interior market; Richard of Devizes, although not an eyewitness, depicts just such a scenario.[80] In the midst of these attacks, the crusaders twice attempted to rush the city and exploit the breaches in the wall: first on 14 June and then again three days later. On both occasions, they were forced to pull back when Saladin's cavalry attacked the camp fortifications on the other side. The Muslims actually had some success on these occasions. In the first attack, they managed to get as far as the Christian tents, which they looted, but the intense heat of the day and a Christian counterattack eventually compelled them to withdraw. The second attack, however, advanced no farther than the ramparts before the Christians launched a cavalry charge that drove them off.[81]

The remainder of June consisted of lighter skirmishes outside the city. There are two reported encounters between what were likely foraging parties and members of Saladin's advance guard. The first, on 22 June, was near Montmusard, when some crusader cavalry and foot soldiers encountered Muslim riders: the result was a few deaths on either side and the capture of an anonymous Christian knight. The second skirmish occurred on the very next day, but on the opposite side of the camp, by the River Belus. Some Christian foot soldiers were caught moving along the water, and again Muslim riders attacked. The two sides reportedly captured one soldier apiece and, after killing them, immolated their bodies – Ibn Shaddād claims to have seen the flames. Certain Muslims also made a habit of sneaking into the crusader camp at night time, snatching supplies out of tents.[82] But these incidents were minor in comparison to the heavy fighting along the ramparts and Acre's walls.

## The beginning of the end

Roger of Howden reported the occurrence of an eclipse of the sun on 23 June.[83] As the light dimmed in the sky, Muslim hopes began similarly to fade, as Saladin welcomed the arrival of what would be his final reinforcements at the siege. They were led by four men who had departed the siege for winter rest but had returned. The lord of Sinjār, Mujāhid al-Dīn Yarunqush, returned and was stationed on Saladin's left flank. Two Egyptian contingents, led by 'Alam al-Dīn Kurjī and Sayf al-Dīn Sunqur al-Dawādār, arrived after 24 June, and a final group of men from Egypt on 28 June. Finally, the lord of Mosul, 'Ala' al-Dın Khurramshah, returned; Saladın actually left the siege on 25 June and rode south to al-Kharrūba to meet him. Upon their arrival, the Mosul troops were stationed on the right flank near Montmusard. The last arrivals came on 9–11 July: Sābiq al-Dīn, lord of Shayzar, returned, as did Badr al-Dīn Dildirim and Asad al-Dīn Shīrkūh.[84] Saladin's army was now at maximum strength, for no more Muslim soldiers would arrive at Acre before its capitulation.

Throughout it all, artillery attacks continued to seriously weaken Acre's walls. The damage to the section near the Cursed Tower was only the beginning; now several other portions of the wall were taking sustained hits, and stones were being knocked out at a steady rate. Breaches appeared, too small to fully exploit, but large enough for a man to squirm through. This was problematic, because the city defenders, whittled down in numbers from both a lack of food and ongoing artillery and missile fire, had become too stretched along the entire length of the northern and eastern walls. Sleep was also at a premium due to the constant need to watch for enemy intrusions.[85] A picture emerges of an exhausted, beleaguered garrison that was nearing total collapse. It had not been resupplied since mid-April, and the French and English ships off the coast ensured that it would not be again. Complaints and accounts of the suffering trickled out of the city, along with the first serious rumors since 1190 of its potential surrender.[86]

Matters swiftly worsened for the Muslims. Starting on 2 July, the crusaders began to assault the walls with contingents of men and other, non-artillery engines in round-the-clock fashion, working in shifts to maintain constant pressure. The defenders gave as well as they could, using their remaining missiles as counter-battery fire within short range. When a Welsh cat was pushed up to the wall, the garrison redirected a catapult and assailed it with rocks. They also dumped some kindling atop it and then phials of naphtha, which incinerated it, along with Philip Augustus' own *cercelia*, which was positioned nearby. It is unclear whether the king was inside at the time, shooting his crossbow at Muslims on the wall; but he was livid on account of its destruction and accused his soldiers of incompetence.[87] In such fashion, the crusader attacks were held somewhat in check.

The Christians had an even savvier trick up their sleeves. While the artillery fire was ongoing, they began to strengthen and heighten the ramparts around the back side of their camp. Essentially, as Acre's walls came down, so the camp walls went up; the net effect was a doubling of the efficacy of the blockade. The better defended the camp became, the less likely it was that Saladin could either dislodge the crusader army or even disrupt its siege operations. Saladin understood the danger clearly, and the building crisis was crystallized for him when he received a desperate dispatch from the Acre garrison on 3 July. In it, the defenders asked again for succor and warned that, should it not come soon, they would surrender the city in exchange for their lives.[88] In response, the sultan urged his men into repeated attacks on the crusader ramparts. Saladin's brother al-'Ādil charged twice, putting himself at great risk, as he and others drew fire away from comrades trying to fill the crusader ditches. Desperation grew among the Muslim cavalry, who took the rare step of dismounting to fight on foot on a day that was apparently blisteringly hot: they fought with blades, axes, and spiked clubs but were either driven back or killed in the ditches by the Christians, who were more used to infantry combat. Missile troops also stood firm in a human wall, calmly draping volleys of arrows and bolts atop the Muslims as they tried to climb out of the ditch. Two particular defenders are celebrated for their bravery and steadfastness. One stood atop the rampart, hurling stones at the Muslims and shrugging off those that hit him in return. Another was a female archer, who wounded several attackers with her bow until she herself was struck down. Nightfall eventually brought an end to the fighting.[89]

With their rear protected from Saladin's attacks, those crusaders besieging Acre were able to ply their craft to tremendous effect. That same day, 3 July, another section of the city's wall collapsed. Two groups of French sappers had been tunneling towards the wall throughout the summer artillery barrage, one towards the already damaged wall adjacent to the Cursed Tower and the other towards a different, unnamed section near another gate. On that day, the second group finally reached their target: propping up the wall with timbers, they set the wood on fire and the stones came crashing down, nearly killing some of the miners in the process. The stones did not fall free and clear, but collapsed into a large mound of rubble that still impeded entry into the city. Led by Conrad of Montferrat, the French grabbed ladders and began to scale the rubble. About 150 crusaders were killed in the scramble, including several elites and also King Philip's marshal Aubery Clement, who had boasted that he would enter the city that day. Aubery was left alone atop the stones when his ladder broke, dropping his comrades back down the pile; he was quickly surrounded by Muslim defenders and cut down. The first group of sappers reached the Cursed Tower soon afterward, but their tunnel was countermined by the garrison and the two groups of diggers actually encountered each other underground. A deal was struck: the French would abandon their mine in exchange for some Christian prisoners.[90] It is unclear whether Philip ever learned of this arrangement. On account of the death of his marshal, however, the king called off the assault for the remainder of the day, and the army mourned.

That afternoon, the emirs in Acre sought parley with Philip Augustus. Emir al-Mashṭūb was granted safe conduct into his presence in the camp, where he proposed the first formal surrender terms since May 1190. The accounts all differ as to the terms of his proposal, but as a minimum he asked Philip to spare the lives of everyone inside the city. The Lyon *Eracles* adds that the Muslims asked to retain their possessions as well, and Ibn al-Athīr claims that al-Mashṭūb also sought permission for the entire populace to rejoin Saladin (certainly an outlandish request, if true). Rigord adds even more – they offered the return of all Christian prisoners taken during the siege; and he and Richard of Devizes both include a Muslim offer of the return of the piece of the True Cross Saladin had taken at the Battle of Hattin in 1187.[91] The actual terms notwithstanding, the fact is that the crusaders' siege had earned them yet another offer of conditional surrender, the third in nearly two years. As before, however, it was refused.

Four reasons for Philip's refusal emerge from the collection of sources, with each one predicated on the differing terms of the offer.

One seems to have been based on pride and/or avarice: he would spare the people's lives but not their possessions; and/or he refused to agree to either unless the city was delivered first.[92] Another is that he refused to allow the garrison to rejoin Saladin, which implies that he would take them prisoner for some stretch of time.[93] A third is that Philip made a counteroffer: in addition to the city, he wanted the return of all Christian prisoners, the True Cross, *and* all the land in the Levant taken by Muslims since the Second Crusade. This latter condition was a flipping of the purported Muslim terms, as described by Rigord and Richard of Devizes, and would have been outlandish and impossible without Saladin's consent. According to Roger of Howden, Philip gave al-Mashṭūb three days to persuade Saladin to accept the counteroffer, but of course the sultan refused.[94] There was no chance at all that Saladin would trade in his conquests – which included Jerusalem itself – to save one coastal city, no matter how vital. The fourth reason for Philip's refusal of al-Mashṭūb's terms is quite different and involves Richard the Lionheart. Richard of Devizes claims that Richard wanted no deal – he wanted to conquer the city outright, which mirrors the way the Christian leaders balked at the terms offered in 1189 and 1190. Moreover, the *Eracles* notes that Richard was not even privy to the discussions between Philip and al-Mashṭūb. As a result, perhaps from anger or just pure stubbornness, he ordered his catapults to shoot at the city during the parley, while al-Mashṭūb was under safe conduct.[95] This seems outrageous, but one wonders why the *Eracles* author would insert such an inflammatory claim if it were not true, especially given the consequences (as we will see).

Al-Mashṭūb returned to Acre with nothing to show for his efforts. He could be rightly incensed about the failed parley and Richard's insults. In anger, he is said to have responded to Philip with hollow threats: "We shall not surrender the city until we are all killed. Not one of us will be killed without first killing fifty of your great men."[96]

But al-Mashṭūb's return was not received well by the Muslims inside the city. They knew full well that the blockade would soon result in their deaths from starvation, if the artillery barrage and crusader tunnels did not permanently breach the walls first. This realization prompted some of them to flee. The very next day, 4 July, a small ship slipped out of Acre's harbor and made its way to a friendly shore near Saladin's army. Aboard were Emir ʿIzz al-Dīn Arsul al-Asadī, Ḥusām al-Dīn Timurtāsh (the son of Emir ʿIzz al-Dīn Jāwūlī), and Sunqur al-Wishāqī.[97]

The course of the parley also caused divisions and infighting in both armies. Richard's purported interference drove a wedge between the two Christian kings that soon got out of hand. The *Eracles* claims that Philip not only allowed al-Mashṭūb to return to Acre safely, but even encouraged him and his retainers to fight their way back, if passage was prevented by Richard's men. The result was a clash between the emir's men and some English soldiers, with many of the latter killed in action. In a furious moment, Philip also ordered an attack on Richard himself and even began donning his armor before his advisers convinced him of the folly of such a course.[98]

Things were not well in Saladin's camp, either. The emirs who had fled Acre immediately went into hiding, suspecting that the sultan would disapprove of their desertion. It was a prescient notion, and one of them was soon discovered and imprisoned. Even worse, Saladin's men began disobeying his orders. On the morning of 4 July, the sultan announced a raid with the purpose of, once again, filling in the crusader ditches; but the soldiers refused to join him, saying: "We shall put Islam at risk. There is no advantage in that."[99] Ibn Shaddād skips lightly over this impertinence, but it reveals the very real frustration among the Muslim rank and file, who had lived with the siege for nearly as long as their Christian counterparts and without significant result. Both armies seem to have sensed that the siege was nearing its end, and there was some reluctance to engage in yet more fruitless labors.

Saladin therefore did not lead his men back into action, but rather entertained a second parley later on 4 July, this one initiated by the crusaders. Now in a position of strength, they attempted to bring the sultan to better terms than those offered by al-Mashṭūb. Saladin may well have welcomed the opportunity. Roger of Howden claims that the sultan had been sending gifts of fresh pears and plums to the crusade leaders ever since Richard the Lionheart had arrived in Acre, in an attempt to bring them to the negotiating table.[100] On this occasion, some crusaders were admitted into Saladin's presence: after giving them some fruit and ice for refreshment, he learned that some Knights Hospitaller would arrive the next day (5 July) to negotiate. There is no evidence that this subsequent meeting ever took place, but Ibn al-Athīr does note the offer Saladin had been prepared to entertain: in addition to Acre's surrender, there would be a prisoner exchange equal to the size of Acre's garrison, plus the return of the True Cross. This offer, like al-Mashṭūb's, was rejected.[101] The confidence of the Christians is obvious: in a dominant position and well defended from the sultan, they felt absolutely no need to settle. And as it turned out, Acre would be theirs only seven days later.

It was impossible for Saladin to ignore the writing on the wall, and so he tried to save his garrison troops in yet another fashion. On 5 July, Saladin sent a swimmer into Acre with orders for the defenders to abandon the city. The plan was for the Muslims to erupt out of the Gate of St Michael on the western edge of the wall, attack the nearest crusaders with speed and intensity, and drive forward through Montmusard. There, Saladin's soldiers would attack from the opposite side, with the anticipated result being a breach on the seaward side of the crusader camp. Acre's residents, unfortunately, would be left to fend for themselves in the aftermath. In this scenario, Saladin was trying to trade the city for his soldiers. Unlike his orders the day before, this plan was actually carried out, assuredly because the garrison was in dire straits, while the men in Saladin's army were not.

Such a plan required coordination and, ideally, a simultaneous attack on Montmusard from the southern and northern sides; but instead, the attacks were carried out in sequence. Saladin's army moved first, with Ṣārim Qaymāz al-Najmī and Emir al-Janāḥ, the brother of al-Mashṭūb, dismounting and rushing the camp ditches with their men. Others, such as ʿIzz al-Dīn Jurdīk al-Nūrī, soon joined the effort. Then the garrison sallied and headed for the rally point but could not reach it. It seems that the Christians knew the plan all along: two sources reveal that a certain anonymous mamluk had slipped out of the city and betrayed the attack to the crusaders. Guards were placed on both sides of the camp and took away the Muslims' initiative. The Christians kept Saladin's men at bay on the northern perimeter and then repelled the garrison as soon as it exited the Gate of St Michael. At length, it retreated back into Acre and the fighting ended.[102]

This failed breakout plan is highly revealing. First, it clearly demonstrates the implacable nature of the fortified crusader camp by 1191. Saladin had tried many times to break through its perimeter without success; here, a concerted, pre-planned, and joint attack on just one specific section also failed. One might argue that such a plan could have succeeded in 1189 or even early 1190, when the constructed defenses were new and untested. Second, the breakout attempt is also evidence that Saladin had abandoned the possibility of holding Acre itself. Had the garrison managed to escape the city would have been left utterly defenseless. Its capitulation would have been swift. Third, it reveals the sultan's feelings towards the city residents. The survival and return of the garrison soldiers was paramount, and he was willing to abandon the people and the port in order to effect it.

Saladin gave up any hope of taking the camp. There was a brief negotiation on 6 July between a group of forty Christians and al-ʿAdl al-Zabadānī, the governor of Sidon, outside the rampart gates, but the discussion was inconclusive. Following this was the last recorded attack on the crusader camp – a general assault on 7 July that, while personally led by Saladin, reads like a desperate move by a leader who had run out of ideas.[103] It achieved nothing. The last we see of Saladin conducting military operations, in fact, is the very next day, 8 July, when he ordered the burning of Haifa and its vineyards and also the uprooting of fruit trees on the Acre plain.[104] Given the state of affairs, his decision seems born more out of anger and frustration than any notion of a viable scorched-earth strategy.

On the same day, Roger of Howden claims that the Virgin Mary appeared to the crusaders, promising that God would deliver the city; subsequently, an earthquake shook Acre.[105] It was an ominous sign for the city: the western kings were determined to achieve their desired terms through force, for the crusading army had kept up the attack on Acre all the while. Catapults continued to shoot at the walls, and a new mine was already being dug towards the Cursed Tower, this time by the English and Normans. The mound of earth excavated by the sappers was piled into a high ridge of dirt, resembling a snake that steadily crept closer to the city. On 11 July, the tunnel reached a point underneath the tower, wooden timbers were set alight, and this time the tower itself came crashing down in a heap of rubble.[106] Richard ordered his men to rush forward and remove the jumbled rocks, so that a clear entrance into the city could be made, offering two gold bezants for each block hauled away. He then upped his price to three and then four bezants. Unfortunately, the tower's collapse seems to have been a bit of a surprise, for there were not enough men in the vicinity to complete the task; it did not help that it fell at about nine o'clock in the morning, while many crusaders were at their tents eating breakfast.[107] Meanwhile, a heavy exchange of crossbow fire took place. Richard himself was still quite ill, but in a famous story he ordered his *cercelia* dragged forward to the walls so that he could shoot his crossbow at the defenders. He hit one Muslim in the chest, killing him, but his foes were equally adept: "Armour, however good, strong or sure was of no use there – double pourpoints and double hauberks – they were of no more use than blue cloth against the framed crossbows, for the bolts were of such heavy caliber."[108]

A group of Pisans managed to scale part of the wall near the ruined tower, but they were driven right back down by the defenders. Some squires with swords tried climbing up the rubble pile, but the Muslims fought back and also laced the pile with Greek Fire, causing the youths to slide back down as well. All told, some forty crusaders were killed in the assault, although the only man identified was a Pisan called Leonard.[109] These were the final Christian casualties before the garrison's surrender – although no one knew it yet, the siege was over.

# AFTERMATH AND REPERCUSSIONS

*"There were never more outstanding warriors or better defenders than these, whatever their beliefs."*[1]

s 12 July dawned, the siege of Acre reached its 653rd day. One of the longest sieges of the middle ages was at last drawing to a close.[2] In the wake of the collapse of the Cursed Tower, the Acre garrison decided to surrender the city to the crusade leaders. A.S. Ehrenkreutz points out the obvious reason: the garrison stopped believing that Saladin could rescue them.[3] There were problems from the very start of this latest round of negotiations, the fifth since 1189. The difficult terms, combined with Saladin's absence from the actual meetings, would result in a partial default for the Muslims and one of the most infamous episodes of Christian–Muslim violence from the entire crusading period – one that has reverberated in religion and politics down to the present day.

The garrison opened negotiations on 12 July by requesting safe conduct for its leaders into and from the crusader camp. This being granted, a meeting took place in the tent of either Philip Augustus or

Robert of Sable, the new Templar master. On one side was Philip, Richard the Lionheart, and most of the notable Christian leaders; among the latter we can assume were men like Conrad of Montferrat, Geoffrey of Lusignan, Henry of Champagne, Duke Leopold, and the respective masters of the Knights Templar and Hospitaller. On the other side were the emirs al-Mashṭūb and Qāraqūsh. Via a translator, the emirs gave their surrender terms.[4]

Beyond the turning over of Acre itself and the return of the piece of the True Cross taken at Hattin, every other term of the agreement differs according to the source one reads. The first question centers on the booty inside the city. Only the Arabic sources claim that the deal allowed the Muslim defenders to leave with their lives, families, *and* property; the western sources state that property and possessions were to be forfeited. Rigord slightly alters this by suggesting that only an acceptable portion of the city's supplies would be received. Second, a prisoner exchange was arranged, in which a certain number of Christian elites and regular soldiers would be set free by Saladin. The number of elites varies between 50 and 2,000. Richard of Templo claims that the first offer was to release 250 elites, but after the crusade leaders balked, the number was increased to 2,000. The kings would be permitted to choose who was to be set free. As for the common men, the numbers range from 500 to 1,500. The Lyon *Eracles* is alone in claiming that all Christian prisoners of any rank were to be released.[5] However, it also makes no mention of the third condition, that of money: 200,000 bezants, to be split between Richard and Philip as they saw fit, according to both Muslim and Christian sources. Interestingly, the Arabic documents describe a second, individual monetary payment of 14,000 bezants to Conrad of Montferrat. Ibn Shaddād claims this was compensation for Conrad's role as an intermediary in the negotiations.[6] Such a role is never mentioned by the Christian authors. Given their collective hatred of the marquis, one could speculate on their hesitancy to credit him with any positive deed.

On the other hand, such a dubious arrangement might also feed their conspiratorial fires.

All of the negotiations took place and concluded on 12 July, marked by Ambroise as the day after the feast of St Benedict of Nursia (actually the feast of the *translatio* of his relics), 11 July.[7] Both sides agreed to terms with oaths, and al-Mashṭūb and Qāraqūsh promised well-born hostages from inside Acre to serve as surety. They would communicate the terms to Saladin, who would then have a set period in which to satisfy the conditions: Ibn Shaddād sets the time at three months; Ibn al-Athīr at two months; Roger of Howden at forty days; and Richard of Templo at only one month.[8] The emirs then returned to the city to break the news to the people there and arrange for their departure. For their part, the western kings ordered an immediate halt to the artillery bombardment, which had apparently continued throughout the negotiations.[9]

### Acre falls

These matters being resolved, the city gates were opened and, at last, the crusaders triumphantly entered Acre. They danced, sang with glee, and thanked God for his blessings. The kings' banners were raised over the walls and towers, and crosses were restored to the rooftops of the churches. Conrad set his own banners atop the main city mosque.[10] Given the length and cost of the siege, the descriptions of Acre's final capitulation in the Christian texts are surprisingly muted and brief. Although the siege had lasted for nearly two years, Acre's fall was, after all, still only the first step in the story of the Third Crusade. Jerusalem had yet to be recovered, and all the authors (writing in hindsight) knew that it never would be in their lifetimes. Moreover, while Acre was of course a valuable prize, Saladin himself had not actually been defeated – his armies remained camped outside the city, as strong and capable as ever. Their presence remained a vivid reminder that God's work had only just begun.

No sooner had the city been surrendered than the griping and in-fighting among the victors began. Many of the regular Christian soldiers were upset at how the city was won, perhaps thinking that it should have been taken in a final, glorious assault. This is reminiscent of the general belief prior to the St James offensive in July 1190 that the elites were avoiding proper combat in exchange for their own safety. Richard of Templo dubs such an attitude foolish – after all, Acre had finally been taken! – but financial considerations help to explain it better.[11] Had the city been taken by storm and/or sacked, the soldiers might have profited by seizing goods for themselves; but instead, the kings divided the spoils between themselves in advance. Rigord tries to put a good spin on this, asserting that the rank and file received a greater share than the elites; and Richard of Devizes claims that, true, half went to the kings, but the other half was divided among the army.[12] None of the witness accounts corroborate this: they instead emphasize how Philip and Richard got everything and then distributed it according to their own designs. Each king entrusted his share to subordinates, who acted as caretakers for the money.[13]

Who got what in terms of property in Acre was an instant controversy. Upon entering, many of the knights immediately found and moved into living quarters that, technically, did not belong to them. Medieval Acre was divided into a number of "quarters," with several of these governed by a separate commune or Order. Considerable research has been conducted on the precise locations of the quarters, their layouts, and the properties held within, both surviving and lost. A basic diagram illustrates the proposed layout of these quarters (Map 4). The named quarters were acquired throughout the twelfth and thirteenth centuries. The oldest claim was that of Genoa (1104), which had contributed to the original Christian capture of the city in that year; thereafter, Venice (after 1110) and Pisa (1168). The Marseille/Provence quarter does not appear on the medieval maps, but it was founded by 1249 and lay somewhere south and west of the

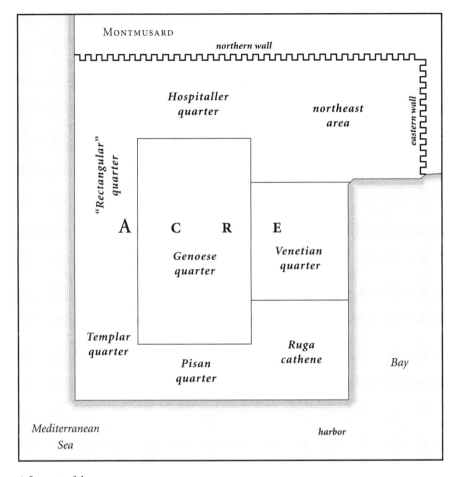

4. Layout of Acre.

Venetian quarter.[14] The Hospitaller quarter was established in 1191, for the Order needed a new administrative headquarters after losing its own in Jerusalem in 1187. The Templars also regained their quarter in the southwest region of the city after the siege's conclusion in 1191.[15] Information for all these quarters is not equal. For example, while a complete inventory for the houses in the Genoese quarter exists, records for the Venetian quarter list only communal property.[16] Even less is known about the Pisan quarter.[17]

Three other areas belonged to no one particular group but rather constituted residential and administrative sectors. The northeast area and the "rectangular" quarter were largely residential. The former contained a number of churches and, on its southern side, by the water, was the crusader arsenal. The latter quarter seems to have been a poorer, though well-defended, residential district, and, later, inside it sat a Dominican monastery.[18] The Quarter of the Chain (*Ruga cathene*) was astride the harbor and served as a customs office; it fell under the jurisdiction of the king of Jerusalem.

Now that Acre was back in Christian hands, the burgesses of the city petitioned the kings, arguing that the properties had been theirs before Saladin had taken the city over four years previously, on 9 July 1187, and should now be returned to them. Richard and Philip agreed that they ought not to be disinherited and ordered the properties returned, albeit with the qualification that the knights could remain as lodgers until the army moved on from the city. The kings themselves took the best lodgings, Philip in the castle in the Hospitaller quarter and Richard with the Templars.[19]

Many of the buildings in the city were in disrepair, having been damaged by the artillery fire; but the churches were in the worst shape because their interiors had been desecrated by the Muslims, with crucifixes, altars, and statues smashed. Theobald, the titular bishop of Acre, received his episcopal chair with the recovery of the city, but he would have much work to do in restoring the condition of the facilities under his direction. Repairs began soon after Acre was retaken: while Richard concerned himself with the rebuilding of the damaged portions of the city wall and the emptying of its moat, several prelates took to restoring and re-consecrating the churches.[20] Yet continuing debates over the spoils of Acre soon led to acrimony and division.

Perhaps the biggest beneficiaries of the victorious siege were the Italians, who received properties in the city, as well as significant financial allowances for their role in both overseas transport and battle.[21] Many of these rights were, in fact, granted during the siege, before Acre was even in Christian hands. The Pisan commune received the most liberties, if not land, as spelled out in great detail in a confirmation grant from Guy and Sibylla in November 1189. In terms of property, the Pisans received back their quarter and those buildings in their possession in 1187, a mill, and the right to maintain their own churches. Other benefits included freedom from all tolls, a curia by which to adjudicate most of their own affairs, the right to collect fees from resident Pisans there (and a corresponding prohibition on Guy of Lusignan from doing the same), the right to garrison Pisan soldiers in the city and at its gates, and freedom from a whole host of ancillary fees on shipwrecks, ovens, baths, and so on.[22] In 1191, Richard the Lionheart made them the patrons of the Hospital of the Holy Spirit in Acre and, crucially, confirmed all of Guy's previous grants to them.[23] This was no doubt due not only to legal considerations, but also to their exceptional contributions during the siege and their newfound loyalty to Richard. The Genoese similarly saw the return of all their property in Acre from before its capture by Saladin, as well as freedom from tolls; this, too, was later confirmed in a charter of Richard's.[24] The king offered future spoils as well: were the Genoese to provide ships for a potential future invasion of Egypt, he would reimburse them half the cost of the galleys and pay one-third of any booty seized during the campaign.[25] Italians from the Amalfi coast were granted freedom from tolls into and out of Acre, a house in the city, and the right to their own local curia.[26] These grants were in addition to other grants to Italians in and around Tyre, which were confirmed by both Guy and Conrad of Montferrat.[27]

Other participants fared somewhat worse. Merchants from Marseille would be free from tolls and embargoes but owed a 1 percent sales tax on seaborne goods. They also received a curia and the right to adjudicate their own matters, save in instances of capital crimes.[28] To the Germans went property for the founding of the

Hospital of St Mary, which had been conceived of during the siege but prevented by the Hospitallers, who claimed a privilege from Rome ordering that all hospitals in Acre must be subject to them.[29] In the end, only the Pisan quarter had direct access to the port, which meant that the three other seafaring communes – Venice, Genoa, and Marseille – would remain locked in protracted competition with each other in Acre.[30]

These grants offer context for the summer divisions among the crusaders. Much of the city had already been distributed prior to the Muslims' surrender, and many of the nobles in camp were left on the outside looking in. They demanded their fair share from the kings, and while promises were apparently made several elites remained disgruntled and some, "compelled by poverty," left the Holy Land entirely.[31] Duke Leopold of Austria left after he was denied any share of the city at all, for he had arrived late to the siege (spring 1191) and had contributed little to the military effort. In an odd incident, his standard was thrown down into mud and trampled, perhaps on the orders of Richard himself; Otto of St Blasien adds the detail of the king also berating the duke in public. Leopold therefore quit the city and crusade entirely, returning home with his men.[32]

The most famous departure, however, was that of Philip Augustus himself. Soon after entering Acre, the French king declared his intentions of returning home, a decision for which he was roundly criticized. Some authors claim illness as his excuse, but while he had indeed been quite sick in fits and starts, Ambroise refused to accept this reasoning. Instead, he declares there to be "no witness that illness gives a dispensation from going with the army of the Almighty King"; further, he argues that Philip's sunken efforts at Acre should have compelled him to stay and finish the job.[33] Richard of Templo claims that Philip was actually healthy at the moment of his decision, and this is corroborated by Rigord (a physician), who notes that the king was cured while in Outremer on 10 August; on the same day, Philip's son Louis was miraculously cured of dysentery back in

France.[34] Ansbert claims that Philip could simply no longer tolerate Richard the Lionheart's arrogance, but in the same sentence he also mentions the death of Count Philip d'Alsace. This is interesting, because William of Newburgh, in the middle of a demeaning passage in which he asserts that Philip simply could not compare to Richard's brilliance and glorious presence, claims that the French king coveted Philip d'Alsace's lands.[35] This view became dominant, not only during the middle ages but in modern scholarship: that Philip returned west to claim lands in Flanders and also to conspire with Prince John against the absent Richard. Indeed, it forms the very background for some of the "Robin Hood" tales.[36] Rigord covers all these possibilities, except the lure of Flanders, and adds the sinister accusation that Richard was secretly conspiring with Saladin.[37]

Richard, for his part, tried to convince Philip to remain in the Levant. Roger of Howden has the English king attempting to swear Philip to a three-year oath to stay, which he refused; Ralph of Diss claims Richard tried to bribe him with half of his gold and wares.[38] Failing this, Richard made his counterpart swear on saints' relics that he would leave English domains in peace once he returned. Whether intentional on Ambroise's part or not, this event draws immediate parallels with the Bayeux Tapestry's depiction of Harold Godwinson making a similar oath to William the Bastard: while the context was different, Philip's later conniving symbolizes treachery at the highest levels.[39] Philip thereafter left five elite men behind in Acre as an assurance and received two galleys from Richard for the voyage home. Most of the French soldiers, however, remained in Acre for the time being, supported by Philip's treasure and food supplies, and Richard hired away all the French archers for his own use.[40] Philip's own nobles – those who had survived, at any rate – also begged him to stay, but to no avail: the French king gifted his share of Acre to Conrad of Montferrat, and then the two of them sailed for Tyre, accompanied by a few soldiers and some Muslim prisoners. He eventually crossed the sea to Apulia, then Rome, and was back home in Paris by Christmas.[41]

There was then the matter of the Muslim residents. As they filed out of Acre and into the plain, streaming towards either Saladin's ranks or locales farther away, Richard of Templo describes their appearance. He compliments them as worthy adversaries and notes their still-fierce resolve; but he was shocked by their physical appearance: strong, clean, and well dressed, they seemed completely undaunted by the turn of events and remained steadfast in their continence. Many of them had swallowed their jewels and coins. There is no indication that all of the residents were expelled, but if any Muslims did remain they surely must have lodged in the "rectangular" quarter, away from the churches. Many of the more notable residents remained as hostages in the city, along with the garrison soldiers, to be released only once Saladin fulfilled the terms of the agreement. Al-Mashṭūb was held by Richard, but Qāraqūsh was taken by Philip and Conrad to Tyre, as was the warrior Muḥammad ibn Bārīk. The Acre captives seem to have been resolute and took it all in their stride.

Not so the Muslims in Saladin's army, beyond the crusader camp: they mourned the loss of the city and cried and despaired over the outcome of their fellows. Ibn Shaddād claims to have personally consoled the sultan, who wept like "a bereft mother or a distracted love-sick girl."[42] Saladin had lost not only the city but also every ship moored in its port. This would have lasting effects: not until the fourteenth century would another Muslim fleet be able to seriously challenge the dominance of western navies in the eastern Mediterranean. An offer of conversion was offered to the prisoners: those who accepted baptism would be set free, and while many Muslims did receive the sacrament, they seem to have done so under false pretences, renouncing Christianity immediately upon joining their fellow Muslims in Saladin's ranks.[43] Ibn Shaddād (who himself authored a separate work on *jihad*) noted that the wiser Muslims kept their mind and prayers on the afterlife, leaving the events on earth to Allah. And while the eventual execution of the resolute

Muslim garrison would greatly anger him, he eventually came to accept the result, offering that God knows best.[44]

## Saladin dithers

Technically, however, the matter of Acre was not yet concluded because no one knew whether or not Saladin would accept, and then fulfill, the terms of the surrender. In the meantime, the military leaders busied themselves with post-siege work. Saladin ordered his heavy baggage moved south once more to Shafar'am, where he would soon return now that matters had concluded in the north. He himself remained outside Acre.[45] Richard ordered his catapults disassembled and packed away for transport, for he would need them later when the crusading army began its march south towards Ascalon.[46]

There seems to have been no removal of the temporary fortifications constructed outside the city, however: although many of the tents were likely packed away, the ditches and ramparts remained in place and under guard. The city could not accommodate the many thousands of crusaders on the scene, and so the bulk of the soldiers remained in residence in the camp. This explains why the Muslims stayed in a fighting disposition: Saladin and his advisers remained on alert, hoping that some of the Christians might be foolish enough to leave the camp and open themselves up to attack. Indeed, such a lapse in caution seems to have occurred on 25 July: Ibn Shaddād reports that a group of crusaders emerged from their camp near Montmusard, for an unstated purpose. Saladin's advance guard alerted the sultan and then attacked, driving off the Christian cavalry and killing about fifty foot soldiers before the lot were able to flee back to a position behind their fortifications.[47]

Saladin himself was in a difficult situation. Acre was in the hands of the crusaders, and so he had now permanently lost local access to the city, as well as many of his emirs and best soldiers within its walls. Moreover, those same emirs had struck a deal without his permission. In an extended and very detailed passage, Ambroise touts a purported understanding between the sultan and his emirs: Saladin expected reinforcements within the week, but if the garrison was pushed to the brink before their arrival, it had leave to surrender.[48] But this is directly contradicted by Ibn Shaddād, who was with the sultan and in a better position to know the truth. He relates that Saladin received a letter from a swimming courier that contained the stipulations of the deal:

> When the sultan had perused their letters and understood the contents, he expressed his great disapproval and was upset by the whole business. He assembled the leaders and the great men of state who were his councillors, informed them of the situation and consulted them about what to do. Their views left him confused, divided in mind and disturbed. He decided to send a letter that night by the swimmer and to condemn their coming to terms in this manner, while he was in a situation as this.[49]

Saladin had two problems with the deal. First, he had never actually given permission to the garrison to surrender. He was still naively optimistic that, with more reinforcements on the way, he could break through the crusader fortifications and relieve the city. He likely had strategic misgivings too, since most of the Egyptian fleet was stuck in Acre's harbor and would now be lost, ruining his carefully constructed plan of control over the Levantine harbors. Taken along with the fleet's previous defeat at Tyre in 1187 and all the losses in the Acre engagements, it was a hard reality to accept.[50]

Second, he could not fulfill the steep terms of the deal because he was broke. Saladin tended to spend or distribute money as soon as he acquired it, leaving no ready hoard from which to draw funds. Moreover, he had the habit of spurning sources of revenue out of pride and piety. At Acre, as we have seen, he had turned down the Abbasid caliph's meager offer of 20,000 bezants back in April 1190.[51]

His tax policies also stunted the inflow of cash. In 1171, he had abolished taxes and customs duties in Egypt that were holdovers from the Fatimid period, partly because some were forbidden in the Koran but also as a means of expressing his goodwill towards the residents and merchants in Cairo. All told, he had discontinued 1 million dinars in annual taxes, as well as 2 million measures of grain.[52] Such decisions affected his bottom line, in both the short and the long term. Simply put, in the summer of 1191, he did not have 200,000 bezants and had no easy way of amassing such a sum within two months.

The sultan tried to buy some time. On 15 July, after making his move south to Shafar'am, three crusader envoys tracked him down, bringing Qāraqūsh's chamberlain along for the journey. They reiterated the treaty terms, spent the night in safety, and in the morning left to visit the Christian prisoners in Damascus, who were set to be freed according to the agreed terms. Knowing that they would be absent for a while, Saladin sent a letter to Acre, asking the kings to specify the number of days he had to make good. Given his reception of the letters from the garrison, as well as the Christian envoy, he obviously already knew how long the term was, but this was a clever way of forestalling the payments while he collected what monies he could.[53]

By 2 August, Saladin was prepared to make good on most of the deal. Some of it had already been fulfilled: after all, Acre had already been turned over and the crusaders had indeed taken all the spoils from within it. The prisoner exchange is more difficult to ascertain because of the wide difference between the numbers in the various sources, as noted above. Saladin had 1,600 Christian prisoners ready for release, which may or may not have been enough. Regarding the money, however, he had only been able to raise half of the required amount, some 100,000 bezants. Saladin apparently wanted to send the prisoners and money along and wait for the Christians to reciprocate by releasing the Acre garrison, particularly the emirs, and the city's more wealthy citizens. But his advisers deemed their sultan far too trusting: they contended that he should hold back until assurances were made, via oaths from the Knights Templar, that the released Muslims would be of sufficient rank and quality, not the poorest and most common – and therefore of little value. He assented and wrote to the Christians, requesting such adjusted terms.[54]

In the end, Saladin never received his assurances, so he in turn refused to send over what money and prisoners he had collected. His apparent reneging on the deal led to the most infamous episode of the siege of Acre – that of Richard the Lionheart executing the whole Muslim garrison in front of the city. The diplomatic back-and-forth over terms and the executions are both well described in the sources, but given the nature of the event and the controversy it elicits even today, it is important to examine the individual elements carefully.

There are numerous notes and accusations that obscure the narrative, with the first question being: which side violated the treaty first? On the matter of the True Cross, the accounts make different claims but ultimately tell a coherent story. The Christian accounts all claim that Saladin delayed handing it over, saying that he needed more time to locate it, but ultimately reneged.[55] Ibn Shaddād, however, reveals that envoys were present in the Muslim camp at Shafar'am between 25 July and 2 August: they had asked to see the True Cross and their request was granted. The Christians prostrated themselves on the ground before it in a dust-filled spectacle, while amused Muslims looked on.[56] The envoys then departed, with some returning to King Richard and at least one to King Philip. Ambroise actually reports that rumors of this story were circulating in camp, but he declares them to have been quite untrue.[57] However, he appears to have been wrong: the True Cross *was* at Shafar'am and some crusaders *did* see it. One wonders about this misunderstanding. It seems unlikely that Ambroise was overtly lying because the mere presence of the valued relic should have excited him. Rather, he simply had no reliable evidence on the point: his information was tertiary, rumors about someone with whom he had not personally spoken.

Likewise, there was confusion about the prisoner exchange. Ambroise writes that Saladin "did not redeem or deliver those who were condemned to death."[58] Implicit in this statement is that the sultan had the crusader prisoners at the ready and could have released them at any time, whether or not they were in the immediate vicinity or at Damascus. It is unclear, though, if the Christian envoys had actually seen these prisoners for themselves. The prisoners were certainly in the area – Ibn al-Athīr writes of their being returned to Damascus once Richard carried out his executions – but obviously not in the sultan's tent, where the envoys had seen the True Cross. Ibn Shaddād speaks only of a flurry of diplomatic activity, in which the figure of 1,600 prisoners was agreed.[59] Nonetheless, there is no reason to believe that the Christians doubted the actual existence of these hostages; their complaint was only the delay in their release. For his part, Saladin would not release them without assurances that the exchanged Muslims were men of rank and wealth, but there is no mention of this condition in any of the Christian sources. Richard of Templo's outline of the terms indicates that Saladin could choose *which* nobles would be released but not that *all* freed hostages would be elites. Yet this new condition was the main sticking point for the sultan: while the True Cross was practically disposable, Saladin insisted on being able to choose those Muslims to be returned to him.

Next was the issue of money. Saladin had collected only half, but the amount was certainly enough for a first payment. There seems to have been no consternation over the amount. The Christian authors were most concerned with the cross and prisoners, probably because those things were real and no one but the kings and possibly a few select magnates would ever see the money. In the Arabic accounts, the crusaders were ready to accept this first payment and release half of their prisoners; the rest would be released once the balance was paid. Again, Saladin would not pay unless he could first choose which prisoners would be set free.[60]

Finally, there is the matter of how much time had elapsed in light of the terms of payment. As noted above, there is confusion over how long Saladin actually had to make good. Ambroise complains that more than two weeks had passed since the deadline, but this was untrue. The deal was concluded on 12 July, and Richard executed the prisoners on 20 August, so at worst Saladin was eight days late – and that is only if the term was one month. If it was forty days, as Howden claims, or two months, as per Ibn al-Athīr, then Saladin was not late at all. Moreover, there may have been some jiggling of the dates of which Ambroise was unaware: Ibn Shaddād claims that the Christian envoys, on the authority of their leaders, had allowed Saladin to pay in three installments over the course of three months.[61] The *Eracles* claims that two meetings were arranged for the payment and prisoner swap but that Saladin was a no-show for both. The latter was particularly grating, for sizable numbers of soldiers and clerics had supposedly walked barefoot to the meeting spot in a show of piety, only to have their hopes dashed.[62]

But while Saladin could perhaps draw out the payment period, the reality was that he was simply in no position to renegotiate the actual terms to which his emirs, for good or for bad, had sworn oaths. The Christian kings held Acre and the Muslim garrison within it, and with an open port and clear momentum they had no incentive to wheel and deal. The sultan's request to choose what prisoners were freed was a new – albeit reasonable – one, and it seems a pity that Qāraqūsh and al-Mashtūb lacked the foresight to make it during the actual negotiation. His insistence on using the Knights Templar to swear oaths was a nonstarter, because they were not willing to stake their reputation on the turbulent moods of the kings.[63] Given that he was asking for something new, he might have shown better faith by releasing some Christians to see how it would be reciprocated; had the crusaders released only poor and downtrodden soldiers, he could have been more certain of their intentions and made a better decision about the remainder of hostages and the other 100,000 bezants. Ibn Shaddād does note that the envoys had brought four important Muslims to Shafar'am in late July, so one could argue that the westerners themselves were displaying good faith in regards to the prisoner swap.[64]

Beyond these issues, we do not even know with whom Saladin was corresponding. Ibn al-Athīr puts some words in the mouths of "their princes," but the sultan only talked personally with the anonymous envoys and then sent letters to "the Templars." Roger of Howden speaks of two proposed conferences, one between Richard and al-'Ādil and another between Richard and Saladin; but neither came to fruition.[65] This is not the stuff of serious, high-level negotiations. Saladin never met with Richard or Philip, and we can justly wonder why.[66]

In the end, Saladin refused to turn over either the True Cross or the bezants and prisoners until his new demand of verification was met; and in doing so, he was clearly the one to break faith over the surrender agreement. This was certainly the conclusion of the Christian chroniclers.[67] One could argue that, since he never agreed to the terms in the first place, it is unfair to blame him. Rigord, in fact, tries to give him such an out, suggesting that Qāraqūsh and al-Mashtūb had been unable to persuade him of the terms.[68] One would be more sympathetic to such an argument had he never tried to meet the terms in the first place but rather refused outright. Instead, he went about collecting money and the equally arduous task of transferring prisoners from Damascus to Shafar'am. This suggests that, despite the steep cost, he intended to meet the contract as best he could but changed his mind later, on the advice of his emirs. Saladin was not a stupid man, and he surely knew that breaking the deal meant forfeiting a chance to have his best fighting men returned safely. Perhaps, as Yaacov Lev has suggested, he was personally indifferent to his own men, which resulted in his "monumental failure" to even attempt to ransom them.[69] Roger of Howden also reports a meeting in early July in which the kings had queried Muslim envoys about the True Cross: if true, then Saladin should not have been blindsided by the request a month later.[70]

## A war crime?

Still, while Saladin was wholly to blame for breaking the agreement, his role is far less controversial than Richard the Lionheart's response. On 20 August, the king assembled a large group of both cavalry and infantry and moved out from the siege camp's fortifications, marching east to Tel al-'Ayyāḍiyya and setting up a temporary array of tents. The Muslim advance guard had apparently moved farther east to Tel Kaysān by that point, so there was room to maneuver and little risk of counterfire. The Muslim garrison was led out alongside the army, its members bound together with ropes: the number ranges from 2,000 to 16,000, but the number appearing in most modern histories is between 2,600 and 3,000. The Muslims were arranged in rows and then executed, either by sword and spear thrusts or clean beheadings. Although Richard is usually singled out for this deed, he had made the decision in council to execute the prisoners and was assisted by Hugh of Burgundy, who coordinated the execution of those Muslims held by the French.

After the wayward Muslims learned what happened, they hurriedly assembled and charged at Richard's men: a disorganized melee raged until nightfall separated the two sides. Richard marched his men back to Acre, and the Muslims counted and collected their dead. In like response, Saladin ordered his Christian prisoners present to be beheaded and also sent the piece of the True Cross back to Damascus.[71] 'Imād al-Dīn relates that Saladin, now having no hostages to ransom (or so he believed, for Richard had spared the lives of a few elites), distributed the 100,000 bezants he had collected among his officers and men according to need.[72]

Opinion concerning Richard's execution of the Muslim garrison in front of Acre has spanned the entire possible range: from those who see fit to convict him of a war crime – entirely in the modern sense of the concept – to those who wish to exonerate him completely.[73] Negative judgments appear in most of the well-known, popularly available crusades histories. Steven Runciman, Jonathan Riley-Smith, and Lyons and Jackson have all dubbed Richard's executions a "massacre," a word hinting at malevolence. Christopher Tyerman goes further by calling the king's actions "butchery" and "an atrocity"; Hans Mayer simply calls it murder. John Gillingham has been the most prominent voice moderating the discussion.[74] Popular culture has chimed in as well, most recently in the "tsk-tsk" rebuke of Russell Crowe's character in Ridley Scott's 2010 movie *Robin Hood*, in which the humble archer dares to "speak truth to power" to King Richard himself:

> When you had us herd two and a half thousand Muslim men, women, and children together; the young woman at my feet, with her hands bound, she looked up at me. It wasn't fear in her eyes, it wasn't anger. It was only pity. She knew that when you gave the order, and our blades would descend upon their heads, that in that moment: we would be godless. All of us. Godless.[75]

Thus, a medieval event has remained in the public eye, even today. It is a controversy as much political as historical, and is considered to have been one of the great sins of the crusading era against the Muslim world.[76] But the historian's ethic demands that we dispense with the presentism that seeks to judge the past by the standards of today and ask two plain and essential questions: why did Richard do it, and was he justified in doing so according to the accepted norms of his time? In order to interpret the event with as much objectivity as possible, one should locate every explanation provided in the extant sources, an admittedly tedious but necessary process.

Leaving aside the later medieval legends about Richard's decision, there are five themes that appear across the contemporary texts, and some authors present more than one reason in the same passage.[77] The first is that Richard executed the Muslims in response to Saladin's breaking of the treaty, either because of the botched prisoner exchange or because of the sultan's refusal to turn over the True Cross.[78] Another is pure anger on the king's part.[79] A third is that Saladin's delay was impeding the crusade itself, which, after all, did not end in Acre, but was directed at the retaking of Jerusalem.[80] A fourth concerns money: Richard wanted the bezants promised and realized he might end up receiving nothing.[81] Finally, there is the notion that Richard executed the Muslims on behalf of either the Christians at Acre or Christianity itself. This last theme can be cast as either revenge, not only for the deaths of Christians in the army but also for the entirety of Muslim rule in Outremer, or religious zeal as Richard sought to prosecute holy war by eliminating the enemies of God.[82]

An alternative to these five motives appears, albeit a slim one: that Saladin had actually executed his own prisoners first. In his *Gesta* (finished in 1192), Roger of Howden claims that Saladin beheaded his Christian prisoners on 18 August, two days before Richard: "Saladinus fecit amputari capita omnium Christianorum captivorum." In his later *Chronica* (finished in 1201) Howden chose to add some background to the story. To wit, Saladin had heard of Richard's plan to execute the Muslim garrison on 20 August and so, through messengers, asked him to delay. Moreover, the sultan informed him that any executions would result in the Christian prisoners dying in a reciprocal move. When he then heard that Richard refused to delay, Saladin moved first and the decapitation of the Christians commenced. Gillingham has attributed these passages to rumors, which may have been fabricated in the crusader camp.[83] That no other source makes such a claim suggests that this may indeed have been the case. Even so, it is curious that Howden repeated the charge in the *Chronica*, which was revised after he was back in the West, where he had access to new sources of information, including Richard I's confidant and clerk, Philip of Poitou, the bishop of Durham.[84] Stranger still, just a few lines afterwards, Howden inserts a letter from Richard to the abbot of Clairvaux, in which the king describes the executions, but does not claim that Saladin acted first. In all likelihood, Howden knew the real story, but nonetheless offered two different versions of the executions in the same book!

We are fortunate to have this letter of Richard's in Howden's *Chronica*, which contains Richard's own recollection of the event. For what it is worth, the king claims that his decision was based on the first justification, that the treaty had been broken:

> . . . shortly after which the noble city of Acre was surrendered to my lord the king of the Franks and ourselves, the lives being saved of the Saracens who had been sent for the purpose of defending and protecting it, and an agreement being fully confirmed on the part of Saladin that he would give up to us the Holy Cross, and one thousand five hundred captives alive, a day being appointed for the due performance of the said covenants. However, the time having expired, and the stipulation which he had agreed to being utterly disregarded, we put to death about two thousand six hundred of the Saracens whom we held in our hands, as we were bound to do; retaining, however, a few of the more noble ones, in return for whom we trusted to recover the Holy Cross and certain of the Christian captives.[85]

This letter, if we believe its contents in any portion, belies the broad, popular understanding that posits Richard as a brute. Amin Maalouf's book, *The Crusades through Arab Eyes*, a widely read but unquestionably biased survey, summarizes the essential parts of such a depiction: Richard was "the prototype of the belligerent and flighty knight whose noble ideals did little to conceal his baffling brutality and complete lack of scruples."[86] Rather, we have here a rational explanation for his actions.

In particular, Richard's claim to have been "bound" (alternatively, to have done "what is proper") to dispatch the garrison is interesting and relates to the legality of his actions. A passage in the Lyon *Eracles*, written years after Richard's letter, includes a purported statement from Emir Qāraqūsh during the surrender negotiations: "If it turns out that Saladin does not do what I have said, we shall remain at your mercy to be treated as slaves."[87] If this is true, that the captive garrison was construed as an enslaved population, what then was Richard's legal obligation towards it? Western norms for the treatment of POWs-turned-slaves in this period are understudied subjects, and it is unclear what the exact customs might have been.[88] Richard was not against releasing captives as a matter of principle, for Ibn Shaddād relates that the king had released to Saladin a Muslim captive from North Africa during a series of abortive negotiations in late June.[89]

Alternatively, Richard's bond might have related to a remark from Richard of Templo, who put some interesting words into the mouths of Saladin's advisers. They urged the sultan to secure terms for the prisoners' release: "Otherwise, under the rights of war, they could be seized and put to a derisive and shameful death, making the Muhammadan law . . . appear worthless."[90] Whether Saladin knew it or not, there was indeed a legal precedent from the Battle of Badr in 624, in which Muhammad himself ordered the execution of two prisoners and numerous other Meccans were executed on his soldiers' own volition. The Hanbali jurist Ibn Qudāma al-Maqdisī, who had fought at the Battle of Hattin, explains that Christian prisoners of war might be set free or ransomed (presuming that they were willing to pay the *jizya*, or head-tax), but could also be enslaved or killed.[91] Thus, both contemporary and Koranic commentary allowed the killing of captives, and Saladin himself took advantage of this many times. Once, in 1183, his brother al-'Ādil suggested they first seek legal advice before commencing with executions; Saladin responded:

"the judgment of God on men like these is not a problem for scholars nor is it obscure. Let the decision to kill them be carried out."[92]

Such an attitude belies the popular modern view of the sultan as a gentler, more tolerant sort of leader, of the kind portrayed in another Ridley Scott movie, *Kingdom of Heaven* (2005).[93] Championed during the Age of Enlightenment and after, he holds a posthumous reputation as the counterpoint to supposed crusader cruelty and fanaticism. This characterization is based not only on his "legendary patience" (in the words of al-Qāḍī al-Fāḍil, a *kātib* who served as Saladin's vizier in Egypt from 1189 to 1192) and apparent generosity – which, at Acre, included his sparing an aged, toothless pilgrim and returning a captured Christian infant to his mother – but also on what has been interpreted as his more measured approach to violence. But Saladin's behavior was not, in fact, much different from that of Richard, despite the sympathetic interpretations of modern writers.[94] He enslaved some 11,000 Christian citizens after taking Jerusalem in 1187 and ordered the beheading of hundreds of Knights Hospitaller and Templar after the Battle of Hattin in the same year.[95] He allowed a group of Sufis to participate in the latter; with the executioners being unaccustomed to such tasks, these decapitations took longer and were more gruesome, and Saladin himself sat and watched the entire proceeding, "his face joyful," according to 'Imād al-Dīn.[96] One can thus make a moral-equivalence argument, that Richard's actions resembled those of his great foe.

However, most modern commentators have been loath to equate the two men with one another. So far as I can tell, there are three reasons for this, none of them mutually exclusive. One is the starkness of the numbers. Perhaps over time Saladin executed 3,000 prisoners (or even more) – but this was not in a single, newsworthy incident. Historians ought to be able to transcend this rhetorical difference. Yet the premise is still uncomfortable for some, and years (or centuries) of holding one individual somehow above another in a moral sense are hard to overcome. Old notions die hard: after all,

Queen Mary of England is still known by the nickname "Bloody" for burning 300 Protestants at the stake for heresy, while her half-sister Elizabeth I largely escapes criticism for having "strangled, disembowelled and dismembered" nearly 200 Catholics for treason.[97]

Second, there has been some confusion over the identities of the Muslims. No source relates the presence of women or children in the group marched to Tel al-'Ayyāḍiyya. In other words, the woman who taught Russell Crowe about atheism is entirely fictional. Rather, the entire group consisted of soldiers from the Acre garrison. This is why Ambroise could quip, "Thus was vengeance taken for the blows and crossbow bolts." Yvonne Friedman has complained about Richard's "butchery of defenseless Muslim captives"; defenseless, yes, but certainly not innocent: they were prisoners of war.[98] It was therefore quite unlike the massacres of Muslims and Jews in Jerusalem in 1099, in which the victims included non-combatants and women and children.[99] As regular soldiers, these men had little hope of being individually ransomed like the elites; indeed, that is why Richard kept the Muslim emirs alive.[100] If they could not be ransomed as a group they would either remain in prison or die. Religious difference could have little bearing on this notion, even during the middle ages. In 1174, for example, common Flemish mercenaries (who were Christian) who participated in the widespread rebellion against Richard's father, Henry II, were starved to death in English prisons while Breton and Norman elites (also Christian) were held but eventually ransomed.[101] In this sense, what Richard did reflected contemporary practice: its perceived criminality only differs in its theatricality and in the overt cultural gap between the executioners and the executed.

Finally – and on this last point, the modern reception of the executions has been overly presentist – acts of violence perpetrated in the name of Christ are condemned by modern commentators as wholly incompatible with "true" or "real" Christianity. There have been demands for Christian leaders to apologize for acts of past violence; once given, they serve to ratify this judgment. Moreover, the concept of "hate crimes" – a wholly contemporary notion – involves the imposition not only of additional legal penalties but also of greater moral outrage. In this sense, Richard's execution of Muslims, who today constitute a minority and therefore marginalized population in the West, is all the more horrific through our modern lenses; that to his action has been attributed a religious motive makes it even worse. If Richard acted as a barbarous Christian, however, one must consider that Saladin had likewise acted as a barbarous Muslim, similarly compelled by his religion.[102]

In the end, all of this posturing about war crimes serves only to obscure the truth of the matter, which is actually rather straightforward. First, Saladin violated the terms of the treaty proposed and settled by his emirs. Second, Richard probably violated the terms as well by executing the garrison before the deadline had passed. By their actions, both leaders knowingly risked forfeiting the lives of their comrades-in-arms. And because both leaders were guilty of executing large numbers of prisoners of war, any condemnation of Richard must fall upon Saladin as well. There is no need to either convict or absolve Richard of any war crime because both leaders were culpable in the events outside Acre in August 1191: Richard executed the Muslim soldiers only after Saladin had left them there to die.

## To Arsur and beyond

Coinciding with the negotiations over surrender terms was a series of departures from Acre. Now that the siege had concluded, individuals and groups of crusaders made plans either to stay on with the continuing campaign or to leave for other locales. With Frederick of Swabia dead and Philip departed, Richard the Lionheart became the single leader of the continuing crusade. The matter of the broken treaty had been settled by his mass execution – although perhaps not to his liking because the Christian prisoners were still in Muslim hands or dead themselves. Before the crusade was over, he would miss their collective presence dearly; but now Richard knew it was time to continue towards Jerusalem. Richard ordered the crusader camp struck and its people relocated into Acre.[103] It must have been a bittersweet experience as the tents and wooden buildings were taken down: although the camp had been a dismal environment, constantly exposed to the elements and frequently under assault, it had nonetheless been the two-year home of thousands of people.

Preparations for the march were extensive. Richard pitched his tent outside the ditches of the camp, posted an infantry guard around the perimeter, and ordered all remaining soldiers to muster near him, save those set to guard the city. This proved somewhat problematic because the men within Acre were not keen on leaving. With the siege concluded, they now preferred to relax and enjoy the pleasures of city life:

> The people were too reluctant because the town was delightful with good wines and girls, some very beautiful. They frequented the women and enjoyed the wine, taking their foolish pleasure, so that there was in the town such unseemliness, such sin and such lust that worthy men were ashamed by what the others were doing.[104]

Eventually, however, they were coaxed out of Acre in different ways. The soldiers refused to leave the area without proper provisioning, which Richard agreed to supply and have transported by sea. The French were more difficult, and he had to persuade some of them with bribes and even threats.[105] To guard against wanton distraction (so to speak), Richard left most of the women in Acre. In an amusing passage, Ambroise reveals that the only women permitted to join the army were elderly pilgrims and laundresses, the latter group being "as good as monkeys at getting rid of fleas." The march was a coordinated effort on land and sea: ten days of supplies were loaded onto ships, which tacked along the coastline in view of the marching men as they slowly moved south towards Jaffa and Ascalon.[106]

While the soldiers were mustering, Richard's camp came under attack. A brace of Muslim riders charged at the infantry guard, scattering them in the initial confusion. Richard raced to his horse and led a counterattack, and the Muslims were soon driven off. A group of Hungarian cavalry, however, pursued the fleeing enemy too far and were encircled and captured when the Muslims circled around in a feigned retreat maneuver. Several men were captured, including a Hungarian count and Richard's Poitevin marshal, Hugh.[107]

Finally, on Friday, 23 August, the mustered crusading army left Acre. It moved south but under duress, for Muslim skirmishers harried the march in small groups. By the end of the day, the army had crossed the River Belus and made camp on the opposite bank. There it remained on the next day, the Feast of St Bartholomew, not moving out again until Sunday, 25 August. The army marched alongside a massive standard, a long ship's mast plated in iron and mounted on a wagon, with Richard's emblem flying at the top. Richard himself led the English cavalry in the vanguard; the center of the army, where the standard rolled along, consisted of Normans; and the French were in the rearguard, led by Hugh of Burgundy.[108]

Once away from Acre, the crusaders encountered more attacks as Saladin mirrored their march south, culminating in the famous Battle of Arsur on 7 September 1191, in which Richard gained a major field victory over the sultan.[109] His army of some 10,000 men finally reached Jaffa three days later; but his subsequent campaigning never reached the final target of the crusade, Jerusalem. The closest the king got to the Holy City was 19 kilometers away, in January 1192, but severe weather and a lack of sufficient forces conspired to keep him from mounting an attack. The crusade ended formally that same year with the Treaty of Ramla, a three-year truce between Richard and Saladin guaranteeing crusader control of the Levantine coast from Acre to Jaffa but leaving Jerusalem to Saladin. Before departing for home, Richard conferred with his nobles and reluctantly agreed to allow Conrad of Montferrat to claim the Jerusalem throne, thereby cutting Guy of Lusignan out of the equation. The latter had the last laugh, however: Richard's ship was wrecked off the coast near Venice and he was arrested by Leopold, whom he had scorned at Acre; while on 28 April 1192, Conrad was murdered in Tyre by two Nizari assassins disguised as monks.[110]

With Jerusalem still in Muslim hands, the Christian kingdom in the East permanently relocated to Acre, where most of the blood of the Third Crusade had been shed. Already the main port of entry for pilgrims, it swiftly became a center of political and ecclesiastical operations. It was also the principal trading and creative center for Christians in the East. Connections with Byzantium were extensive, and a general construction boom accompanied the retaking of the city.[111] Relics from across the Holy Land were brought to Acre, and in the thirteenth century eight indulgences were issued for pilgrims who visited particular sites within it.[112] Today, Acre is a fertile area for archaeological excavations, and although little trace of the original crusader walls remains a number of house foundations have been found, as well as an underground tunnel running under the Pisan and Templar quarters.[113]

The city remained important to both crusaders and pilgrims for the next century, and it served as the seat of both the Kingdom and Patriarchate of Jerusalem until it finally fell to the Ayyubid's successors, the Mamluks.[114] In 1291, the Mamluk sultan al-Malik al-Ashraf Khalīl bombarded the city walls with his trebuchets until the towers fell. Soldiers entered the city and eliminated all Christian resistance. The Templar quarter was the last to fall: after some knights were given safe conduct but then treacherously beheaded, the remaining brothers resisted until the mamluks mined their tower walls. A lone eyewitness to the event, the so-called "Templar of Tyre," provides the last glimpse of Christian Acre:

...the Saracens entered the tower with so many men that the supports in the mine gave way, and the tower collapsed, and those brethren of the Temple and the Saracens who were inside were killed. Moreover, when the tower collapsed, it fell outwards toward the street, and crushed more than two thousand mounted Turks. And so this city was taken, abandoned, on Friday the eighteenth day of May in the said year, and the Temple compound ten days later, in the manner which I have described to you.[115]

Combat and siege, parley and betrayal, execution and conquest: as the 1200s neared their close, Acre fell in a manner similar to that in which it had been captured a century before.

# CONCLUSION

*"For all who died there, and for all who went there, for the great and the lesser, who supported the army of God."*[1]

The siege of Acre was a lengthy and complicated military event. More than just an assault on a fortified city, it involved a whole series of diverse engagements on both land and sea. The initiative and momentum shifted back and forth between the Christian and Muslim armies, with a common theme being each side's almost complete inability to follow up major victories with a final, devastating attack. At every turn commanders made poor decisions, moved too hastily against a set army, squandered golden opportunities with an overabundance of caution, and lost or redirected resources to less important goals and remote possibilities. Soldiers and leaders arrived and departed with time and the seasons, and petty squabbling between allies cost both armies valuable time and energy. In the end, one side outlasted the other, and the Christians, who had sat ensconced within ditches and ramparts that Saladin himself had permitted them to construct, finally collapsed the Cursed Tower and thereby persuaded Acre's garrison to capitulate. Although the siege took nearly two years to complete, its success propelled Richard the Lionheart and the soldiers of the Third Crusade onward on the quest for Jerusalem. Nonetheless, the tremendous numerical toll at Acre, combined with the departure of Philip and the ill-fated imperial expedition, resulted in Richard's commanding a force that he believed was insufficient to retake the Holy City itself. The siege of Acre, therefore, determined the ultimate fate of the Third Crusade.

As a military event, the siege of Acre must be regarded as the ideal snapshot of twelfth-century warfare, broadly construed. It featured soldiers from three continents and diverse areas therein: northern and southern Europe, Syria and Mesopotamia, Egypt and the Maghreb. The greatest warriors of the day either participated in the siege or died on their way to it, and many met their end on the Acre plain. We read of the signature tactics of East and West – charges of heavy cavalry, feigned retreats, fighting marches – and imagine the strikes from the latest advances of military technology manifest in massive siege towers, battering rams, and trebuchets. Four heads of state converged on the same field of battle, a rare occurrence in the twelfth century indeed: Guy of Lusignan, king of Jerusalem; Philip Augustus, king of France; Richard the Lionheart, king of England; and Saladin, sultan of Egypt and Syria. In short, it was an epic event, and one in which thousands of men and women died to win this vital port on the Levantine coast.[2]

## Command and control

A major reason the Third Crusade still draws widespread interest was the presence of some of the crusading era's most famous leaders. Saladin and Richard the Lionheart, in particular, have captured the imaginations of historians, amateurs, and enthusiasts in a way that few other figures have. Numerous biographies and studies of both men abound, and the litany of arguments over their careers and legacies is well-trodden ground. Here, we are obligated to ask whether or not their deeds at the siege of Acre specifically complement their fine, warlike reputations: historical, mythological, or otherwise.[3] A quick review reveals that both of their reputations must necessarily suffer in light of what happened there and that their enduring fame as military commanders was achieved at other times and in places other than Acre.

One inescapable takeaway is that Saladin's inability to defeat the Christians at Acre was mostly of his own making. Over the course of two years, he had multiple opportunities that he declined to exploit, especially at the outset of the siege. He passed up an opportunity to catch Guy of Lusignan's army marching south from Tyre in August 1189, when it was trapped along the Mediterranean Sea on the Scandelion Pass. In early September of the same year, he had the Toron surrounded on at least two sides, but instead of attacking Guy atop the hill his soldiers engaged along Haifa Bay, seeking to open a passage into Acre itself. In mid-September, Taqī al-Dīn broke through the crusader ranks by Montmusard and did open a path to the city – but then he and Saladin agreed to delay their attack for a day. When fighting recommenced on 19 September, a half-hearted effort to draw the crusaders out from their tents with showers of arrows failed; Saladin's own sally from Acre was beaten back into the city. Thereafter, there were no more immediate assaults on the position. Another opportunity arose when the Christians mobilized on 4 October and pushed into Saladin's camp. For whatever reason, the sultan or his commanders either did not or could not mobilize the Muslim left wing in time to fully entrap the routed crusaders, and Geoffrey of Lusignan was able to rally enough men to hold the camp and avoid complete destruction.

In late October 1189, Saladin made more mistakes. He extended the radius of his army vis-à-vis the Christian camp in an attempt to lure them out into ambushes, when perhaps he should have pressed his advantage in numbers and morale with direct assaults. (He made the same mistake again in July 1190.) Once given space and time, the crusaders instead remained in camp and began digging protective ditches and building ramparts. Ignoring the advice of his emirs, Saladin still eschewed direct assaults and the Christian defense improved substantially; in the process, he willingly surrendered the supply path into the city that Taqī al-Dīn had opened just one month earlier.

Over the course of 1190, the Muslim attacks on the ramparts were scattershot: daily assaults around the perimeter and occasional concerted rushes on certain portions of the ramparts, but no direct, large-scale assault focused on smashing through. He might have focused on a single section of rampart: the crusaders were camped along the entire length of Acre's stone walls, and with numbers on his side he might have found some success. Despite the influx of new crusaders from the sea, Saladin seems never to have been badly outnumbered, but he insisted on mirroring his enemies by maintaining an encirclement of left–center–right formation. A telling example of his stubbornness came in the spring of 1190. After sending divisions of his army north to protect against Frederick Barbarossa, Saladin concentrated on shifting soldiers from the left and center wings into the depleted right. In other words, his priority was to maintain his encircling position, not to break the crusader defenses. It was a strategy of exhaustion, and perhaps he was counting on starvation and disease to do his work for him. But although untold numbers of crusaders died in the winters of 1189–90 and 1190–91, conditions were never quite bad enough to compel their surrender, and deliveries of food and fresh soldiers always seemed to arrive just in time.

Other mistakes and setbacks followed. Saladin was unable to contain and crush the St Martin offensive in November 1190. Most crucially, he could not stop the fighting retreat along the west bank of the River Belus. The Christians were hemmed in on three sides, and all Saladin had to do was send his entire right wing of cavalry north along the river: because the retreat was slow, his riders would have reached the Doc bridge first, and – had they crossed and then rode south – the Christians would have been completely entrapped. But Saladin replicated his containment tactics at Acre: most of his right wing paced the Christian march north from the opposite bank of the Belus, shooting arrows in a harassing attack. Only a few Muslims actually went as far north as the bridge, and Geoffrey of Lusignan and company were able to smash through them in a cavalry charge. The Christians then crossed the bridge and returned to camp. Thus, the sultan simply was not aggressive enough on the attack. A month later, Saladin swapped out the Acre garrison, replacing the battle-hardened veterans with new soldiers who, while capable, were simply not acclimatized to the defensive routines. That operation was long, costly, and demoralizing.[4]

The deleterious impact of Saladin's errors, both individually and viewed collectively, was apparent in the response of his own soldiers. The Acre garrison repeatedly considered surrendering to the crusaders and actually entered into real negotiations five times: October 1189, May 1190, twice in early July 1191, and, finally, in late July 1191. No doubt the Christian leaders were foolish to pass over the initial opportunities. Particularly in 1189 and 1190, their desire to either win stronger terms or to glory in outright, bloody conquest meant that they willingly extended the duration of the siege, which ultimately (and needlessly) cost thousands of crusaders their lives. In time, the Acre garrison clearly lost faith in Saladin's ability to save them; by late July 1191, it had stopped asking for the sultan's permission to surrender and abruptly informed him that it would do so without his blessing. In the same month, while Saladin attempted, once more, to alleviate pressure on Acre by attacking the Christian camp, his own soldiers baldly refused his orders; others sneaked out of camp and deserted. It was a sharp fall for a man who had, I agree, "exhibited generalship of a very high order" just four years previously, at the Battle of Hattin.[5]

We now move to consider King Richard's exploits at Acre. Over the course of 200 years, British historians have confirmed Richard's legendary reputation as the quintessential medieval general. In 1778, David Hume's *History of England* laid out a classic and enduring depiction:

> The most shining part of this prince's character are his military talents. No man, even in that romantic age, carried personal courage and intrepidity to a greater height; and this quality gained him the appellation of the lion-hearted, *coeur de lion*. He passionately loved glory, chiefly military glory; and as his conduct in the field was not inferior to his valour, he seems to have possessed every talent necessary for acquiring it.[6]

A century later, William Stubbs pursued this same glory angle, writing that Richard "would fight for anything whatever, but he would sell everything that was worth fighting for. The glory he sought was victory rather than conquest."[7] The same point had been driven home in Sir Walter Scott's novel *Ivanhoe* (1819):

> ...the personal glory which he acquired by his own deeds of arms, was far more dear to his excited imagination, than that which a course of policy and wisdom would have spread around his government.[8]

Such interpretations help explain why Richard balked at the initial negotiations between al-Mashṭūb, Qāraqūsh, and Philip in early July 1191: he, like the leaders at Acre before him, eschewed negotiations because he wanted to take the city by force of arms alone.

However, these nineteenth-century views of Richard the Lionheart have not held their ground. In the twentieth century, the earlier English histories gradually began to be viewed as incomplete. The Victorian texts became quaint and idealistic, often built upon teleological assumptions. The later works, often influenced by the German/Rankean tradition, were judged to be rather more rigorous in their scrutiny of documents – *wie es eigentlich gewesen* – but they nonetheless trended toward nationalistic impulses. Some authors were denounced outright.[9] Since then, Richard's military career has been characterized somewhat differently, and in 1984, Gillingham convincingly argued that Richard "was very far from the impetuous leader of romantic legend."[10]

So what place should the siege of Acre hold in the military career of this warrior-king? Richard was at Acre for less than two months, and in that time he missed half of the assaults against its walls due to illness. On the other hand, his catapults, sappers, and soldiers were highly effective in their attacks. It was Richard, not Philip Augustus, who struck fear into the hearts of the Muslims, or at least that is what the Arabic sources claim. Suspending old and new notions of his prowess, however, it was not Richard himself who turned the tide at Acre, but rather Philip. Philip altered the course of the siege by undermining the city wall and negotiating terms with the garrison while Richard convalesced. Yet Philip did not finish the job himself because Richard soon recovered and added his own resources to the siege works.

I would therefore argue that Richard did not "win" the siege of Acre when his men collapsed the Cursed Tower. Acre was taken through the combined efforts of a diverse range of knights and soldiers (some of them encamped before the city for two years) and through hardship and glory. They were led by an array of commanders who kept the army from falling apart. Arriving near the end, Richard played an important role; but more crucial was the infusion of his men. Bolstered by the reserves from England and the continent, the Christian army was able both to maintain its camp perimeter against Saladin's army and to inflict enough damage on Acre's walls to secure a victory. As regards Richard's reputation as a crusader, that was won not at Acre, but rather at Arsur and Jaffa. The latter, in particular, was a seminal moment: one year after Acre, in August 1192, Richard and fewer than 2,000 soldiers ably defended the city against Saladin's advance. As Smail has remarked, "his personal prowess on that day helped him to win immortality," and Christopher Tyerman agrees that Jaffa "secured . . . [his] legendary status as a warrior and general."[11]

At the same time, there were several commanders at Acre who led with aplomb, but who have lingered in the shadows of Saladin and Richard the Lionheart. Taqī al-Dīn must be considered to have been the finest and most capable Muslim general at Acre. Commanding Saladin's right wing, he led the breakthrough in Montmusard that opened a passage into the city in September 1189. On 4 October, he was driven back by the crusader left wing but held his men together enough so that they never crumbled; once the counterattack began, he was able to regroup and force his enemy first into their comrades in the center and then backwards into their camp. He successfully recruited additional reserves in Syria and persuaded Sanjar Shāh to end his 1190 defection and return his men to the siege. The emirs Qāraqūsh and Ḥusām al-Dīn Abū'l-Hayjā led the Acre garrison in 1189 and 1190, until the latter was removed in Saladin's reorganization. Together, they found ways to neutralize the crusader siege engines with counter-battery fire, Greek Fire, and cavalry sorties at key moments. In 1191, it was Qāraqūsh who spearheaded the negotiations with kings Philip and Richard.

For the Christians, three names shine brightly in the siege sources. Count Henry of Champagne redirected the focus of the Christian forces away from Saladin's army and towards the siege works. His catapults and battering rams inflicted the initial blows that were exploited later by others. Although he and his fellows were unable to prevent the sergeants from leading the disastrous St James offensive, he ensured the survival of his army by keeping the nobles and knights behind the battlements. Henry also led the magnificent fighting retreat in early November 1190, in which he engaged Muslim forces on four consecutive days while on the march and saved his army from encirclement and near destruction. Likewise, Geoffrey of Lusignan proved a fine leader: protecting the camp and rescuing defeated comrades in 1189, commanding alongside Count Henry on the St Martin offensive, and leading key cavalry charges in times of great need. Finally, some respect must be paid to Philip Augustus, who is routinely overshadowed by his English peer, Richard. It was Philip's artillery that first seriously damaged Acre's walls, and his French sappers were the first to undermine the wall by the Cursed Tower. He pressed his attacks both with and without the support of Richard. While the English king lay ill, Philip's attacks proved strong enough to compel Qāraqūsh to consider surrendering a week before Richard became seriously involved.[12]

However, not all of the successes and failures at Acre were credited to the decisions of commanders and the exploits of soldiers. Although in this book I have emphasized operational, organizational, logistical, strategic, tactical, and technological aspects of the siege, not every medieval source viewed the action through a similarly functional lens. Rather, they frequently attributed victory and defeat at Acre to the role of the divine, as had authors and warriors alike since the beginning of the crusade period.[13] Many events were testament to God's will cooperating with human agency to bring about victory in battle. Given that the Third Crusade featured contests between the armies of Christianity and Islam, one might expect serious differences in the way faith inspired, conditioned, and limited combat and diplomacy. Yet in many ways the Latin, Old French, and Arabic sources express shared notions about the role of God on the battlefield and the need for faith during the conduct of war.

Both sides believed that they, and only they, were God's chosen warriors. There are several examples of the "soldier of God" motif: Ambroise dubbed the crusaders the army of God; Jesus himself was thought to have inspired his knights to fight; Duke Frederick of Swabia is depicted as an athlete of God; and Hubert Walter, though a bishop, was, by his virtues, made a knight.[14] In similar fashion, the Muslims were soldiers of Islam.[15]

Distinctions were also made between the respective armies. Ambroise twice juxtaposes the Christians and the Muslims: the former were the people of God, while the latter were "the scum of the earth" and "the accursed race, whom God curses with his own mouth."[16] Richard the Lionheart himself, in his letter to Clairvaux copied by Roger of Howden, refers to holy sites that "the enemies of the Cross of Christ" had desecrated.[17] Saladin himself claimed that he was willing to die, so long as "God's enemies perish," too.[18] In this way, both Muslims and Christians rushed to arms in like manner, fearing defeat, but confident that their efforts would serve the will of God and the propagation of right belief.

## Leaving Acre

Like all significant military events, there will always be more to say about the siege of Acre, different angles to pursue, and competing interpretations to advance. The complexity of the siege narrative is striking and lends itself to constant study and revision. All told, the event featured eight set-piece battles in the open field. Notions that there were no formal battles during the Third Crusade – except for Arsur – are therefore erroneous.[19]

Complementing these major engagements were twenty-six skirmishes that were important enough to merit special mention in the sources and an uncountable number of other minor fights and daily attacks on the crusader ramparts. Included among the latter were over a dozen sorties by the Acre garrison, launched out of its gates against, and often into, the Christian camp. In response, there were twelve extended periods of crusader siege attacks against the city of varying method and intensity. Finally, in the waters of Haifa Bay and the Mediterranean Sea, ten naval encounters took place between individual ships or whole fleets from Italy, Cyprus, Lebanon, and

Egypt. As the respective armies trudged away from Acre in late August 1191, marching south towards Arsur, we can only imagine how many Christian and Muslim soldiers looked back over their shoulders at the peninsula that had occupied so much of their lives. The feeling must have been bittersweet – and the memory of their fallen companions who never saw inside its walls, much less those of Jerusalem, doubly so. Yet, long as the siege might have been, it was only the first encounter of the Third Crusade.

Different dimensions of medieval warfare were on full display at Acre. In terms of military technology, Acre is an exhibition of the advanced methods and contrivances of the twelfth century: a variety of mechanical devices, such as artillery, siege towers, cats, rams, and fortified ships; chemical and biological warfare in the Muslim use of Greek Fire and the pollution of water supplies with corpses; and ingenuity of construction in the crusader ramparts and sapping efforts of Christians and Muslims alike. Military organization and logistics at Acre can be closely studied for both the eastern and western armies: how soldiers mustered and marched, labored and rested, and traded and consumed. A wide variety of tactics play out in the narrative. At siege, we see how both Christians and Muslims attacked fortifications and repelled the enemy. In the field, we read about where and how troops were stationed, formed up, attacked, counterattacked, and broke. The two sides sometimes moved sharply and decisively to exploit weaknesses in the lines of the other; at other times, both sides cracked from assault. Moments of high drama and combat were balanced by periods of downtime and considerable suffering. Clear, level-headed command was often counterbalanced by panicky, too-cautious, or too-aggressive decision-making in the heat of combat, and the morale of both elite and common warriors is dealt with in the sources. To those present, nothing at Acre was certain: neither the state nor the size of the armies; neither the abilities nor the politics of their leaders; neither the arrival of reinforcements nor at times even the next meal.

On a strategic level, the siege offers lessons in the need for decisiveness and clear objectives. Saladin's inefficient strategy of exhaustion for breaking the siege has already been discussed. The Christian dithering was equally problematic. Alternating between attacks on the city and Saladin's encircling force, the crusade leaders lost sight of their primary objective of Acre itself. In 1189, this amounted to an effort at "shoving off" Saladin's men, in order to gain room to operate; but the reverse occurred when the 4 October battle was lost. While Henry of Champagne temporarily redirected the army's energies back towards Acre in 1190, he was similarly drawn away from the city via the St Martin offensive. The ebb and flow of these operations must be read in human terms. The thousands of soldiers could not so easily fight a major battle one day, and then, with little turnaround, simply pivot to the full-on conduct of siege operations the next. The confused prioritizing on both sides resulted in a costly affair that took longer than anyone expected. No wonder Philip Augustus was astounded on his arrival in the spring of 1191 to see the city still untaken and asked – in modern parlance – "what have you been *doing* all this time?"

Following Philip's and Richard's arrival, the Christians finally solved the puzzle, splitting the army between siege and rampart defense but relinquishing the initiative to Saladin: in other words, consigning half their men to offense and the other half to defense. Military historians tend to be fond of leadership studies, and no doubt debate over the choices made by commanders on all sides will endure.

Fortunately, there is much grist for this mill. The depth and detail of our extant sources and the interpretive questions surrounding two years' worth of engagements and interactions – in the context of both Christian and Islamic holy war, no less – all preclude simple retellings of the siege of Acre in 1189–91. No single source reveals this panoply of engagements; rather, all the narratives from both the western and eastern perspectives must be consulted and scrutinized in order to determine its order and magnitude. Modern historians are fortunate to possess reams of information and the material findings of extensive and ongoing archaeological excavation of Old Akko, the Toron, and their surrounds. More will be discovered and said about medieval Acre, and likely soon.[20]

"At Acre, by the time September was set, the sun had put all the air to the sword ..."[21] So said Milo, the abbot of St Mary-of-the-Pine in Poitiers in Maurice Hewlett's novel, *The Life and Death of Richard Yea-and-Nay.* The evocative passage was later recalled by none other than T.E. Lawrence, that doughty champion of Arabic peoples and civilization, as he experienced the intensity of the Middle East's summer heat in 1917.[22] He had visited Acre eight years earlier and knew well the nature of the city and the lifestyle of its residents. As we similarly recall the labors of the thousands who fought and died at Acre, the image of both sun and blade seems fitting indeed.

# APPENDICES

## Appendix A: Description of Acre

In all the coastal region of the Levant, construed as the region stretching in a crescent from Asia Minor to Egypt, David Jacoby has dubbed Acre (modern Akko) "the most exciting city for the historian of the middle ages."[1] Extensive archaeological excavation and surveying of the city have taken place, much of which led to its 2001 designation as a UNESCO World Heritage Site.[2] Since then, new findings have constantly been made, and archaeologists seemingly learn more about the city with each passing day.

Some twelfth- and thirteenth-century descriptions and depictions of the city have survived along with the material remains. There is a good description of the city and its surroundings in Richard of Templo's version of *Itinerarium peregrinorum*:

> The city is triangular in shape: narrower on the west, more extended on the east. More than a third of its perimeter, on the south and west, is enclosed by the flowing waves. Its harbour is not as good as it should be. It often fails to protect vessels wintering there so that they are smashed to pieces, because the outcrop of rock which runs parallel to the shore is too low to break the force of waves in a storm.[3]

The walls ensconcing the peninsula today do not date back to the crusader period, or even the Napoleonic period.[4] They are primarily of nineteenth-century Ottoman build and can be deceiving at first glance. For example, the current western wall along the Mediterranean did not exist at all in the twelfth century; instead, Acre's northern wall ran west and terminated in a tower at the sea's edge.[5] Fortunately, there are three illustrations of Acre that appear in medieval manuscripts, and all of them highlight its fortifications (see Plates 3 and 4).[6] The thirteenth-century maps of Pietro Vesconte and Paulinus of Puteoli show eleven or twelve towers, including the *Turris maledicta* (the Cursed Tower) at the juncture of the northern and eastern walls.[7]

The maps also show roads leading up to towers with gates drawn upon them. Identifying all the gates on the original wall is tricky and has been the source of some debate. On the northern wall we know the names of five gates. From the western edge (along the sea) these are the Gates of St Michael, of the Bathhouse, of the Hospital (or St John), of Mary (or Our Lady), and of the English (or St Hugh). This wall ends with the Cursed Tower. The eastern wall sprang from that tower and ran south, punctured by Pilgrim's Gate (later St Nicholas) and then the gate of Geoffrey le Tor.[8] On the eastern wall was the Ox Spring Tower, which may have stood over this last gate.[9] Once the city was retaken, the Christian residents renamed some gates, and more entrances appeared as the walls were expanded and new walls added in the thirteenth century.[10]

The foundations of the crusader walls have not yet been excavated, although some remaining elements have been found: notably, a section on the northern side upon which the Ottoman structure was built and the remains of a tower 170 meters northeast of the northeast corner of the present-day wall (see Plate 5).[11] Excavated pieces of minor arts and catapult stones and the discovery of stone foundations suggest that the eastern crusader wall lay farther east, perhaps 450 meters outside the current wall and covering a good deal of the distance between it and the Toron. It sat partially on a ridge, was sloped to form a glacis, and was probably fronted by a water-filled moat.[12]

To the east and beyond the walls of Old Akko lay the Toron and other natural features, which Richard also describes:

> A city called Ptolemais was formerly situated on top of Mount Turon, which lies in the vicinity of the city . . . The river which flows to the city is called the Belus. It has a narrow bed and is not deep, but Solinus claims no little glory for it, including it among the wonders of the world and stating that it has sands like glass . . . Mount Carmel rises loftily on the south side of the city.[13]

Perched on the remains of a Canaanite capital and Phoenician seaport, the Toron lies a little over a kilometer as the crow flies from the base of the hill to where the peninsula meets the water.[14] Under foot on the modern walking trails lie thousands of shards of Hellenistic-era pottery, strewn about and trodden into the dirt like so many discarded trinkets. Rising above the hill itself, a black-steel statue of Napoleon Bonaparte sits astride his bucking Marengo, forever gazing upon the city that so frustrated him during his own siege of 1799.

The rest of the city surroundings can easily be spied from the hilltop (see Plate 6). South of the Toron flowed the River Na'man, or Belus, which emptied below Acre's harbor. The general region to the east of the city, broadly referred to as the Acre plain, stretches about 10 kilometers to the foothills of the hilly regions of Galilee and was filled, at the time, with gardens, vineyards, and farms.[15] Farther south and across the bay, Mount Carmel rises sharply from the sea: once the sparring ground of Elijah and the priests of Baal, today it is home to the port of Haifa, the third-largest city in Israel. To the east across the Acre plain lie woods and rolling hills that ascend towards the rough heights of Upper Galilee, with roads trekking east and southeast towards Tiberias and Nazareth. Not far to the north awaits Lebanon: Tyre, Tripoli, and the ancient roads to Asia Minor.

**Appendix B: Engagements at/near Acre, 1189–91**

The siege of Acre was a scene of constant military operations. The sources agree that Saladin's army attacked the crusader camp routinely, often on a daily basis; likewise, siege operations against the city were ongoing across the two years. It is therefore difficult to quantify the exact number of engagements. Here, I have tallied every action that is specifically noted in the texts. There is some subjectivity in my determination of "type" of engagement: the narratives do not always permit a clear-cut distinction between a "skirmish" and a "battle," so I have differentiated the two by listing as battles only set-piece field actions. "Victories" indicate that a particular military objective was met (such as ending an assault by destroying equipment or holding the field after battle).

| Date | Type | Location | Initiator | Result |
|------|------|----------|-----------|--------|
| 1189 (22–28 Aug.) | Skirmish | Scandelion Pass | Saladin's army | Inconclusive |
| 1189 (1 Sept.) | Siege | Acre | Christians | Defeat |
| 1189 (2 Sept.) | Skirmish | The Toron | Saladin's army | Victory: opened route to city |
| 1189 (mid-Sept.) | Skirmish | Acre bay shore | Saladin's army | Defeat |
| 1189 (15 Sept.) | Battle | Montmusard | Saladin's army | Inconclusive |
| 1189 (16 Sept.) | Battle | Montmusard | Saladin's army | Victory: opened route to city |
| 1189 (16 Sept.) | Sortie | Montmusard | Acre garrison | Victory: camels seized |
| 1189 (17 Sept.) | Battle | Montmusard | Saladin's army | Defeat |
| 1189 (19 Sept.) | Skirmish | Montmusard | Acre garrison | Defeat |
| 1189 (22 Sept.) | Battle | Crusader camp | Christians | Defeat |
| 1189 (29–30 Sept.) | Skirmish | River Belus | Saladin's army | Victory: successful ambush |
| 1189 (4 Oct.) | Battle | Acre plain | Christians | Defeat |
| 1189 (4 Oct.) | Sortie | Crusader camp | Acre garrison | Inconclusive |
| 1189 (31 Oct.) | Naval | Haifa Bay | Muslims | Victory: ships ran the blockade |
| 1190 (March) | Skirmish | Acre plain | Christians | Inconclusive |
| 1190 (March) | Naval | Mediterranean Sea | Christians | Victory: ships sunk |
| 1190 (early May) | Siege | Acre | Christians | Defeat |

**Appendix B: (cont.)**

| Date | Type | Location | Initiator | Result |
|---|---|---|---|---|
| 1190 (12 May) | Skirmish | Crusader camp | Saladin's army | Defeat |
| 1190 (12 May) | Sortie | Crusader camp | Acre garrison | Defeat |
| 1190 (14–15 June) | Naval | Haifa Bay | Muslims | Victory: ships ran the blockade |
| 1190 (25 July) | Battle | Acre plain | Christians | Defeat |
| 1190 (25 July) | Sortie | Crusader camp | Acre garrison | Inconclusive |
| 1190 (August) | Siege | Acre | Christians | Inconclusive |
| 1190 (2–3 Sept.) | Sortie | Crusader camp | Acre garrison | Victory: catapults burned |
| 1190 (late Sept.) | Naval | Tower of Flies | Christians | Defeat |
| 1190 (2 Oct.) | Sortie | Crusader camp | Acre garrison | Inconclusive |
| 1190 (mid–Oct.) | Skirmish | Tel al-ʿAyyāḍiyya | Christians | Defeat |
| 1190 (15 Oct.) | Siege | Acre | Christians | Defeat |
| 1190 (15 Oct.) | Sortie | Crusader camp | Acre garrison | Victory: rams burned & captured |
| 1190 (17 Oct.) | Naval | Tower of Flies | Christians | Defeat |
| 1190 (2 Nov.) | Sortie | Crusader camp | Acre garrison | Defeat |
| 1190 (12–15 Nov.) | Sortie | Crusader camp | Acre garrison | Inconclusive |
| 1190 (12 Nov.) | Skirmish | Tel al-ʿAjūl | Christians | Inconclusive |
| 1190 (13 Nov.) | Battle | Recordane | Christians | Inconclusive |
| 1190 (Nov.–Dec.) | Sorties* | Crusader camp | Acre garrison | Inconclusive |
| 1190 (14 Nov.) | Fighting march | River Belus | Christians | Victory: army returns to camp |
| 1190 (15 Nov.) | Fighting march | Doc bridge | Christians | Victory: successful ambush |
| 1190 (24 Nov.) | Skirmish | Montmusard | Saladin's army | Victory: partial wall collapse |
| 1191 (1–5 Jan.) | Siege | Acre | Christians | Victory: partial wall collapse |

**Appendix B: (cont.)**

| Date | Type | Location | Initiator | Result |
|---|---|---|---|---|
| 1191 (1–5 Jan.) | Sorties | Crusader camp | Acre garrison | Inconclusive |
| 1191 (11 Jan.) | Naval | Acre harbor | Christians (defectors) | Victory: ship looted |
| 1191 (22–23 Jan.) | Naval | Acre harbor | Christians | Defeat |
| 1191 (2 March) | Naval | Acre harbor | Muslims | Victory: ship captured |
| 1191 (31 March) | Skirmish | Unknown | Saladin's army | Inconclusive |
| 1191 (14 May) | Skirmish | Crusader camp | Saladin's army | Victory: camp raided |
| 1191 (26 May) | Naval | Mediterranean Sea | Christians | Defeat |
| 1191 (30 May) | Siege | Acre | Christians | Victory: partial wall collapse |
| 1191 (4–5 June) | Skirmishes | Crusader camp | Saladin's army | Victory: siege attacks aborted |
| 1191 (7 June) | Naval | Mediterranean Sea | Christians | Victory: ship sunk |
| 1191 (8 June) | Ravaging | Haifa and Acre plain | Muslims | Inconclusive |
| 1191 (11 June) | Siege | Acre | Christians | Defeat |
| 1191 (11 June) | Skirmish | Crusader camp | Saladin's army | Defeat |
| 1191 (11 June) | Sortie | Crusader camp | Acre garrison | Victory: engines burned |
| 1191 (14 June) | Siege | Acre | Christians | Defeat |
| 1191 (14 June) | Skirmish | Crusader camp | Saladin's army | Victory: camp looted |
| 1191 (17 June) | Siege | Acre | Christians | Defeat |
| 1191 (17 June) | Skirmish | Crusader camp | Saladin's army | Defeat |
| 1191 (22 June) | Skirmish | Montmusard | Saladin's army | Defeat |
| 1191 (23 June) | Skirmish | River Belus | Saladin's army | Inconclusive |
| 1191 (2 July) | Siege | Acre | Christians | Inconclusive |
| 1191 (3 July) | Skirmish | Crusader camp | Saladin's army | Defeat |

**Appendix B: (cont.)**

| Date | Type | Location | Initiator | Result |
|---|---|---|---|---|
| 1191 (3 July) | Siege | Cursed Tower | Christians | Victory: partial wall collapse |
| 1191 (3 July) | Sortie | Crusader camp | Acre garrison | Inconclusive |
| 1191 (5 July) | Skirmish | Montmusard | Saladin's army | Defeat |
| 1191 (5 July) | Sortie | Montmusard | Acre garrison | Defeat |
| 1191 (6 July) | Battle | Crusader camp | Saladin's army | Defeat |
| 1191 (11 July) | Siege | Cursed Tower | Christians | Victory: partial wall collapse |
| 1191 (25 July) | Skirmish | Montmusard | Saladin's army | Victory: fifty crusaders killed |
| 1191 (20 Aug.) | Skirmish | Tel al-'Ayyāḍiyya | Saladin's army | Inconclusive |
| 1191 (21–22 Aug.) | Skirmishes | Crusader camp | Saladin's army | Inconclusive |
| 1191 (23 Aug.) | Skirmish | River Belus | Saladin's army | Inconclusive |

**Total known engagements:**   **75**

| | |
|---|---|
| Skirmishes: | 26 |
| Battles: | 8 |
| Fighting marches: | 2 |
| Ravaging: | 1 |
| Naval actions**: | 10 |
| Siege attacks: | 12 |
| Sorties: | 16 |
| Outright Muslim victories: | 14 |
| Outright Christian victories: | 8 |

\* Pluralized to indicate the occurrence of at least two engagements.
\*\* Either warship vs. warship or attacks on merchant vessels.

## Appendix C: Commanders from battle of 4 October 1189

| | Troop Makeup | Commanders/Principals |
|---|---|---|
| **Christian Left** | Italy | Conrad of Montferrat |
| | | Gerardo of Ravenna |
| **Christian Center** | Catalonia | Andrew of Brienne |
| | France | Gerard of Ridefort |
| | Germany | Ludwig III of Thuringia |
| | Knights Templar | |
| **Christian Right** | France | Guy of Lusignan |
| | Pisa | |
| | Knights Hospitaller | |
| **Crusader Camp/ Reserve** | France | Geoffrey of Lusignan |
| | Flanders | James of Avesnes |
| **Acre Garrison (Muslim)** | | Bahā' al-Dīn al-Asadī Qāraqūsh |
| | | Ḥusām al-Dīn Abū'l-Hayjā |
| **Advance Guard (Muslim)** | | 'Īsā Ḍiyā al-Dīn al-Hakkārī |
| **Far Right (Muslim)** | Hama | Taqī al-Dīn |
| **Center Right (Muslim)** | Aleppo | Al-Afḍāl 'Alī |
| | Damascus | Al-Ẓāhir Ghiyāth al-Dīn Ghazī |
| | Mosul | Ḥusām al-Dīn ibn Lājīn |
| | Diyār Bakr | Qaymāz al-Najmī |
| | Nablus | Quṭb al-Dīn ibn Nūr al-Dīn |
| **Center (Muslim)** | *'askar* & *ḥalqa* | Ṣalāḥ al-Dīn |
| **Center Left (Muslim)** | Sinjār | Mujāhid al-Dīn Yarunqush |
| | Kurds | Mujallī ibn Marwan |
| | Edessa, Harran & Irbil | Muẓaffar al-Dīn ibn Kūkbūrī ibn Zayn al-Dīn |
| | Kurds | Sayf al-Dīn 'Alī ibn Aḥmad al-Mashṭūb |
| | Mamluks | |
| **Far Left (Muslim)** | Asadiyya | Sayf al-Dīn Yāzkūj |
| | Mamluks | Ruslān Bughā |

**Appendix D: Participants at Acre**

The following is a list of known participants at the siege, both Christian and Muslim. It only includes individuals who can be definitively placed at Acre, and not those who crusaded but never reached the city or who joined the crusade or Saladin's ranks after the armies moved south of Acre in late August 1189. For the Christians, I have rendered names into modern, anglicized forms for consistency where possible, but in other cases I have copied the format employed by the sources from which they came.

| Muslims | Source |
| --- | --- |
| Al-ʿAdl al-Zabadānī, governor of Sidon | Ibn Shaddād |
| Al-Afḍāl ʿAlī of Damascus, Saladin's son | Gibb, "Aiyūbids" |
| ʿAlāʾ al-Dīn Khurramshāh ibn ʿIzz al-Dīn Masʿūd ibn Mawdūd, son of the lord of Mosul | Ibn Shaddād |
| ʿAlam al-Dīn Kurjī | Ibn Shaddād |
| ʿAlam al-Dīn Qaiṣar, emir from Ascalon | *Ymagines* |
| ʿAlam al-Dīn Sulaymān ibn Jandar, emir from Aleppo | Ibn al-Athīr |
| Ali, chemist from Damascus | Ibn al-Athīr |
| Al-Amjad Bahrām Shah of Baalbek, Saladin's grandnephew | Gibb, "Aiyūbids" |
| Anonymous, from Mazandaran | Ibn Shaddād |
| Anonymous, descendant of Muhammad | Ibn Shaddād |
| Arghush, mamluk | Ibn Shaddād |
| Asad al-Dīn Shīrkūh, Saladin's uncle | Ibn Shaddād |
| Ayaz the Tall, Saladin's guard | Ibn Shaddād |
| Al-ʿAzīz ʿUthmān of Egypt, Saladin's son | Gibb, "Aiyūbids" |
| Badr al-Dīn, prefect of Damascus | Ibn Shaddād |
| Badr al-Dīn Dildirim al-Yārūqī, lord of Tel Bāshir | Ibn Shaddād |
| Bahāʾ al-Dīn al-Asadī Qāraqūsh, emir | Ibn Shaddād |
| Bahāʾ al-Dīn Ibn Shaddād, *qāḍī* | Self |
| Grair, an archer | *Estoire* |
| Ḥusām al-Dīn Abūʾl-Hayjā "the Fat," emir | Ibn al-Athīr |
| Ḥusām al-Dīn Bishāra, lord of Banyas | Ibn Shaddād |
| Ḥusām al-Dīn Husayn ibn Bārīk al-Mihrānī | Ibn Shaddād |
| Ḥusām al-Dīn ibn Lājīn, lord of Nablus | Ibn Shaddād |
| Ḥusām al-Dīn Luʾlu, emir | Ibn Shaddād |
| Ḥusām al-Dīn Ṭimurtāsh, son of Emir ʿIzz al-Dīn Jāwūlī | Ibn al-Athīr |
| Ḥusām al-Dīn Ṭumān | Ibn Shaddād |
| Ibn al-Jāwalī the Elder | Ibn Shaddād |
| ʿImād al-Dīn al-Iṣfahānī, *kātib* | Abu Shāma |
| ʿImād al-Dīn Zankī ibn Quṭb al-Dīn Mawdūd ibn Zankī, lord of Sinjār | Ibn Shaddād |
| ʿĪsā Ḍiyā al-Dīn al-Hakkārī, jurist | Ibn Shaddād |
| Ismāʿīl al-Mukkabbis | Ibn Shaddād |
| ʿIzz al-Dīn Arsul al-Asadī, emir | Ibn al-Athīr |
| ʿIzz al-Dīn ibn al-Muqaddam, lord of Kafarṭāb and Baʾrīn | Ibn Shaddād |
| ʿIzz al-Dīn Jurdīk al-Nūrī | Ibn Shaddād |

**Appendix D: (cont.)**

| Muslims | Source |
| --- | --- |
| ʿIzz al-Dīn Masʿūd ibn Mawdūd ibn Zankī, Atabeg lord of Mosul | Ibn Shaddād |
| Jamal al-Dīn Abū ʿAlī ibn Rawāḥa al-Hamawī, scholar and poet | Ibn al-Athīr |
| Al-Janāḥ, emir and brother of al-Mashṭūb | Ibn Shaddād |
| Khalil al-Hakkārī, chamberlain | Ibn al-Athīr |
| Lord of al-Shaqīf Arnūn (Belfort) | Ibn Shaddād |
| Majd al-Dīn ibn ʿIzz al-Dīn Farrūkhshāh ibn Shāhinshāh, lord of Baalbek | Ibn al-Athīr |
| Al-Malik al-ʿĀdil Sayf al-Dīn Abū Bakr ibn Ayyūb, Saladin's brother | Ibn Shaddād |
| Al-Malik al-Ashraf Muḥammad, Saladin's son | Ibn Shaddād |
| Al-Malik al-Muẓaffar Taqī al-Dīn ʿUmar, Saladin's nephew and lord of Hama | Ibn Shaddād |
| Al-Malik al-Ṣāliḥ Ismāʿīl, Saladin's son | Ibn Shaddād |
| Al-Malik al-Ẓāfir Khiḍr, Saladin's son and lord of Busra | Ibn Shaddād |
| Al-Manṣūr Muḥammad of Hama, Saladin's grandnephew | Gibb, "Aiyūbids" |
| Al-Muʿaẓẓam Fakhr al-Dīn Tūrānshāh, Saladin's son | Ibn Shaddād |
| Muḥammad ibn Bārīk | Ibn Shaddād |
| Muʿizz al-Dīn Sanjar Shāh ibn Sayf al-Dīn Ghazī ibn Mawdūd bin Zankī, lord of al-Jazīra | Ibn Shaddād |
| Mujāhid al-Dīn Yarunqush, from Sinjār | Ibn Shaddād |
| Al-Mujāhid Shīrkūh II of Homs, Saladin's first cousin once-removed | Gibb, "Aiyūbids" |
| Mujallī ibn Marwan, emir | Ibn al-Athīr |
| Muẓaffar al-Dīn Kūkbūrī ibn Zayn al-Dīn, lord of Edessa, Harran and Irbil | Ibn Shaddād |
| Nāṣir al-Dīn ibn Taqī al-Dīn, lord of Manbij | Ibn Shaddād |
| Qāraqūsh, soldier | Ibn Shaddād |
| Qaymāz al-Ḥarrāni, guard | Ibn Shaddād |
| Qūsh, chamberlain to Emir Qāraqūsh | Ibn Shaddād |
| Quṭb al-Dīn ibn Nūr al-Dīn, lord of Ḥiṣn Kayfā | Ibn Shaddād |
| Ruslān Bughā, mamluk | Ibn Shaddād |
| Sābiq al-Dīn ʿUthmān ibn al-Dāya, lord of Shayzar | Ibn Shaddād |
| Ṣalāḥ al-Dīn | All |
| Sarāsunqur, mamluk | Ibn Shaddād |
| Sārim Qaymāz al-Najmī, *tawashi* | Ibn Shaddād |
| Sayf al-Dīn ʿAlī ibn Aḥmad al-Mashṭūb, Kurdish chief | Ibn Shaddād |
| Sayf al-Dīn Sunqur al-Dawādār, from Egypt | Ibn Shaddād |
| Ṣayf al-Dīn Yāzkūj, mamluk | Ibn Shaddād |
| Shams al-Dīn, al-ʿĀdil's son | Ibn Shaddād |
| Sunqur al-Ḥalabī, from Egypt | Ibn Shaddād |
| Sunqur al-Wishāqī | Ibn al-Athīr |
| Usāma, governor of Beirut | Ibn al-Athīr |

**Appendix D: (cont.)**

| Muslims | Source |
|---|---|
| Ya'qūb al-Ḥalabī of Aleppo, commander of the *jandarīyaa* | Ibn al-Athīr |
| Ẓāhir al-Dīn, governor of Jerusalem | Ibn al-Athīr |
| Ẓāhir al-Dīn Ibn al-Balankārī, from Mosul | Ibn Shaddād |
| Al-Ẓāhir Ghiyāth al-Dīn Ghāzī of Aleppo, Saladin's son | Gibb, "Aiyūbids" |
| Zayn al-Dīn Yūsuf ibn Zayn al-Dīn 'Alī ibn Baktakīn, lord of Irbil | Ibn Shaddād |

Others (anonymous or unknown)[1]

| Christians | Source |
|---|---|
| Abbot of Châlons | *Itinerarium2* |
| Abbot of Ford | *Itinerarium2* |
| Abbot of Mount Olivet | *Howden2* |
| Abbot of Mount Sion | *Howden2* |
| Abbot of St Pierre of Lesterps | *Howden2* |
| Abbot of the Temple of Our Lord | *Howden2* |
| Adam Brion, Templar seneschal | *RRRH* 1327 |
| Adam of Leun | *Howden2* |
| Adam of Villebon, chamberlain of Philip II | *Howden2* |
| Adelhard, cardinal bishop of Verona | *Itinerarium2* |
| Ado Puntiel | *RRRH* 1304 |
| Aimericus, royal constable | *RRRH* 1279 |
| Aimery of Lusignan | Painter |
| Aimon of Aix, Templar seneschal | *RRRH* 1297 |
| Alan of Fontaines | *Itinerarium2* |
| Albero of Zemling, *ministeriale* | Ansbert |
| Albert of Horn, *ministeriale* | Ansbert |
| Albrecht Rode | Cushing |
| Aldebrand, count (unknown) | *Itinerarium2* |
| Alice, daughter of Guy and Sibylla | *Howden2* |
| Amalric, royal constable | *RRRH* 1285 |
| Ambroise | Self |
| Amfrid of Turon | *Ymagines* |
| Andrew of Brienne, lord of Ramerupt | *Estoire* |
| Andrew of Chaveney | *Estoire* |
| Anonymous, *Itinerarium1* author | Self |
| Anonymous, from the Camville family (1st) | Sayers |
| Anonymous, from the Camville family (2nd) | Sayers |
| *Anonymous1* author (Monachus/Haymar) | Self |
| *Anonymous2* author | Self |
| *Anonymous3* author | Self |

**Appendix D: (cont.)**

| Christians | Source |
|---|---|
| Anselm, royal constable | *RRRH* 1285 |
| Anselm Bellus, consul of Pisa | *RRRH* 1327 |
| Anselm of Lucca, Hospitaller | *RRRH* 1276[2] |
| Anselm of Marseille | *RRRH* 1279 |
| Anselm of Montreal and his retainers | *Howden2* |
| Ansold Boniucini, castellan of Tyre | *RRRH* 1277 |
| Archbishop of Petra (unknown) | *Howden1* |
| Atho of St Saveur | *RRRH* 1277 |
| Aubery Clement, marshal of France | *Estoire* |
| Baldwin, archbishop of Canterbury | *Estoire* |
| Baldwin, brother of Ansold Boniucini | *RRRH* 1277 |
| Baldwin, count (unknown) | *RRRH* 1277 |
| Baldwin Guerico | Mack |
| Baldwin of Bethune | Bennett[3] |
| Baldwin of Carew | *Estoire* |
| Baldwin of Cyprus, consul of Pisa | *RRRH* 1327 |
| Baldwin of Dargus | *Estoire* |
| Baldwin of Jerusalem, scribe of the Hospital in Tyre | *RRRH* 1288 |
| Baldwin of Verdun | Bennett |
| Balian of Ibelin | *RRRH* 1272 |
| Bandinus, chancellor of Conrad of Montferrat | *RRRH* 1298 |
| Bari, nephew of William, archbishop of Rheims | *RRRH* 1298 |
| Bartholomew, archbishop of Tours | *Howden2* |
| Bartholomew, lord of Vignory | Bouchard[4] |
| Bartholomew of Tegrin, consul of Pisa | *RRRH* 1327 |
| Basac (unknown) | *RRRH* 1279 |
| Belmustus, brother of Hugh Lecarius | *RRRH* 1277 |
| Berengar of Legsby | Tyerman, *England* |
| Berengaria of Navarre, wife of King Richard I | *RRRH* 1279 |
| Bernard, count (unknown) | *Itinerarium2* |
| Bernard, Templar and viscount of Tyre | *RRRH* 1333 |
| Bernard Galti | Röhricht[5] |
| Bernard of La Carra, bishop of Bayonne | *Howden2* |
| Bernard of St Valery-sur-Somme | *Itinerarium2* |
| Berthold, duke from Germany (unknown) | *Howden2* |
| Berthold of Worms, *ministeriale* | Ansbert |
| Bertram of Wissel | Cushing |
| Bertrand Aundi | *RRRH* 1279 |
| Bertrand Caminali | *RRRH* 1279 |
| Bertrand Sardus of Marseille | *RRRH* 1279 |
| Bertrand of Verdun, seneschal of Ireland | *Estoire* |
| Bertulf, count (unknown) | *Itinerarium2* |

**Appendix D: (cont.)**

| Christians | Source |
|---|---|
| Bishop of the Forest (unknown) | *RRRH* 1307 |
| Bishop of Hebron (titular; unknown) | *Howden2* |
| Bishop of St George (probably Lydda; unknown) | *Howden2* |
| Bishop of Tiberias (unknown) | *Howden2* |
| Boves of Estables | *RRRH* 1288 |
| Boves of Joigny | *Howden2* |
| Brothers of Tournebu (Eure), unspecified number | *Estoire* |
| Castellan of Ypres | *Howden2* |
| Chaplain of Archbishop Baldwin | *Epistolae Cantuarienses* |
| Chotard of Loreora | *Estoire* |
| Clarembald of Montcaulon | *RRRH* 1304 |
| Clarembald of Noyers, Hospitaller | *RRRH* 1288 |
| Conrad, marquis of Montferrat | Various |
| Cornelius Majal | *RRRH* 1325 |
| Daughter of Isaac Comnenus (unknown) | *Howden2* |
| Desiderius, bishop of Toulon | *Itinerarium2* |
| Diepold, bishop of Passau | Ansbert |
| Dietmar, freedman | Ansbert |
| Dietrich Vorrad | Cushing |
| Dominic Contarini, legate of the doge of Venice | *RRRH* 1298 |
| Drogo fitz Ralph | Tyerman, *England* |
| Drogo of Amiens | *Itinerarium2* |
| Drogo of Merlou | *Howden1* |
| Elias Rutze of Lübeck | Cushing |
| Engeram of Fiennes | *Itinerarium2* |
| Erard, marshal of Champagne | Edbury[6] |
| Erard III, count of Brienne | *Howden2* |
| Erard of Châtinay | *Itinerarium2* |
| Ernald of Grandeville | *Estoire* |
| Erthaudus, Templar | *RRRH* 1297 |
| Escorfaz (unknown) | *RRRH* 1307 |
| Eustace of Burnes | Tyerman, *England* |
| Femiano (unknown) | *RRRH* 1279 |
| Ferrand, knight | *Itinerarium2* |
| Florence of Hangy | *Ymagines* |
| Frederick, duke of Swabia | Various |
| Frederick, son of Berthold V of Meran | *Howden1*[7] |
| Frederick of Nusse | Cushing |
| Fulcone of Castello | Mack |
| Fulk Rostangi | *RRRH* 1279 |
| Garnier of Creato, lord of Montreal | *RRRH* 1288 |

**Appendix D: (cont.)**

| Christians | Source |
|---|---|
| Garnier of Nablus, master of the Hospital | *RRRH* 1327 |
| Gaucher of Châtillon-sur-Marne | *RRRH* 1304 |
| Gautbert of Aspremont | *Itinerarium2* |
| Gautbert of St Quintino, Templar | *RRRH* 1304 |
| Gautier le Beau, viscount of Acre | *RRRH* 1327 |
| Gautier of Braholget, Hospitaller | *RRRH* 1288 |
| Gawain of Cheneche | *RRRH* 1272 |
| Gazellus of Tyre | *RRRH* 1271 |
| Geoffrey, count of Perche (son of Rotrou III) | *RRRH* 1308 |
| Geoffrey, son of Geoffrey Tortus | *RRRH* 1271 |
| Geoffrey Tortus | *RRRH* 1272 |
| Geoffrey of Bruyere | *Howden2* |
| Geoffrey of Joinville | *Itinerarium2* |
| Geoffrey of La Celle | *Estoire* |
| Geoffrey of Lusignan, lord of Jaffa and Ascalon | Various |
| Geoffrey of Rançon | *Estoire* |
| Gerald Aldreer | *RRRH* 1279 |
| Gerald Tatti | *RRRH* 1279 |
| Gerald of Furnival | Tyerman, *England* |
| Gerard, bishop of Ravenna | *Itinerarium2* |
| Gerard, chaplain of Richard I | *RRRH* 1320 |
| Gerard, provost of St Donatian and chancellor of Philip of Alsace | *Crusade Charters* 125 |
| Gerard of La Barte, archbishop of Auch | *Howden1* |
| Gerard of Ridefort, grand master of the Temple | Various |
| Gerbert, grand preceptor of the Temple | *RRRH* 1297 |
| Gilbert Malet | Tyerman, *England* |
| Gilbert Malmain | *Itinerarium2* |
| Gilbert Pipard | Tyerman, *England* |
| Gilbert Talbot, lord of Linton | *Estoire* |
| Gilbert of Tillieres-sur-Avre | *Itinerarium2* |
| Giles of Corbeil, physician | Mitchell[8] |
| Grawz of Bétpaumes | *RRRH* 1306 |
| Guy, lord of Vergy | Bouchard |
| Guy, lord of Vignory | Bouchard |
| Guy II, lord of Dampierre | *Ymagines* |
| Guy III, butler of Senlis | *Estoire* |
| Guy Spinola | Mack |
| Guy of Chappes | Edbury |
| Guy of Châtillon-sur-Marne | *Itinerarium2* |
| Guy of Choily | *RRRH* 1297 |
| Guy of Dancy | *Howden2* |

**Appendix D: (cont.)**

| Christians | Source |
| --- | --- |
| Guy of Germinio | RRRH 1297 |
| Guy of Lusignan, king of Jerusalem | Various |
| Guy of Mézières | *Itinerarium2* |
| Guy of Pierre-Pertuis | Bouchard |
| Guy of Pierre-Pertuis' nephew | Bouchard |
| Hellin of Wavrin, seneschal of Flanders | *Estoire* |
| Henfridus of Montreal | RRRH 1285 |
| Henry I, count of Bar-le-Duc | *Estoire* |
| Henry II of Champagne, count of Troyes | Various |
| Henry fitz Nicholas | *Estoire* |
| Henry of Arzilliers | RRRH 1304 |
| Henry of Bardewieck | Cushing |
| Henry of Bockholt | Cushing |
| Henry of Cannelli, chamberlain of Conrad of Montferrat | RRRH 1298 |
| Henry of Modlin, *ministeriale* | Ansbert |
| Heraclius, patriarch of Jerusalem | Various |
| Hertald, Templar | RRRH 1304 |
| Hervey IV, count of Nevers | *Itinerarium2* |
| Hubert Mordenz | RRRH 1307 |
| Hubert Vulpes | RRRH 1325 |
| Hubert Walter, bishop of Salisbury | *Ymagines* |
| Hugh III, duke of Burgundy | *Eracles* |
| Hugh IV, count of St Pol | *Estoire* |
| Hugh IX of Lusignan, count of LaMarche | *Estoire* |
| Hugh Lecarius | RRRH 1277 |
| Hugh Martini, marshal | RRRH 1327 |
| Hugh of Choily | RRRH 1297 |
| Hugh of Coy (Coify-le-Haut?) | RRRH 1304 |
| Hugh of Ferri | RRRH 1279 |
| Hugh of Gournay | *Howden2* |
| Hugh of La Fierté | *Estoire* |
| Hugh of Landricourt | RRRH 1304 |
| Hugh of Poitou, marshal of Richard I | *Itinerarium2* |
| Hugh of Puchperg, *ministeriale* | Ansbert |
| Hugh of St Maurice | RRRH 1291 |
| Hugh of Tabari | *Ymagines* |
| Hugh of Tiberias | RRRH 1327 |
| Hugh of Vallières | RRRH 1306 |
| Humbert of Argentoil | RRRH 1288 |
| Humphrey of Toron | Gillingham, *Richard I* |
| Humphrey of Veilly | *Howden2* |
| Isabella, wife of Conrad of Montferrat | Various |

**Appendix D: (cont.)**

| Christians | Source |
|---|---|
| Ivo of Vieuxpoint | *Itinerarium2* |
| James of Avesnes, lord of Condé and Guise | *Howden2* |
| James of Clare, consul of Pisa | *RRRH* 1327 |
| Joan, sister of Richard I | *Howden2* |
| John, bishop of Brescia | *Itinerarium2* |
| John, bishop of Evreux | *Estoire* |
| John, constable of Chester | *Howden2* |
| John, count of Loegria | *Itinerarium2* |
| John, count of Ponthieu | *Itinerarium2* |
| John, count of Sées | *Itinerarium2* |
| John, count of Vendôme | *Howden2* |
| John, son of Femiano | *RRRH* 1279 |
| John Crispin of Lübeck | Cushing |
| John Morecini, legate of the doge of Venice | *RRRH* 1298 |
| John Stralera | *RRRH* 1277 |
| John of Arcis-sur-Aubé | *Itinerarium2* |
| John of Bridgeport, physician | Mitchell |
| John of Burgundy | *RRRH* 1323 |
| John of Hessle | Sayers |
| John of Lambert | *Howden2* |
| John of Montmirail | *Itinerarium2* |
| John of Morwick, canon of York | Sayers |
| John of Neele, castellan of Bruges | *Itinerarium2* |
| John of Preaux (Seine-Inferior), knight of King Richard I | *Estoire* |
| John of St Albans | Mitchell |
| Jordan of Hommet, constable of Sées | *Estoire* |
| Joscelin, archbishop of Tyre | *RRRH* 1298 |
| Joscelin, count (unknown) | *Itinerarium2* |
| Joscelin, royal seneschal | *RRRH* 1279 |
| Joscelin of Apulia | *Howden2* |
| Joscelin of Montoire-sur-le-Loire | *Howden2* |
| Joscelin of Munmorec | *Howden1* |
| Joseph, physician | Mitchell |
| Knights named Torolens (unspecified number) | *Estoire* |
| Lambert of Barro | *RRRH* 1291 |
| Leonard, from Pisa (unknown) | *Howden2* |
| Leopold V, duke of Austria | Various |
| Lethard II, bishop of Nazareth | *Howden2* |
| Lord of Comté, in Burgundy (unknown) | *Itinerarium2* |
| Lord of Wancy (unknown; Wanchi-Capval?) | *Howden2*[9] |
| Louis of Arceles | *Itinerarium2* |
| Lovell of Châtillon-sur-Marne | *Itinerarium2* |

**Appendix D: (cont.)**

| Christians | Source |
|---|---|
| Ludwig III, landgrave of Thuringia | *Estoire* |
| Malger, master | Mitchell |
| Manassier of Bar, bishop of Langres | Baldwin |
| Manassier of Garlande | *Itinerarium2* |
| Manassier of Villegruis | *RRRH* 1305 |
| Maraduc, archer from Wales | *Estoire* |
| Maria, daughter of Guy and Sibylla | *Howden2* |
| Maurin, consul of Genoa | *RRRH* 1314 |
| Maurin, son of Rodoani of Platea Longa | *RRRH* 1320 |
| Mayno Bertlune of Lübeck | Cushing |
| Monaldus, bishop of Fano | *Howden2* |
| Mother of the viscount of Châtillon | *Howden2* |
| Narjot of Toucy | *Itinerarium2* |
| Nephew of Knut VI, king of Denmark (unknown) | *Itinerarium2* |
| Nicholas, count of Hungary | *Itinerarium2* |
| Nicola Embriaco | Mack |
| Nigel of Mowbray | Sayers |
| Obertus, seneschal of Conrad of Montferrat | *RRRH* 1333 |
| Octavian, bishop of Therouanne | *Itinerarium2* |
| Odart of Alneto | *RRRH* 1304 |
| Odarus, marshal of Campania | *RRRH* 1291 |
| Odo, bishop of Beirut | *Howden2* |
| Odo, bishop of Sidon | *Howden2* [10] |
| Odo of Choily | *RRRH* 1297 |
| Odo of Gunesse | *Howden2* |
| Oger, grand preceptor of the Hospital in Jerusalem | *RRRH* 1288 |
| Oger of St Chéron | Edbury |
| Ortlieb of Winkel, *ministeriale* | Ansbert |
| Osbert of La Mare | Tyerman, *England* |
| Otho of Tresoni | *Ymagines* |
| Otto III, count of Guelders | *Itinerarium2* |
| Otto of La Fosse | *Itinerarium2* |
| Otto of Tabari | *Ymagines* |
| Pain of Haifa | *RRRH* 1333 |
| Peter, archbishop of Arles-le-Blanc | *Howden2* |
| Peter, bishop of Tripoli | *RRRH* 1323 |
| Peter, royal chancellor and archdeacon of Tripoli | *RRRH* 1272 |
| Peter, Templar prior | *RRRH* 1303 |
| Peter Aunda | *RRRH* 1279 |
| Peter Mignot, household of King Richard I | *Howden2* |
| Peter Turkinus | *RRRH* 1291 |
| Peter of Ate, Hospitaller | *RRRH* 1288 |

**Appendix D: (cont.)**

| Christians | Source |
|---|---|
| Peter of Barres | *Itinerarium2* |
| Peter of Bétpaumes | *RRRH* 1306 |
| Peter of Falcone, consul of Pisa | *RRRH* 1327 |
| Peter of Preaux (Seine-Inferior), knight of King Richard I | *Estoire* |
| Peter of Vilerbetun | *RRRH* 1306 |
| Philip II, king of France | Various |
| Philip Morosini | *RRRH* 1323 |
| Philip of Alsace, count of Flanders | *Eracles* |
| Philip of Chartres | *Howden2* |
| Philip of Dreux, bishop of Beauvais | *Howden2* |
| Philip of Lalande | *RRRH* 1306 |
| Philip of Poitou, clerk of King Richard I | Tyerman, *England* |
| Pippin, consul of Pisa | *RRRH* 1327 |
| Ponce of Reuest | *RRRH* 1279 |
| Priest who blesses a trebuchet (unknown) | *Estoire* |
| Priest with a crossbow (unknown) | *Itinerarium2* |
| Prior of the Holy Sepulchre (unknown) | *Howden2* |
| Rainard of Grancy | Bouchard |
| Ralph, lord of Issoudun | *Ymagines* |
| Ralph, parson of Croxby | Tyerman, *England* |
| Ralph, scribe | *RRRH* 1305 |
| Ralph, viscount of Châteaudun (Eure-et-Loire) | *Estoire* |
| Ralph I, count of Clermont | *Estoire* |
| Ralph II, bishop of Bethlehem | *RRRH* 1298 |
| Ralph Besace, physician | Mitchell |
| Ralph fitz Godfrey, chamberlain of King Richard I | Tyerman, *England* |
| Ralph Teisson, lord of St Saveur-le-Vicomte | *Estoire* |
| Ralph of Alta Ripa, archdeacon of Colchester | *Itinerarium2* |
| Ralph of Aubeni | *Howden1* |
| Ralph of Coucy | *Crusade Charters* 116 |
| Ralph of La Rucoira | *RRRH* 1307 |
| Ralph of Mauleon | *Estoire* |
| Ralph of Tabari | *Ymagines* |
| Ralph (or Reginald) of Tiberias | Edbury |
| Ralph of Tilly | *Howden2* |
| Ranulf of Bradford | Tyerman, *England* |
| Ranulf of Glanville, justiciar of England | *Itinerarium2* |
| Raymond II, viscount of Touraine | *Itinerarium2* |
| Raymond Babin | *RRRH* 1279 |
| Raymond of Bone Done | *Eracles* |
| Raymond of Nefra | *RRRH* 1276 |
| Raymond of Posqueires | *RRRH* 1279 |

**Appendix D: (cont.)**

| Christians | Source |
|---|---|
| Raymond of Saona | *RRRH* 1279 |
| Rayner of Gibelto | *RRRH* 1276 |
| Reginald, bishop of Chartres | Baldwin |
| Reginald, lord of Sidon | *RRRH* 1285 |
| Reginald of Magny, marshal of Henry of Champagne | *Howden2* |
| Relis, Templar seneschal | *RRRH* 1333 |
| Rericus of Corteno, Templar seneschal | *RRRH* 1306 |
| Richard I, king of England | Various |
| Richard of Camville, justiciar of Cyprus | *Howden2* |
| Richard of Clare | *Howden2* |
| Richard of Legsby | Tyerman, *England* |
| Richard of Templo | Self |
| Richard of Turnham | Tyerman, *England* |
| Richard of Vernon, knight | *Itinerarium2* |
| Robert, prior at Acre | *RRRH* 1325 |
| Robert, treasurer | *RRRH* 1325 |
| Robert II, count of Dreux | *Howden2* |
| Robert IV, earl of Leicester | *Estoire* |
| Robert Mordenz | *RRRH* 1307 |
| Robert Scrope of Barton-on-Humber | Tyerman, *England* |
| Robert Trussebot, knight | *Itinerarium2* |
| Robert Vulpes, consul of Pisa | *RRRH* 1327 |
| Robert of Boves | *Itinerarium* |
| Robert of Châtillon-sur-Seine | *RRRH* 1304 |
| Robert of La Mare, lord of East Anglia | *Estoire* |
| Robert of Lain, Hospitaller | *RRRH* 1288 |
| Robert of Lalande | *Howden2* |
| Robert of Milly | *RRRH* 1291 |
| Robert of Neuborg (Eure) | *Estoire* |
| Robert of Sable, grand master of the Temple | *Eracles* |
| Robert of Vieuxpoint | *RRRH* 1307 |
| Robert the Constable, seneschal of William of Mandeville | *Howden2* |
| Robert the Huntsman of Pontefract | Tyerman, *England* |
| Rodaun family, one brother of | Ansbert |
| Roger, abbot (unknown) | *Howden2* |
| Roger, duke of Apulia | *Howden2* |
| Roger, parson of Howden | Self |
| Roger, preceptor of the Hospital | *RRRH* 1333 |
| Roger Marchel, keeper of the seal | Bennett |
| Roger of Glanville | *Howden2* |
| Roger of Harcourt, knight of King Richard I | *Estoire* |
| Roger of Polebare | *Howden2* |

**Appendix D: (cont.)**

| Christians | Source |
| --- | --- |
| Roger of Saty | *Estoire* |
| Roger of St Cheron | *RRRH* 1291 |
| Roger of Tosny (Eure) | *Estoire* |
| Roger of Waurin, bishop of Cambray | *Ymagines* |
| Rory, Templar | *RRRH* 1297 |
| Rosso della Volta | Mack |
| Rotrou III, count of Perche | *Estoire* |
| Rudwin of Gars, *ministeriale* | Ansbert |
| Ruffino della Volta | Rigord |
| Selletus, consul of Pisa | *RRRH* 1327 |
| Sibrand, master of the Hospital of St Mary of the Germans | *RRRH* 1285 |
| Sibylla, queen of Jerusalem | Various |
| Siegfried II, count of Moerl and Kleeburg | Ansbert |
| Simon, soldier of Bishop's Villa | *Crusade Charters* 108 |
| Simon of Wale | Sayers |
| Simone Doria | Mack |
| Spezzapietra della Volta | Mack |
| Stephen, count of Sancerre | *Estoire* |
| Stephen John | *RRRH* 1279 |
| Stephen Longchamp | *Howden1* |
| Stephen of Corboli, Hospitaller | *RRRH* 1288 |
| Stephen of Pierre-Pertuis | *RRRH* 1288 |
| Stephen of Thornham, marshal and treasurer of Richard I | Bennett |
| "Sturmann" | Cushing |
| Stuteville family members (unspecified number) | *Estoire* |
| Sylvester, seneschal of Baldwin of Canterbury | *Howden1* |
| Theobald, bishop of Acre | *RRRH* 1327 |
| Theobald, seneschal of King Philip II | Rigord |
| Theobald I, count of Bar-le-Duc | *Itinerarium2* |
| Theobald V, count of Blois | *Estoire* |
| Theobald of Monfaucon, archbishop of Besançon | *Itinerarium2* |
| Thomas, chamberlain | *RRRH* 1323 |
| Thorel of Mesnil, knight | *Estoire* |
| Treasurer of Philip II (unknown) | Ibn Shaddād |
| "Tumme" | Cushing |
| Ubaldo, archbishop of Pisa | *Howden2* |
| "Vifhusen" | Cushing |
| Villani of Nuilly | *RRRH* 1304 |
| Viscount of Châtellerault | *Itinerarium2* |
| Viscount of Châtillon | *Howden2* |
| "Vlekke" | Cushing |

**Appendix D: (cont.)**

| Christians | Source |
|---|---|
| "Vromold" | Cushing |
| Walchelin of Ferrieres-St Hilary | *Ymagines* |
| Waleran of Ford | Tyerman, *England* |
| Walter, lord of Sombernon | Bouchard |
| Walter Durus, marshal of Conrad of Montferrat | *RRRH* 1298 |
| Walter of Arzilliers | *Itinerarium2* |
| Walter of Kyme | Sayers |
| Walter of Moy | *Howden2* |
| Walter of Oyri | *Estoire* |
| Walter of Ros | Sayers |
| Walter of Scrope | Sayers |
| Walter the Englishman | *RRRH* 1279 |
| Warin fitz Gerald, household of Richard I | *Estoire* |
| "Wickede" | Cushing |
| Wife of Femiano | *RRRH* 1279 |
| William, bishop of Asti | *Itinerarium2* |
| William, butler of Senlis[11] | *Howden1* |
| William, castellan of Pecquigny | *Howden1* |
| William, count of Joigny | Edbury |
| William, priest | Mitchell |
| William, viscount of Châtel Eraud | *Ymagines* |
| William II, chamberlain of Tancarville | *Estoire* |
| William II, count of Chalon-sur-Saône | *Itinerarium2* |
| William Bernard, archbishop of Aire | *Howden2* |
| William Bloez | *Estoire* |
| William Goeth | *Itinerarium2* |
| William Malet | *Estoire* |
| William Marcel | *Estoire* |
| William Ricius, consul of Genoa | *RRRH* 1333 |
| William the Strong | *RRRH* 1327 |
| William Tiberias | *RRRH* 1272 |
| William of Arzilliers | *RRRH* 1304 |
| William of Barres | *Eracles* |
| William of Buhchat | *RRRH* 1306 |
| William of Corsera | *RRRH* 1307 |
| William of Ferrers, earl of Derby | *Itinerarium2* |
| William of Forz of Olrun | *Howden1* |
| William of Garlande, knight | *Estoire* |
| William of La Mare | *Itinerarium2* |
| William of Mello | *Estoire* |
| William of Olcimiano | *RRRH* 1277 |
| William of Posqueres | *RRRH* 1279 |

**Appendix D: (cont.)**

| Christians | Source |
| --- | --- |
| William of Preaux (Seine-Inferior), knight of King Richard I | *Estoire* |
| William of Roches | *Estoire* |
| William of Tabari | *Ymagines* |
| William of Villehardouin, marshal of Henry of Champagne | Howden1 |
| William of Villiers, preceptor of the Hospital in Acre | *RRRH* 1327 |

# NOTES

## Introduction

1. Bradford B. Broughton, *The Legends of King Richard I Coeur de Lion: A study of sources and variations to the year 1600* (The Hague, 1966), 42–3 and 61–2.
2. Cf. Acts 21:7, Judges 1:31 and 1 Maccabees 5:15–22, 11:22–4, 12:45–8.
3. On Jerusalem's being "the centre of the world" in the eleventh century, see Jonathan Riley-Smith, *The First Crusade and the Idea of Crusading* (Reprint, London, 2003), 20–1.
4. The differences, or lack thereof, between the two are examined in Christopher Tyerman, *The Invention of the Crusades* (London, 1998), 27–9.
5. The sole exception is Ibn Shaddād, who claims to have thrown stones at the crusaders at one point during the siege. The value of witness accounts is explored in J.F. Verbruggen, *The Art of Warfare in Western Europe during the Middle Ages, from the Eighth Century to 1340*, trans. S. Willard and Mrs. R.W. Southern, 2nd ed. (Woodbridge, 1997), 16–18.
6. On the main issues, such as the propensity of witnesses to report miraculous events and/ or to incorporate information from secondary and anonymous sources, see Elizabeth Lapina, "'Nec signis nec testis creditur': the problem of eyewitnesses in the chronicles of the First Crusade," *Viator* 38 (2007), 117–39; and Yuval Noah Harari, "Eyewitnessing in the accounts of the First Crusade: The *Gesta Francorum* and other contemporary narratives," *Crusades* 3 (2004), 77–99.
7. John France, *Victory in the East: A military history of the First Crusade* (Cambridge, 1994), 24–5. In particular, religion seems to have strengthened hostile attitudes of the armies towards each other, which often engendered greater degrees of violence; see Malcolm Barber, "The Albigensian Crusades: Wars like any other?" in *Dei gesta per Francos: Etudes sur les croisades dédiées à Jean Richard*, ed. M. Balard, B.Z. Kedar, and J. Riley-Smith (Aldershot, 2001), 54–5.
8. Such studies are periodically cited throughout this book, but on some more recent contributions see Jay Rubenstein, "In search of a new crusade: A review essay," *Historically Speaking* (April 2011), 25–7.

9. The most comprehensive military narratives of the siege to date are R. Rogers, *Latin Siege Warfare in the Twelfth Century* (Oxford, 1992), 212–35; and Malcolm C. Lyons and D.E.P. Jackson, *Saladin: The politics of the holy war* (Cambridge, 1982), 295–334. See also John Gillingham, *Richard I* (New Haven, 1999), 155–71; and Sidney Painter, "The Third Crusade: Richard the Lionheart and Philip Augustus," in *A History of the Crusades*, Volume II: *The Later Crusades, 1189–1311*, ed. K. Setton, R.L. Wolff, and H.W. Hazard (Madison, 1969), 45–85.

10. Certainly more complex than previous short treatments have allowed; see, for example, the three pages in R.C. Smail, *Crusading Warfare, 1097–1193*, 2nd ed. (Cambridge, 1995), 187–9; the single paragraph in Niall Christie, *Muslims and Crusaders: Christianity's wars in the Middle East, 1095–1382, from the Islamic sources* (New York, 2014), 47; or the single sentence in Jonathan Phillips, "The Latin East: 1098–1291," in *The Oxford History of the Crusades*, ed. J. Riley-Smith (Reprint, Oxford, 2002), 132. In fairness, Professor Phillips is presently preparing a comprehensive history of the Third Crusade with a fuller consideration of Acre.

11. Adrian Boas, "Some reflections on urban landscapes in the Kingdom of Jerusalem: archaeological research in Jerusalem and Acre," in *Dei gesta per Francos*, 242.

## Chapter I  Target Acre

1. *Itinerarium2*, 1.32.

2. On the location of this particular piece of the True Cross up to the Battle of Hattin, see Alan V. Murray, "'Mighty against the enemies of Christ': The relic of the True Cross in the armies of the Kingdom of Jerusalem," in *The Crusades and their Sources: Essays presented to Bernard Hamilton*, ed. J. France and W.G. Zajac (Aldershot, 1998), 217–38.

3. Surveyed in John France, *Great Battles: Hattin* (Oxford, 2015), 102–4.

4. Ibn al-Athīr, 325.

5. For a series of maps of these regions set in context, see Jonathan Riley-Smith (ed.), *The Atlas of the Crusades* (New York, 1991).

6. France, *Great Battles: Hattin*, 105–6.

7. On the details of the succession dispute, see Bernard Hamilton, *The Leper King and his Heirs: Baldwin IV and the crusader Kingdom of Jerusalem* (Cambridge, 2000), 217–21; and on the political difficulties of Guy before the Battle of Hattin, R.C. Smail, "The predicaments of Guy of Lusignan, 1183–87," in *Outremer: Studies in the history of the crusading Kingdom of Jerusalem presented to Joshua Prawer*, ed. B.Z. Kedar, H.E. Mayer, and R.C. Smail (Jerusalem, 1982), 159–76.

8. Balian had escaped from Hattin; see Peter W. Edbury, *John of Ibelin and the Kingdom of Jerusalem* (Woodbridge, 1997), 17.

9. For the text of this bull, see J. Bird, E. Peters, and J.M. Powell (eds), *Crusade and Christendom: Annotated documents in translation from Innocent III to the fall of Acre, 1187–1291* (Philadelphia, 2013), 4–9.

10. This sequence is described in detail in John D. Hosler, *Henry II: A medieval soldier at war, 1147–1189* (Leiden, 2007), 166–8; see also Alan Forey, "Henry II's crusading penance for Becket's murder," *Crusades* 7 (2008), 153–64.

11. Hosler, *Henry II*, 168–70. The writer Gervase of Canterbury estimated a much higher total amount, but his figures have been qualified; see John D. Hosler, "Henry II, William of Newburgh, and the development of English anti-Judaism," in *Christian Attitudes towards the Jews in the Middle Ages: A casebook*, ed. M. Frassetto (New York, 2007), 170, and the studies cited therein.

12. Christopher Tyerman, *God's War: A new history of the crusades* (Cambridge, 2006), 376–99, provides a detailed survey of the preaching of the crusade in different European locales, as well as matters of recruitment.

13. "Audita tremendi," in *Crusades and Christendom*, 8. The Latin original is in *Opera omnia Urbani III, Gregorii VIII, Romanorum pontificum epistolae et privilegia*, in *Patrologia Latina*, ed. J.-P. Migne, vol. 202 (Paris, 1855), 1542a: "Non est quidem novum, quod terra illa judicio divino percutitur, sed nec insolitum, ut flagellate et castigata misericordiam consequantur. Poterit Dominus quidem sola eam voluntate servare, sed non habemus ei dicere cur ita fecerit. Voluit enum forsitan experiri, et in notiam ducere aliorum, si quis sit intelligens aut requirens Deum, qui oblatum sibi paenitentiae tempus hilariter amplectatur . . ."
14. Ibn al-Athīr, 369 (cf. Koran 13.13, in which Allah smites with thunder and lightning); Ibn Shaddād, 104–6.
15. On the extent of Saladin's conquests, see Lyons and Jackson, *Saladin*, 279–94.
16. Edbury, *John of Ibelin*, 19–20.
17. *Howden2*, 3.126; *Estoire*, lines 2738–50; *Itinerarium2*, 1.26; Benjamin Z. Kedar, "The Patriarch Eraclius," in *Outremer*, 203.
18. Ibn al-Athīr, 2.364; Ibn Shaddād, 96.
19. *Itinerarium2*, 1.27.
20. D.S. Richards, "A consideration of two sources for the life of Saladin," *Journal of Semitic Studies* 25:1 (1980), 50 and 61. Both he and the other Muslim witness, 'Imād al-Dīn, saw Saladin's reign as a peak moment in Islamic history, equaled only by the Golden Age (of Muhammad and the four rightly guided caliphs); see Konrad Hirschler, *Medieval Arabic Historiography: Authors as actors*, Routledge Studies on the Middle East (Abingdon, 2006), 85.
21. On his contribution to knowledge of the First Crusade, see Konrad Hirschler, "The Jerusalem conquest of 492/1099 in the medieval Arabic historiography of the crusades: From regional plurality to Islamic narrative," *Crusades* 13 (2014), 65–73.
22. However, his younger brother, Ḍiyā' al-Dīn Naṣr Allāh, did serve Saladin and also the sultan's son al-Afḍāl 'Alī; see Ibn al-Athīr, 1.1.
23. Hamilton A.R. Gibb, "The Arabic sources for the life of Saladin," *Speculum* 25:1 (1950), 58–72. His critiques of military events are nonetheless very useful, for he often points to deficiencies and mistakes in strategy and tactics that a writer in the sultan's immediate presence might well ignore. A recent biography is François Micheau, "Ibn al-Athīr," in *Medieval Muslim Historians and the Franks in the Levant*, ed. A. Mallett (Leiden, 2015), 52–83. Short defenses of al-Athīr include Richards' introductions in Ibn al-Athīr, 1.2–5 and 2.3–4; F. Gabrieli (ed. and trans.), *Arab Historians of the Crusades* (Reprint, Berkeley, 1984), xxvii–xxviii; and Lyons and Jackson, *Saladin*, 1 n.3. For an overview of all three Muslim writers, see Carole Hillenbrand, *The Crusades: Islamic perspectives* (New York, 2000), 180–2.
24. Ibn al-Athīr, 2.364–5; Ibn Shaddād, 96–7; 'Imād al-Dīn, 4.412. Muslim baggage trains needed to be kept close by the army because, in addition to supplies, the heavy armor was kept there; see Hamilton A.R. Gibb, *Studies on the Civilization of Islam*, ed. S.J. Shaw and W.R. Polk (Boston, 1962), 84–5.
25. Ibn al-Athīr, 2.365.

### Chapter II  The siege begins, 1189

1. *Eracles*, 4.17.128: "par diverses manieres de fors batailles tres passa le tens."
2. *Eracles*, 4.10.118–19; Newburgh, 1.348. *Anonymous2*, 252, pegs the total force size at this time to 12,000; this source, "Libellus de expugnatione terrae sanctae per Saladinum," borrows from Ambroise in places; see *Estoire*, 17.
3. Survey details of the city from A. Kesten, *Acre: The old city, survey and planning* (Tel Aviv, 1962), 13–15.
4. David Jacoby, "Montmusard, suburb of crusader Acre: The first stage of its development," in *Outremer*, 205–8.

5. For a discussion of these defensive arrangements, see Denys Pringle, "Town defences in the crusader Kingdom of Jerusalem," in *The Medieval City Under Siege*, ed. I.A. Corfis and M. Wolfe (Woodbridge, 1995), 81–4.

6. On this wall, see Benjamin Z. Kedar, "The outer walls of Frankish Acre," *Atiqot* 31 (1997), 160–1. These details are in the verse account *Anonymous3*, lines 620–32; the quote is from P.W. Edbury (trans.), *The Conquest of Jerusalem and the Third Crusade: Sources in translation* (Aldershot, 1998), 81.

7. *Estoire*, lines 2836–44.

8. Ibn Shaddād, 97–8; Ibn al-Athīr, 2.365; ʿImād al-Dīn, 4.413; *Estoire*, lines 2888–9; *Itinerarium2*, 1.27: "et qui venerant obsessuri tenetur obsessi."

9. *Eracles*, 4.16.127: "que il savoit que mestier lor estoit as armes et as cors."

10. *Itinerarium2*, 1.27.

11. As a work of poetry that was meant for oral readings, Ambroise dramatizes the actions in many cases and employs literary devices such as parallelism for emphasis and effect, but there is nonetheless a high level of detail. A Norman, Ambroise probably traveled to Acre with Richard the Lionheart's army and thus witnessed only the final summer of the siege. Richard did not copy directly from Ambroise but rather rewrote portions and enhanced certain themes and descriptions. See M. Ailes and M. Barber (ed. and trans.), *The History of the Holy War: Ambroise's Estoire de la Guerre Sainte*, 2 vols (Woodbridge, 2003), 1–3 and 12–23 for discussion of the author and his work. On his reliability, see Peter Damian-Grint, *The New Historians of the Twelfth-Century Renaissance: Inventing vernacular authority* (Woodbridge, 1999), 76–9. Major portions of Richard's *Itinerarium*, therefore, can be checked against the other two accounts for accuracy; see H.J. Nicholson (trans.), *The Chronicle of the Third Crusade: The Itinerarium peregrinorum et gesta regis Ricardi*, Crusade Texts in Translation (Farnham, 1997), 6–14, for questions of compilation and authorship.

12. *Eracles*, 4.16.127.

13. The letter is printed in *Ymagines*, 2.70–71.

14. *Anonymous3*, lines 687–90; *Eracles*, 4.17.127; *Estoire*, lines 2848–51; *Itinerarium2*, 1.28: "in consiliis Nestor." The ships are alternatively called cogs (a single-masted sailing ship with a flat bottom made from heavy timbers) or snacks (an *esnecca*, a long galley with oars and a sail); see N.A.M. Rodger, *Safeguard of the Sea: A naval history of Britain, 660–1649* (New York, 1997), 47 and 62–3.

15. *Itinerarium2*, 1.43; Coggeshall, 1.252.

16. *Ymagines*, 2.70.

17. Ruthy Gertwagen, "The crusader port of Acre: Layout and problems of maintenance," in *Actes du Colloque de la Society for the Study of the Crusades and the Latin East (Clermont-Ferrand, 22–25 juin 1995)*, ed. M. Balard (Paris, 1996), 555–9.

18. Gertwagen, "Crusader port of Acre," 558–60. On harbor chains in general, see Benjamin Z. Kedar, "Prolegomena to a world history of harbour and river chains," in *Shipping, Trade and Crusade in the Medieval Mediterranean: Studies in honour of John Pryor*, ed. R. Gertwagen and E. Jeffreys (Farnham, 2012), 3–37.

19. David Jacoby, "Crusader Acre in the thirteenth century: Urban layout and topography," *Studi medievali*, 3rd ser. 20:1 (1979), 11–12; John H. Pryor, "A medieval siege of Troy: The fight to the death at Acre, 1189–1191 or the tears of Ṣalāḥ al-Dīn," in *The Medieval Way of War: Studies in medieval military history in honor of Bernard S. Bachrach*, ed. G.I. Halfond (Aldershot, 2015), 99.

20. Adrian Boas, *Crusader Archaeology: The material culture of the Latin East* (London, 1999), 35. On the possibility of a second, inner harbor within the first, see Boas, "Urban landscapes," 249–50.

21. Ibn Shaddād, 97; John H. Pryor, *Geography, Technology, and War: Studies in the maritime history of the Mediterranean, 649–1571* (Cambridge, 1988), 129. The terminology for the numerous vessels that appeared during the siege varies considerably in the sources; for

the principal western types in the Mediterranean, see John E. Dotson, "Ship types and fleet composition at Genoa and Venice in the early thirteenth century," in *Logistics of Warfare in the Age of the Crusades*, ed. J.H. Pryor (Aldershot, 2006), 63–75.

22. These were Nicola Embriaco, Fulcone da Castello, Simone Doria, Baldovino Guerico, and Spezzapietra and Rosso della Volta; see Merav Mack, "A Genoese perspective of the Third Crusade," *Crusades* 10 (2011), 49.

23. *Estoire*, lines 2810–79; *Itinerarium2*, 1.26; *Howden2*, 3.126; *Anonymous1*, 3.cviii, lines 51–75.

24. *Newburgh*, 1.349. On the borrowing, see John Gillingham, "Two Yorkshire historians compared: Roger of Howden and William of Newburgh," *Haskins Society Journal* 12 (2002), 20–5.

25. On such disputes and issues see Clifford J. Rogers, *Soldiers' Lives throughout History: The middle ages* (Westport, 2007), 66–7; and John France, *Western Warfare in the Age of the Crusades, 1000–1300* (Ithaca, 1999), 210.

26. *Eracles*, 4.17.127 ("par quei nus ne doit douter que Deu n'eust envoié celui secors en confort a ceaus qui se fierent en sa misericorde"); *Estoire*, lines 2836–937 ("Si orez com[e] Deus reguarde; / Cels qu'il velt [aveir] en sa guarde"); *Itinerarium2*, 1.27 ("In hoc itaque articulo positos visitavit eos Oriens ex alto"), cf. Luke 1:78.

27. *Blasien*, 36.54.6–10. Communications between Acre and Saladin were also conducted via letters, carried by men swimming across the harbor or in small boats, and by carrier pigeons; see 'Imād al-Dīn, 4.442 and 4.470; and Ibn Shaddād, 121. In 1191, the garrison began hoisting a basket on a flagpole attached to the top of the church of St Lawrence in the city; see *Eracles*, 5.14.156. The use of both smoke signals and pigeons is recommended in the military manual of al-Ansari (d. 1408); see *A Muslim Manual of War*, ed. and trans. G.T. Scanlon (Reprint, Cairo, 2012), 47–9; and also Susan Edgington, "The doves of war: The part played by carrier pigeons in the crusades," in *Autour de la Première Croisade: Actes du colloque de la Society for the Study of the Crusades and the Latin East*, ed. M. Balard (Paris, 1996), 167–75.

28. *Itinerarium2*, 1.27.

29. Ibn Shaddād, 87; *Eracles*, 4.17.128; *Itinerarium2*, 1.27.

30. *Itinerarium2*, 4.8: "Turcorum etiam moris est, ut quando persenserint se fugantes a persequendo cessare, tunc et ipsi fugere cessabunt, more muscae fastidiosae, quam si abegeris avolabit, cum cessaveris redibit, quamdiu fugaveris fugiet, cum desieris praesto est. Non secus est de Turcis: cum persequi desistens reverteris, tunc Turcus insequitur, si fugaveris fugiet."

31. *Estoire*, lines 2952–3049; *Itinerarium2*, 1.28.

32. *A Muslim Manual of War*, 100–2.

33. Ibn Shaddād, 98; Ibn al-Athīr, 2.365–6.

34. Ibn Shaddād, 99.

35. Ibn Shaddād, 98–9. Ibn al-Athīr's account is much shorter and lacks operational detail.

36. Saladin's male relatives feature prominently at Acre. His sons were all major governors: al-Afḍāl 'Alī of Damascus, al-Ẓāhir Ghiyāth al-Dīn Ghāzī of Aleppo, and al-'Azīz 'Uthmān of Egypt, as well as his brother al-'Ādil, grand-nephews al-Manṣūr Muḥammad (of Hama) and al-Amjad Bahrām Shah (of Baalbek), and first cousin once-removed, al-Mujāhid Shīrkūh II of Homs. See Hamilton A.R. Gibb, "The Aiyūbids," in *A History of the Crusades*, Volume II: *The Later Crusades, 1189–1311*, ed. H.W. Hazard, K.M. Setton, and R.L. Wolff (Madison, 1969), 693.

37. *Estoire*, lines 2900–7; *Itinerarium2*, 1.28; Ibn al-Athīr, 2.366; Ibn Shaddād, 99.

38. *Estoire*, lines 2911–15 ("Aincees fud puis chose seüe / Qu'entre toz cels qui Deu / [mescreoient / N'ot meillor gent qu[ë] il estoient / Por vile guarder e defendre / E por chastel a force prendre"); *Itinerarium2*, 1.28 ("quia virtus et in hoste laudatur").

39. 'Imād al-Dīn, 4.415. 'Imād al-Dīn avoids panegyric and is thought to offer an objective history, and Abu Shāma strove to preserve it by clearly differentiating the excerpted

passages from his own musings. See Hamilton A.R. Gibb, *The Life of Saladin, from the Works of 'Imad ad-Din and Baha' ad-Din* (Oxford, 1973), 2–4. For a recent biography of the secretary, see Lutz Richter-Bernburg, "'Imād al-Dīn al-Iṣfahānī," in *Medieval Muslim Historians and the Franks*, 29–51. In general, see D.S. Richards, "Biographies of Ayyubid sultans," in *Ayyubid Jerusalem: The holy city in context, 1187–1250*, ed. R. Hillebrand and S. Auld (London, 2009), 441–55.

40. Ibn Shaddād, 99.
41. Ibn Shaddād, 99.
42. In the Levant, at least; for the larger infantry role in Spain, see David Nicolle, *Crusader Warfare*, Volume II: *Muslims, Mongols and the Struggle against the Crusades* (London, 2007), 134–5. This occasion might also lead us to question Gibb's assessment that infantry appears "in the sources only in connection with siege operations, either as defenders or attackers"; see *Studies on the Civilization of Islam*, 84. For the extant treatise on Muslim bows and tactics from the period, see Nabih Amin Faris (ed. and trans.), *Arab Archery: An Arabic manuscript of about A.D. 1500, "A Book on the Excellence of the Bow & Arrow" and the description thereof* (Princeton, 1945).
43. Montmusard itself was fortified in the years after the siege, probably between 1198 and 1212; see Jacoby, "Suburb of crusader Acre," 212–13.
44. On the strengths and weaknesses of these methods, see Charles R. Bowlus, "Tactical and strategic weaknesses of horse archers on the eve of the First Crusade," in *Autour de la Première Croisade*, 159–216.
45. Smail, *Crusading Warfare*, 76.
46. Ibn Shaddād, 98.
47. Ibn Shaddād, 99–100.
48. Ibn Shaddād, 100.
49. Ibn Shaddād, 100; Ibn al-Athīr, 2.366. Yaacov Lev, "Infantry in Muslim armies during the crusades," in *Logistics of Warfare in the Age of the Crusades*, 195, interprets this event as Bedouins acting more or less as auxiliary infantry.
50. *Eracles*, 4.18.128–9. The fullest, although not necessarily the closest to the original exemplar from which it was derived. There are a large number of studies on the Old French continuations of William of Tyre. The new starting point is Philip Handyside, *The Old French William of Tyre* (Leiden, 2015). For the essential differences between the four versions (the Lyon *Eracles*, the Colbert-Fontainebleau *Eracles*, the *Chronique d'Ernoul et de Bernard le Trésorier*, and the abrégé (abbreviated) *Eracles*), see Peter W. Edbury, "New perspectives on the Old French continuations of William of Tyre," *Crusades* 9 (2010), 107–13; and Edbury, "The Lyon Eracles and the Old French continuations of William of Tyre," in *Montjoie: Studies in crusade history in honour of Hans Eberhard Mayer*, ed. B.Z. Kedar, J. Riley-Smith, and R. Hiestand (Aldershot, 1997), 139–53. On other questions, including the *Eracles'* authorship, see John H. Pryor, "The *Eracles* and William of Tyre: An interim report," in *The Horns of Hattin: Proceedings of the Second Conference of the Society for the Study of the Crusades and the Latin East, Jerusalem and Haifa 2–6 July, 1987*, ed. B.Z. Kedar (Jerusalem and London, 1992), 270–93. A Latin *Continuation* survives as well, which is partly original but also draws from the *Itinerarium*, Roger of Howden, and William of Newburgh; see M. Salloch (ed.), *Die lateinische Fortsetzung Wilhelms von Tyrus* (Leipzig, 1934); and Hamilton, *The Leper King*, 12–13.
51. *Anonymous3*, lines 719–34; *Itinerarium2*, 1.29; *Estoire*, lines 3114–37.
52. Ibn al-Athīr, 2.366–7. He usefully relates the position of each contingent in October: one was in Antioch, positioned to prevent advances towards Aleppo; a second was in Homs, guarding against attacks from Tripoli; a third was outside Tyre; a fourth was still in Egypt, garrisoned at Alexandria and Damietta; and other assorted soldiers were simply on hiatus after having served out their terms with Saladin earlier in the year.

53. Richard of Templo first states that there were two ranks, missile troops and everyone else; but later in the passage he clarifies that the infantry rank split to allow the cavalry through. There were thus three ranks, not two; see *Itinerarium2*, 1.29. R.C. Smail believed there to have been four main crusader divisions, but I count only three; see *Crusading Warfare*, 187.

54. *Ymagines*, 2.70.

55. After the battle, Guy purportedly exchanged letters with Saladin: the latter accused the king of breaking his oath not to take up arms against him, but Guy responded that his sword was never used; see *Eracles*, 4.20.131.

56. *Eracles*, 4.18.129; *Estoire*, lines 2962–3; *Itinerarium2*, 1.29; *Ymagines*, 2.70. Ibn Shaddād, 100, claims that Guy processed in front of the army, led by four priests carrying a book of the gospels before him.

57. Both men are commended in *Anonymous3*, lines 789–94. See *Estoire*, 74 n.229 on the mosque and its location.

58. *Ymagines*, 2.70. The letter of Theobald offers a confusing version of the army arrangement, splitting the leaders and men into four "squadrons." It can be reconciled with the other accounts save for its placement of the Pisans, which he claims, against the others, marched alongside the landgrave. Charles Oman also saw four divisions, not three; see his *A History of the Art of War in the Middle Ages*, Volume I: *378–1278 AD* (Reprint, London, 1998), 335. His account is breathless and does not take into account the sheer length of the battle; nonetheless, the significance of the battle clearly drew his interest and I have not found another comparable narrative since its original publication in 1924.

59. A *tawashi* was a highly paid soldier who brought to war his own horses, pack animals, and a slave to carry weapons. This is in contrast to a *qaraghulam*, which received a lower payment and possessed inferior arms and armor; see Yaacov Lev, *Saladin in Egypt* (Leiden, 1999), 143–4. In 1181, Saladin's Egyptian army of 8,640 included 6,976 *tawashis* and 1,153 *qaraghulams*, so the elite soldiers represented over 80 percent of the men.

60. Saladin himself was Kurdish; on Kurds in Ayyubid armies, see Anne-Marie Eddé, "Kurdes et Turcs dans l'armée ayyoubide de Syrie du nord," in *War and Society in the Eastern Mediterranean, 7th–15th Centuries*, ed. Y. Lev (Leiden, 1996), 226–7.

61. Ibn al-Athīr, 2.367; Ibn Shaddād, 100–1. On the *halqa*, see Lev, *Saladin in Egypt*, 156.

62. *Ymagines*, 2.70. Benjamin Kedar is thus mistaken that "the first major open battle" after Hattin was Arsur in September 1191; rather, it was this engagement on 4 October. See "King Richard's plan for the battle of Arsūf/Arsur, 1191," in *The Medieval Way of War*, 117.

63. Ibn al-Athīr, 2.366; *Estoire*, lines 2978–9.

64. Ibn Shaddād, 101.

65. *Ymagines*, 2.71.

66. Ibn al-Athīr, 2.367; Ibn Shaddād, 101.

67. *Itinerarium2*, 1.29: "Stabant Turci pro castrorum defensione unanimes, et cum nostri propius accessissent, laxato peditum praecedentium cuneo, equos in hostem audacter admittunt. Versus in fugam Gentilis castra deserit." Oman gets this detail wrong, claiming that the infantry passed through intervals in the infantry line; see *Art of War*, 337.

68. The dead named in the Arabic accounts are: the Emir Mujallī ibn Marwan; the governor of Jerusalem Ẓāhir al-Dīn, who was brother to the jurist 'Īsā, who had commanded Saladin's advance guard; the chamberlain Khalil al-Hakkarī; the scholar and poet Jamal al-Dīn Abū 'Alī ibn Rawāḥa al-Hamawī; and Ismā'īl al-Mukkabbis. See Ibn al-Athīr, 2.367–8; and Ibn Shaddād, 102–3.

69. Smail, *Crusading Warfare*, 187–8.

70. Ibn al-Athīr, 2.367–8; 'Imād al-Dīn, 4.424; *Howden2*, 3.126.

71. *Eracles*, 4.18.129; *Itinerarium2*, 1.29: "Christicolae a persequendo desistunt, et spoliis inhiant: papilionum praeciduntur funes, et ipsius Soldani tentoria comes de Baro animosus invadit . . . Parte alia, dum Alemanni ad praedas hiantius convolant."
72. Ibn Shaddād, 103; Ibn al-Athīr, 2.368.
73. 'Imād al-Dīn, 4.424.
74. For example, Ibn Shaddād, 126–7 and 157.
75. *Itinerarium2*, 1.29. Oman missed this development; see *Art of War*, 338.
76. Ibn al-Athīr, 2.368; *Ymagines*, 2.71.
77. *Eracles*, 4.18.129; *Itinerarium2*, 1.29; Ibn Shaddād, 102–4.
78. *Itinerarium2*, 1.29; Ibn al-Athīr, 2.368; Ibn Shaddād, 103–4; *Ymagines*, 2.71; *Howden2*, 3.126.
79. *Eracles*, 4.18.129: "Li Sarrasin en ocistrent tant que li flums corut de sanc."
80. Ibn Shaddād, 103–4; Ibn al-Athīr, 2.368.
81. *Itinerarium2*, 1.30: "Rex etiam Guido Marchiso, cum ab hostibus opprimeretur, accessit adjutor, et licet injuriae praecesissent et simultas subisset, humanitatis tamen obsequium praebuit indigno et eripuit periturum. Frater regis Gaufridus de Lizenan, videns aciem turbari et omnes de fuga contendere, castrorum curam quam defensandam susceperat festinus deserit, et de fratris salute sollicitus, refugos detenturus procurrit. Orerum miseranda mutatio!" See also *Estoire*, lines 3012–15.
82. *Eracles*, 4.19.130: "dont il ot le jor le loz de toz ceaux de la herberge, que il avoit plus fait de sa main que tuit li autre n'avoient fait."
83. *Itinerarium2*, 1.30 (". . . quem adeo supra omnes Francos virtus extulerant, ut ei militiae primatu concesso, caeteri de laude secunda certarent . . . gloriam quam casus obtulerant, ignavia declinavit"); *Estoire*, lines 3008–11 ("La fud ocis Andreu de Braine - / Qui ja s'alme ne seit en paine, / Car tels chevalers ne murut / Ne tantes genz ne socurut"). The Brienne family participated in the Fifth Crusade as well, and Erard II's youngest brother John of Brienne became king of Jerusalem in 1210; see Guy Perry, "'Scandalia . . . tam in oriente quam in occidente': the Briennes in East and West, 1213–1221," *Crusades* 10 (2011), 63–77.
84. The other knight died as a result; see *Itinerarium2*, 1.30.
85. *Ymagines*, 2.71; *Anonymous1*, 3.cix, lines 85–92; *Estoire*, lines 3016–29; *Itinerarium2*, 1.29: "'Absit!' inquit, 'ut vertatur in opprobrium et Templariis in scandalam, ut fugiendo dicar vitam servasse et commilitones meos caesos reliquisse.'" Gerard was replaced as Templar master by Robert of Sable; see Edbury, *Conquest of Jerusalem and the Third Crusade*, 86.
86. Ibn al-Athīr, 2.368. I see no evidence that Gerard's Templars faced Taqī al-Dīn's right wing, *contra* Michael Markowski, "Richard Lionheart: Bad king, bad crusader?" *Journal of Medieval History* 23:4 (1997), 363.
87. 'Imād al-Dīn, 4.425; *Howden2*, 3.126; Turcopoles were local archers recruited and paid to fight in crusading armies. A letter from Patriarch Heraclius to Pope Clement III reports that twenty Templar knights were killed; see *RRRH*, no. 1269.
88. Ibn al-Athīr, 2.368. He also states that three of the crusader prisoners were women, who had been wearing armor and fighting on horseback; on the subject, see Helen Nicholson, "Women on the Third Crusade," *Journal of Medieval History* 23:4 (2013), 335–49. On women and war in the period in general, see Martin Aurell, "Les femmes guerrières (XIe et XIIe siècles)," in *Famille, violence et christianisation au Moyen Age: Mélanges offerts à Michel Rouche* (Paris, 2005), 319–30.
89. Ibn Shaddād, 104.
90. *Ymagines*, 2.71.
91. *Howden1*, 2.94; *Howden2*, 3.21.
92. Thus, while he reports some events in Acre before his arrival, he is most valuable for Richard's deeds in Cyprus and the events of the summer of 1191. See also John Gillingham, "Roger of Howden on Crusade," in *Richard Coeur de Lion: Kingship, chivalry and war in the twelfth century* (London, 1994), 148–9.

93. Paul M. Cobb, *The Race for Paradise: An Islamic history of the crusades* (Oxford, 2014), 197. Both Ibn Shaddād and Ibn al-Athīr spend more time describing how Saladin arranged for the return of stolen camp property (by fellow Muslims) than casualty figures.

94. Ibn al-Athīr, 2.369; 'Imād al-Dīn, 4.427; *Estoire*, lines 3072–93; *Itinerarium2*, 1.31.

95. Ibn al-Athīr, 2.369; Ibn Shaddād, 104–6. The latter claims he attended the council himself.

96. Ibn Shaddād, 106.

97. Ibn al-Athīr, 2.369; Ibn Shaddād, 104–6. *Howden2*, 3.127, claims that the Muslim army still stretched from Castle l'Eveque to Doc.

98. Here I am referring to the original, militant form of *jihad*, the so-called "lesser jihad"; the so-called "greater *jihad*," or internal struggle/conversion, has to my knowledge never been applied to Saladin's efforts at Acre because he clearly sought violent engagement with the Christian besiegers. The distinction between the two forms of *jihad* is, in any case, overblown and has been politicized over time; on the concept's evolution in medieval Sunni jurisprudence and the bearing of modern politics and apologetics on the issue, see David Cook, *Understanding Jihad* (Berkeley, 2005), 32–48; and, on Saladin and *jihad* specifically Hillenbrand, *Crusades: Islamic perspectives*, 175–86.

99. Ibn Shaddād, 156–7. This is extensively discussed in Peter Partner, "Holy war, crusade and *jihād*: An attempt to define some problems," in *Autour de la Première Croisade*, 338–41.

100. Partner, "Holy war, crusade and *jihād*," 338–9; Cook, *Understanding Jihad*, 60. On this crucial last point, see Paul E. Chevedden's provocative essay, "The Islamic view and the Christian view of the crusades: A synthesis," *History* (2008), 181–200. For the classic comparison of *jihad* and crusade, see Emmanuel Sivan, *L'Islam et la Croisade: Idéologie et propagande dans les réactions Musulmanes aux croisades* (Paris, 1968).

101. See Hadia Dajani-Shakeel, "*Jihād* in twelfth-century Arabic poetry: A moral and religious force to counter the crusades," *Muslim World* 66 (1976), 96–113.

102. Cobb, *Race for Paradise*, 30.

103. Although we must simultaneously admit that Saladin spent more of his military career fighting other Muslims than Christians; see John France, *Perilous Glory: The rise of western military power* (New Haven, 2011), 122. Indeed, as noted in Dajani-Shakeel, "*Jihād* in twelfth-century Arabic poetry," 111, his war against the Zangids was seen as having distracted from his pursuit of holy war. Still, as Lyons and Jackson point out in their influential study, whether called against internal or external foes *jihad* worked to "canalize energy and direct it outward"; see *Saladin*, 371.

104. Ibn Shaddād, 119 and 139; Lev, "Infantry in Muslim armies," 195–6.

105. Ibn Shaddād, 152–5 and 138.

106. Ibn Shaddād, 149–51 (cf. Koran 9.120) and 112. This runs counter to the Muslim strategist al-Harawi's belief that the crusaders "desire the things of this world and are indifferent to the things of the next"; see William J. Hamblin, "Saladin and Muslim military theory," in *Horns of Hattin*, 237–8. Al-Harawi does, however, except the militant Orders in this regard.

107. *Eracles*, 6.1.176: "Nos some venu por Deu et por le sauvement de nos armes."

108. *Estoire*, lines 3695–724; *Itinerarium2*, 1.56: "Vulnere lethali transfodit in inquine Turcum."

109. Coggeshall, 1.255; *Anonymous2*, 255; *Itinerarium2*, 1.53: "Sic his datur triumphare qui in Deo spem ponunt."

110. On the intersections between the expectations of the writers and actual deeds in combat, see John D. Hosler, "Knightly ideals at the siege of Acre, 1189–1191," in *Chivalric Identity in the High Middle Ages*, ed. X. Baecke, D. Crouch, and J. Deploige (Leuven, forthcoming); and Richard Abels, "Cultural representation and the practice of war in the middle ages," *Journal of Medieval Military History* 6 (2008), 1–31.

111. *Itinerarium2*, 1.31.

112. *Itinerarium2*, 1.31; *Anonymous1*, 3.cix, lines 93–100. Ibn Shaddād, 100, tells a curious story about a western ship transporting horses; one horse sprang into the water and swam towards the harbor, where it was caught by Muslims in Acre. On these types of ships, see John H. Pryor, "Transportation of horses by sea during the era of the crusades: Eighth century to 1285 A.D.," *The Mariner's Mirror* 68 (1982), 19–21.
113. *Howden2*, 3.127.
114. 'Imād al-Dīn, 4.428. In this way, the siege of Acre bore some resemblance to the Arabic siege of Constantinople in 717, during which the brother of Caliph Sulayman, Maslama, dug trenches behind and between his army and the city's western wall; see Robert G. Hoyland, *In God's Path: The Arab conquests and the creation of an Islamic empire* (Oxford, 2015), 175. Ibn al-Athīr, 2.366, mistakenly claims that work on the ditches began on 19 September. Given the importance of the fortifications, the dates in the western sources should be preferred.
115. Blasien, 36.54.3–4.
116. Contra Blasien, 36.54.12–15, who claims the crusaders made routine sorties but that Saladin refused battle. For descriptions of the digging and building, see *Eracles*, 4.17.128; *Estoire*, lines 3055–71 and 3094–113; *Itinerarium2*, 1.31; *Howden2*, 3.128; Coggeshall, 1.252; and *Anonymous2*, 252.
117. *Eracles*, 4.17.128. They still had the cisterns in the city for water, however; on these, see Boas, "Urban landscapes," 256–7.
118. On the marquis, see *Itinerarium2*, 1.31 and 1.33; on the catapults, *Howden2*, 3.128. A flour mill may also have been constructed within the camp.
119. Ibn Shaddād, 108–9; Ibn al-Athīr, 2.369.
120. Pryor, "Medieval siege of Troy," 115.
121. These included issues of logistics, ship design, contrary winds, and wave strength; see Ruthy Gertwagen, "Harbours and facilities along the Eastern Mediterranean sea lanes to Outremer," in *Logistics of Warfare in the Age of the Crusades*, 96–103.
122. *Itinerarium2*, 1.33.
123. *Estoire*, line 3138; and *Itinerarium2*, 1.33, both state 31 October, although one recension of the latter gives the date as 26 December. Ibn al-Athīr, 2.370, reads 26 November. Ibn Shaddād, 106, does not give a date because he had left the sultan's presence, traveling around Syria and Iraq asking different magnates for extra troops.
124. Ibn al-Athīr, 2.370.
125. 'Imād al-Dīn, 4.430–1; Ibn al-Athīr, 2.370; Ibn Shaddād, 108. Monachus sets the date as "Die prima Domini post Nativitatem"; see *Anonymous1*, 3.cx, lines 114–21.
126. Pryor, *Geography, Technology, and War*, 125. On images of the galleys at Acre, see Richard W. Unger, "Difficult sources: Crusader art and the depiction of ships," in *Shipping, Trade and Crusade in the Medieval Mediterranean*, ed. R. Gertwagen (New York, 2012), 93.
127. A sort of skiff, called a *galliot* in *Itinerarium2*, 1.33; and Coggeshall, 1.253.
128. Lev, "Infantry in Muslim armies," 198.
129. Ibn Shaddād, 108.

## Chapter III  Spring and summer, 1190

1. *Itinerarium2*, 1.38: "Sic ergo duae mundi partes tertiam impetunt: et adversus Europa confligit, quae sola nec tota Christi nomen agnovit."
2. Ibn al-Athīr, 2.372; Ibn Shaddād, 107–8; 'Imād al-Dīn, 4.440–1.
3. Tyerman, *God's War*, 415.
4. Nicholson, *Chronicle of the Third Crusade*, 87 n.166. See also *Anonymous2*, 253.
5. This is also the conclusion of A.S. Ehrenkreutz, who dubs this sortie as one of only two undertaken during the entire siege; see "The place of Saladin in the naval history of the Mediterranean Sea in the middle ages," *Journal of the American Oriental Society* 75:2 (1955), 113.

6. *Estoire*, lines 3267–77: "Adonc vos peüst sovenir / De formiz ki de formilliere / S'en issent devant e deriere." He describes their ships being draped in four fabrics: silk, baize (heavy felted wool), buckram (stiff linen), and samite (heavy, twill-like silk). The heavy cloth may have been for decoration, but the baize may also have been wetted to protect against incendiaries. Thanks to Mary E. Hosler for advice on these fabrics.

7. Aly Mohamed Fahmy, *Muslim Sea Power in the Eastern Mediterranean, from the Seventh Century to the Tenth Century A.D.* (New Delhi, 1966), 167–8.

8. *Itinerarium2*, 1.34; see the original passage in *Itinerarium1*, 34.17–20. On this issue, see Richard Abels and Stephen Morillo, "A lying legacy? A preliminary discussion of images of antiquity and altered reality in medieval military history," *Journal of Medieval Military History* 3 (2005), 1–13; and Bernard S. Bachrach, "'A lying legacy' revisited: the Abels-Morillo defense of discontinuity," *Journal of Medieval Military History* 5 (2007), 153–93.

9. Ehrenkreutz, "Saladin in naval history," 106 n.66; V. Christides, "Navies, Islamic," in *Dictionary of the Middle Ages*, ed. J. Strayer, 13 vols (New York, 1987), 9.76. On these fire ships specifically, see Douglas Haldane, "The fire-ship of Al-Sāliḥ Ayyūb and Muslim use of 'Greek fire,'" in *The Circle of War in the Middle Ages: Essays on medieval and naval history*, ed. D.J. Kagay and L.J. Andrew Villalon (Woodbridge, 1999), 137–44.

10. On the respective recipes and delivery methods, see John Haldon and M. Byrne, "A possible solution to the problem of Greek fire," in *Byzantinische Zeitschrift begründet von Karl Krumbacher*, ed. H.-G. Beck et al. (München, 1977), 92 and 98; and John Haldon, Andrew Lacey, and Colin Hewes, "'Greek fire' revisited: Recent and current research," in *Byzantine Style, Religion and Civilization: in Honour of Sir Steven Runciman*, ed. E.M. Jeffreys (Cambridge, 2006), 291. There were known sources of petroleum in the region, one of them being in the region of Hīt on the Euphrates River, which had supplied asphalt and naphtha since Assyrian times; see Fahmy, *Muslim Sea Power*, 158–9. There are two eleventh-century Arabic recipes for naphtha, written by Mardi ibn 'Ali al-Tarsusi; see "The Army of the Fatimid Caliph," in *Islam: From the Prophet Muhammad to the Capture of Constantinople*," ed. and trans. B. Lewis (New York, 1974), 223. On the jars, see Boas, *Crusader Archaeology*, 179–80.

11. *Estoire*, lines 3270–303; *Itinerarium2*, 1.34. See Ruthy Gertwagen, "A chapter on maritime history: Shipping and nautical technology of trade and warfare in the medieval Mediterranean, 11th–16th century," in *Maritimes Mittelalter: Meere als Kommunikationsräume*, ed. M. Borgolte and N. Jaspert (Ostfildern, 2016), 135–6, who explains the difference between ancient rams and medieval spurs, and the change in hull design that necessitated adaptation of both the weapon and its application.

12. *Itinerarium2*, 1.34.

13. *Itinerarium2*, 1.34: "Mulieres igitur nostrae Turcos caesarie rapta protrahentes, capite detruncabant, probose tractantes et abjectius jugulantes. Quarum quanto manus infirmior, tanto poena dilatione mortis protractior; cultellis enim non gladiis amputabant capita eorum." See also *Estoire*, lines 3304–7.

14. Curiously, it is passed over quickly in Natasha R. Hodgson, *Women, Crusading and the Holy Land in Historical Narrative* (Woodbridge, 2007), 48. There is likely more to interpret here from a gender perspective: male authors disparaging female violence of a type that was celebrated when perpetrated by males?

15. *Estoire*, lines 3372–89: "A vive force en la chaane."

16. *Anonymous1*, 3.cxiv, lines 225–32. *Itinerarium2*, 1.37, claims that the starvation was so severe that the Muslims were forced to eat horse meat and also pork, in disregard of Koranic prohibitions.

17. Ibn al-Athīr, 2.374; Ibn Shaddād, 112–13; *Itinerarium2*, 1.39. *Anonymous1*, 3.cxiv, lines 233–44, dates the wreck of the Muslim ships rather to a later action on 1 July.

18. Their arrangement is provided by 'Imād al-Dīn, 4.443.

19. ʿImād al-Dīn, 4.443–4; Ibn al-Athīr, 2.372; Ibn Shaddād, 109–13. I have preferred the dates and order of Ibn Shaddād, who by this time had returned to Saladin's presence. On Saladin's angry response to this gift, see Lyons and Jackson, *Saladin*, 310–11.
20. *Estoire*, lines 3344–54 ("Une hisduse gent oscure, / Contre Deu e contre nature, / A roges chapels en lor testes - / Onc Deus ne fist plus laides bestes. / De cels i aveit grant plenté, / Od felenesse volenté, / Que de la gent qui ondeioient / E des chapels qui rojoient, / Sembloient cersiers meürs"), and 3362–7 ("Cil as roches chapels aveient / Une enseigne ou tuit se teneient: / Ço esteit l'enseigne Mahumet, / Qui esteit portraite en somet, / En qui nun se vindrent combatre / Por la cristienté abatre").
21. Black Africans were not unknown to crusaders by 1190, especially those in Egypt. King Amalric led five expeditions there in the 1160s and there are western accounts of blacks in the Fatimid court. See Bernard Hamilton, "The crusades and northeast Africa," in *Crusading and Warfare in the Middle Ages, Realities and Representations: Essays in honour of John France*, ed. S. John and N. Morton (Farnham, 2014), 169–70.
22. *Itinerarium2*, 1.38.
23. For the Battle of the Blacks, see: A.S. Ehrenkreutz, *Saladin* (Albany, 1972), 263–73; Jere L. Bacharach, "African military slaves in the medieval Middle East: The cases of Iraq (869–955) and Egypt (868–1171)," *International Journal of Middle East Studies* 13:4 (Nov. 1981), 487–8; Lev, "Infantry in Muslim armies," 192–3; Lev, *Saladin in Egypt*, 141; and Bernard Lewis, *Race and Slavery in the Middle East: An historical inquiry* (Oxford, 1990), 67–8.
24. Lyons and Jackson, *Saladin*, 307. The origin, training, organization, and armament of these men from North Africa are surveyed in B.J. Beshir, "Fatimid military organization," *Zeitschrift Geschichte und Kultur des Islamischen Orients* 55 (Jan. 1978), 37–49. The club reference is curious, but on their use of staffs and maces see Claude Cahen, "Un traité d'armurerie composé pour Saladin," *Bulletin d'études orientales* 12 (1947–8), 139–40.
25. France, *Great Battles: Hattin*, 82. This number comes by way of Saladin's formal review of his army in 1187; on the various Muslim traditions for this, see C.E. Bosworth, "Recruitment, muster, and review in medieval Islamic armies," in *War, Technology and Society in the Middle East*, ed. V.J. Parry and M.E. Yapp (London, 1975), 59–77 and especially 74–7 for non-Abbasid traditions.
26. Gibb, *Studies on the Civilization of Islam*, 77.
27. Drawn from Gibb, *Studies on the Civilization of Islam*, 81, and detailed in preceding pages. The lords and soldiers of the agriculturally rich lands of the Jazīra were critical to the military success of the Ayyubids in general and Saladin specifically; see John France, "Egypt, the Jazira and Jerusalem: Middle Eastern tensions and the Latin states in the twelfth century," in *Crusader Landscapes in the Medieval Levant: The archaeology and history of the Latin East*, ed. M. Sinibaldi, K.J. Lewis, B. Major, and J.A. Thompson (Cardiff, 2016), 153–4.
28. For a reckoning of Saladin's relative troop strength between Hattin and Arsur, see John France, "'Crusading' warfare in the twelfth century," in *The Crusader World*, ed. A.J. Boas (London and New York, 2016), 75–8.
29. Gibb, *Studies on the Civilization of Islam*, 76; Lev, *Saladin in Egypt*, 143; Nicolle, *Crusader Warfare*, 66.
30. The variety and relative strength of these auxiliary groups are surveyed in Gibb, *Studies on the Civilization of Islam*, 81–3. On the iqta system and its relation to western customs of military organization and recruitment, see A.K.S. Lambton, "Reflections on the Iqtā," in *Arabic and Islamic Studies in Honour of Hamilton A.R. Gibb*, ed. G. Makdisi (Leiden, 1965), 358–76; and Nicolle, *Crusader Warfare*, 80–1. On rates of pay for enrolled iqta soldiers, see Gibb, *Studies on the Civilization of Islam*, 76.
31. Benjamin Z. Kedar, "A western survey of Saladin's forces at the siege of Acre," in *Montjoie*, 113–22.

32. For a taxonomy of artillery of the period, see David S. Bachrach, "English artillery 1189–1307: The implications of terminology," *English Historical Review* 121:494 (2006), 1415–17, which identifies *balistae* as spanned crossbow-type weapons, *mangonelli* as torsion engines, and *petrariae* as traction lever engines.

33. He may have been named Haymar (Aimery) and if so, was probably the same Haymar who was also the bishop of Caesarea and patriarch of Jerusalem.

34. *Estoire*, lines 3186–219; *Anonymous1*, 3.cix, lines 101–4; *Anonymous3*, lines 940–6. The anonymous sources' use of the vague term *machinas* is frustratingly typical of the period; on this problem, see John D. Hosler, "Identifying King Stephen's artillery," *Journal of Conflict Archaeology* 10:3 (2015), 192–203.

35. Vinegar had been used since ancient times to ward off fire; see J.R. Partington, *A History of Greek Fire and Gunpowder* (Cambridge, 1960), 5. On the build and mechanics of siege towers, see Rogers, *Latin Siege Warfare*, 253; on their usage over time, Kelly DeVries and Robert Douglas Smith, *Medieval Military Technology*, 2nd ed. (Toronto, 2012), 170–5; and for a general overview, Jim Bradbury, *The Medieval Siege* (Woodbridge, 1992), 241–50.

36. *Estoire*, lines 3396–403; *Itinerarium2*, 1.36; *Anonymous1*, 3.cxiii, lines 201–8; Coggeshall, 1.253; *Anonymous2*, 253; Ibn al-Athīr, 2.372–3; ʿImād al-Dīn, 4.448; Ibn Shaddād, 110.

37. Ibn al-Athīr, 2.373; Ibn Shaddād, 110; *Estoire*, lines 3402–4; *Itinerarium2*, 1.36. Moats in the region could be quite deep; see Boas, *Crusader Archaeology*, 120.

38. Blasien, 36.53.15–21; *Itinerarium2*, 1.36; Ibn al-Athīr, 2.372; Ibn Shaddād, 109–10.

39. He is identified by ʿImād al-Dīn, 4.448.

40. These may well have been neither tension nor torsion devices but rather lever-operated "traction" trebuchets, which appear in Armenian, Greek, and Syriac sources in the eleventh and twelfth centuries or, arguably, much earlier. See George T. Dennis, "Byzantine heavy artillery: The Helepolis," *Greek, Roman, and Byzantine Studies* 39 (1998), 99–115, particularly 107–14; and Paul E. Chevedden, "The hybrid trebuchet: The halfway step to the counterweight trebuchet," in *On the Social Origins of Medieval Institutions: Essays in honor of Joseph F. O'Callaghan*, ed. D.J. Kagay and T.M. Vann (Leiden, 1998), 203–7. On the description of rope-pulled or "traction" trebuchets in the manual of al-Tarsusi, see Donald R. Hill, "Trebuchets," *Viator* 4 (1973), 99–104; and W.T.S. Tarver, "The traction trebuchet: A reconstruction of an early medieval siege engine," *Technology and Culture* 36:1 (Jan. 1995), 148–52.

41. Similar versions of the story appear in all three major Arabic sources: Ibn Shaddād, 110–11; Ibn al-Athīr, 2.373–4; and ʿImād al-Dīn, 449–50, who claims that seventy crusaders died in one of the towers. See also Partington, *Greek Fire and Gunpowder*, 24–5. That Ali claimed to have devised a new recipe and technique seems to have escaped Alfred Crosby, an Americanist quick to disparage the "dull-minded Franks" who had – rather logically – assumed his pots had misfired; see Alfred W. Crosby, *Throwing Fire: Projectile technology through history* (Cambridge, 2002), 89.

42. Ralph had numerous court connections from which he acquired his information on foreign affairs; see Antonia Gransden, *Historical Writing in England c. 550 to c. 1307* (London, 1974), 230–1.

43. *Itinerarium2*, 1.36; Newburgh, 1.348; *Ymagines*, 2.84; *Estoire*, lines 3424–7; Coggeshall, 1.253; *Anonymous2*, 253; *Anonymous1*, 3.cxiii, lines 213–16: "Lamentantur milites, plangunt servientes, / Et suspirant pedites prae dolore flentes . . ."

44. Ibn Shaddād, 111.

45. *Itinerarium2*, 1.38; *Anonymous1*, 3.cxiii, lines 217–24.

46. *Estoire*, 82; *Itinerarium2*, 104.

47. *Estoire*, 82–3; *Itinerarium2*, 105.

48. *Itinerarium2*, 107–8.

49. Ibn Shaddād, 160.

50. *Estoire*, 84; *Itinerarium2*, 111–12.

51. Ibn Shaddād, 100 and 146. See Carol Sweetenham, "What really happened to Eurvin de Créel's donkey? Anecdotes in sources for the First Crusade," in *Writing the Early Crusades: Text, transmission and memory*, ed. M. Bull and D. Kempf (Woodbridge, 2014), 75–88.
52. *Itinerarium2*, 1.38.
53. *Estoire*, lines 3342–3.
54. *Itinerarium2*, 1.38.
55. Ibn Shaddād, 55.
56. 'Imād al-Dīn, 4.454–5 and 4.456–8. Ibn al-Athīr, 2.376, gives the defection of Qilij's sons and their men as the reason.
57. Ibn al-Athīr, 2.376. The old myth that Saladin concocted an alliance with the Byzantine emperor Isaac II Comnenus, in which the latter agreed to attack and diminish the German forces as they advanced through his lands, has now been thoroughly demolished; see Savvas Neocleous, "The Byzantines and Saladin: Opponents of the Third Crusade?" *Crusades* 9 (2010), 87–106.
58. Ibn Shaddād, 116. A mild illness struck the Muslim army in general in early summer 1190.
59. Ekkehard Eickhoff, *Friedrich Barbarossa im Orient: Kreuzzug und Tod Friedrichs I* (Tübingen, 1977), 77; Daniel P. Franke, "Crusade, empire, and the process of war in Staufen Germany, 1180–1220," in *The Crusader World*, 131. Ibn Shaddād, 126, apparently read reports that numbered the Germans at anywhere between 5,000 and 200,000. Other exaggerated figures are detailed in Tyerman, *God's War*, 418.
60. For rates of speed, see John W. Nesbitt, "The rate of march of crusading armies in Europe," *Traditio* 19 (1963), 178–80; on the supplies and coins, Alan V. Murray, "Finance and logistics of the crusade of Frederick Barbarossa," in *In Laudem Hierosolymitani: Studies in crusades and medieval culture in honour of Benjamin Z. Kedar*, ed. I. Shagrir, R. Ellenblum, and J. Riley-Smith (Aldershot, 2007), 357–68.
61. Dana Cushing, *A German Third Crusader's Chronicle of his Voyage and the Siege of Almohad Silves, 1189 AD/Muwahid Xelb, 585 AH: De itinere navali* (Antimony Media, 2013), xcviii–cv. A fifteenth-century source mentioned by Cushing, the *Deutschordenschronik*, claims that they were joined by cogs bearing burghers from Bremen and Lübeck; if so, they would have arrived between the landings of Conrad of Montferrat and the Muslim reinforcements. For the Anglo-Norman role in the expedition to Silves, see Lucas Villegas Aristizábal, "Revisión de las crónicas de Ralph de Diceto y de la gesta regis Ricardi sobre la participación de la flota angevina durante la Tercera Cruzada en Portugal," *Studia historica* 27 (2010), 153–70.
62. For the most recent detailed chronology of Barbarossa's crusade, see John B. Freed, *Frederick Barbarossa: The prince and the myth* (New Haven, 2016), 486–512. *Anonymous1*, 3.cxiv–cxvii, lines 245–332, is the most concise and detailed non-imperial account; see also *Anonymous3*, lines 1397–408.
63. Freed, *Frederick Barbarossa*, 512.
64. *Estoire*, lines 3240–52: "Dendez Acre tel joie en orent / Des noveles quant il les sorent / Qu'il tombouent e thabourent, / Si qu'autre rien ne labourent; / Si veneient sor les toreles / A noz genz dire les noveles, / Que Salahadins bien saveit / E qui mandé le lor aveit; / Si crioient a voiz hauciee / De sum les murs meinte fiee, / E firent dire as reneiez, / 'Vostre empererë est noiez.' / Lors ot en l'ost tele tristesce / E tel deheit e tel destresce . . ." Additional flourishments are added in *Itinerarium2*, 1.24.
65. *Howden1*, 2.89; *Howden2*, 3.171; Rigord, 110. All of these accounts contain errors; Rigord calls the duke Henry, and Roger of Howden calls him Conrad.
66. Ansbert, 92.14–31. Ansbert is mainly concerned with the generation of Frederick Barbarossa's campaign and recedes into vagaries after the emperor's premature death in the spring of 1190. He picks up again with greater interest in 1192, when Richard the Lionheart became the prisoner of Duke Leopold of Austria; in this sense, Acre is some-

thing of a lacuna in the text. On Ansbert, see G.A. Loud (trans.), *The Crusade of Frederick Barbarossa: The history of the expedition of the Emperor Frederick and related texts* (Farnham, 2013), 1–3.

67. ʿImād al-Dīn, 4.458–9; Ibn Shaddād, 120 and 126.

68. Tyerman, *God's War*, 428. Ibn Shaddād, 125, claims that Frederick had taken Antioch "deceitfully and with guile"; for some discussion of the politics involved, see *Itinerarium2*, 1.44. On Antioch in general, see Andrew D. Buck, *The Principality of Antioch and its Frontiers in the Twelfth Century* (Woodbridge, 2017).

69. *Itinerarium2*, 1.44–5; Ibn Shaddād, 128. See also *Anonymous1*, 3.cxvii–cxviii, lines 332–53; and *Anonymous2*, 255.

70. Ibn Shaddād, 125; ʿImād al-Dīn, 4.459; Ibn al-Athīr, 2.376.

71. Ansbert, 93.19–22; Blasien, 35.51–52.26–27; *Eracles*, 5.3.141; Gilbert of Mons, *Chronicle of Hainaut*, trans. L. Napran (Woodbridge, 2005), 129. See also Gerald of Wales, "De principis instructione liber," in *Giraldi Cambrensis opera*, ed. G.F. Warner, 8 vols, Rolls Series (London, 1891), 8.3.23; and in English, Gerald of Wales, "Giraldus Cambrensis concerning the instruction of princes," in *The Church Historians of England*, trans. J. Stevenson, vol. 5:1 (London, 1858). On his life and works, see Robert Bartlett, *Gerald of Wales, 1146–1223* (Oxford, 1982). Gerald is well known for his witness account of Archbishop Baldwin of Canterbury's tour through Wales, in which he preached the Third Crusade; see "Itinerarium Kambriae," in *Giraldi Cambrensis opera*, vol. 7.

72. See in general *Anonymous2*, 253. There was at least one shipment from Gaeta in 1190, organized by the Genoese ship owner Bernardo Riccio, but it must have landed elsewhere, perhaps in Tyre; see Mack, "A Genoese perspective of the Third Crusade," 55.

73. Based on the historical exchange table in M. Adler, *The Jews in Medieval Europe* (London, 1939), which converts the bezant (worth two shillings) to three pounds sterling in 1939.

74. Modern values calculated on "Historical UK inflation rates and calculator," http://inflation.stephenmorley.org/ (accessed 6 August 2016).

75. A bezant was a gold coin of about 93 percent fineness; see B.J. Cook, "The bezant in Angevin England," *Numismatic Chronicle* 159 (1999), 255. In normal times, one gold bezant could be enough to purchase a draft horse, as opposed to a gallon of milk at Acre in 1190! See K. Hodges, "List of price of medieval items," http://medieval.ucdavis.edu/120D/Money.html (accessed 17 August 2016).

76. The sources give different currencies for each item; see *Eracles*, 5.10.150; *Howden2*, 3.171; *Anonymous1*, 3.cxii, lines 157–92. For their conversion into bezants, I have used Peter Spufford, *The Handbook of Medieval Exchange*, Royal Historical Society Guides and Handbooks (London, 1986), 295 (for the value of a bezant to shillings and pennies in 1162) and 297 (for the "Acre" bezant to sous and deniers in 1210). For more typical prices of goods in the period, see D.L. Farmer, "Some price fluctuations in Angevin England," *Economic History Review* 9:1 (1956), 34–43.

77. Ibn al-Athīr, 2.379, names specifically the emir Usāma, governor of Beirut, and the Kurdish chief al-Mashṭūb as two men who arranged for shipments of food to be delivered and sold to the crusaders.

78. These numbers are all taken from John Pryor's summation of the different calculations provided in essays in his edited collection; see "Digest," in *Logistics of Warfare in the Age of the Crusades*, 281–3.

79. Kedar, "The Patriarch Eraclius," 203.

80. *Itinerarium2*, 1.40; *Eracles*, 5.10.150–51; *Anonymous3*, lines 1277–324. There is no indication, however, that any of the soldiers were actually excommunicated, either before or after the St James affair. Certainly matters never reached the level of Innocent III's excommunication of the crusading host during the Fourth Crusade; see *The Deeds of Pope Innocent III, by an Anonymous Author*, trans. J.M. Powell (Washington, DC, 2004), 126.

81. Coggeshall, 1.254; *Itinerarium2*, 1.40: "Plebs rerum novarum cupida, principum incusat ignaviam, et pari desiderio aestuans, se vicissim invitat ad pugnam" ("The common people, greedy for excitement, began to accuse the princes of being cowards and started agitating for a fight") and "Principes quidem, quantum possunt, ausus vulgi temerarios laborant comprimere" ("The princes tried to restrain the rash daring of the common crowd as far as they could"). On the translation of constable, see R.E. Latham (ed.), "Greg/arius," *Revised Medieval Latin Word List from British and Irish Sources* (Reprint, Oxford, 1994), 216; on their rank and duties, see Clifford J. Rogers, "Constables," *The Oxford Encyclopedia of Medieval Warfare and Military Technology*, ed. C. Rogers (Oxford, 2010), 1.423–4. See also the terminology in *Anonymous2*, 254: "vulgus tumultuans sine consilio principium." On the too-common habit of translating *miles* as "knight," see John D. Hosler, *John of Salisbury: Military authority of the twelfth-century renaissance* (Leiden, 2013), 12–19.

82. *Itinerarium2*, 1.40: "Nihil tamen vel illorum dissuasio, vel hujus interminatio proficit; vincit enim furor consilium, rationem impetus, imperium multitudo. Vulgus, quocunque impellitur, temeritatem virtutem putat, id optimum quod optat judicans, et rerum exitu non expendens, corrigentem refugit, et regentem contemnit."

83. 'Imād al-Dīn, 4.467.

84. Richard of Templo copies the incorrect remark in his source that the Muslim right flank was still commanded by Taqī al-Dīn and posted his position as being on the road to Castle Imbert (Akhzib), about 9 miles to the north of Akko; see *Itinerarium2*, 1.40; and *Itinerarium1*, 40.24–5.

85. *Estoire*, lines 3476–9; Ibn al-Athīr, 2.376-7; Ibn Shaddād, 118.

86. *Eracles*, 5.10.151; *Itinerarium2*, 1.40; *Howden2*, 2.172.

87. Ibn Shaddād, 118.

88. *Estoire*, lines 3476–9.

89. Ibn Shaddād, 118; similar remarks concerning Allah's intervention in battle appear in 99, 104, 108 (cf. Koran 33.25, in which Allah turns back unbelievers), 122–3, 127–8, 130, and 161 (nearly verbatim from Koran 3.54). For the Christian variation of weapons separating body from soul, see Hosler, *John of Salisbury*, 133–4.

90. Ibn al-Athīr, 2.376-7. He also claims that the Egyptian troops had actually ridden behind the crusaders, separating them from their camp, but no other source mentions it. In either case, the Arabic sources contradict Amin Maalouf's claim that the German problem had "paralysed Saladin for several months, preventing him from joining the decisive battle," because here, not even a month after sending his emirs north to block the German advance, the sultan is clearly participating in major combat at Acre; see *The Crusades through Arab Eyes*, trans. J. Rothschild (New York, 1984), 207.

91. *Anonymous1*, 3.cxviii, lines 369–72.

92. *Itinerarium2*, 1.40: "Audito fremitu, et strage conspecta, principes nostri dissimulant: duri certe, inhumani et impii, qui fratres suos coram se trucidari conspiciunt, nec opem perituris impendunt, quibus hoc solum fuit pro crimine contra factam inhibitionem a castris exisse. Porro caeteris ex ignavia potius quam offensa haesitantibus . . ."

93. *Estoire*, lines 3480–5; *Howden2*, 3.70; *Anonymous2*, 254; *Itinerarium2*, 1.40: "scientia scilicet praecluem et armis insignem." See R.L. Nicholson, *Joscelyn III and the Fall of Crusader States, 1134–1199* (Leiden, 1973), 187.

94. *Itinerarium2*, 1.40; Ibn al-Athīr, 2.367–77; Ibn Shaddād, 118–19; the latter claims that Saladin had personally ordered that none were to be spared.

95. *Eracles*, 5.10.151; *Itinerarium2*, 1.40; *Anonymous1*, 3.cxviii, line 364; "Epistolae Cantuarienses," in *Chronicles and Memorials of the Reign of Richard I*, ed. W. Stubbs, 2 vols, Rolls Series (London, 1864–5), 2.329; Ibn al-Athīr, 2.367–77; Ibn Shaddād, 19–20. Once again, the latter's numbers are to be preferred because the *qāḍī* claims not only to have spoken with the Muslims charged with counting the dead, but also to have personally ridden among the bodies afterward. He also, once again, claims that

female warriors were counted among the crusader ranks, with four of them taking part in the fighting. However, he also makes the outrageous claim that, over the entire course of fighting, only ten Muslims were killed. On such underreporting of casualties in a victory, see Bernard S. Bachrach, "Early medieval demography: Some observations on the methods of Hans Delbrück," in *The Circle of War in the Middle Ages*, 3–20.

96. On the subject of medieval conceptions of cowardice in war, see Richard Abels, "'Cowardice' and duty in Anglo-Saxon England"; Steven Isaac, "Cowardice and fear management: The 1173–74 conflict as a case study"; and Stephen F. Morillo, "Expecting cowardice: Medieval battle tactics reconsidered," *Journal of Medieval Military History* 4 (2006), 29–49, 50–64, and 65–73, respectively.

97. *Itinerarium2*, 1.40: "si caput nacta."

98. "Epistolae Cantuarienses," 2.329: "Milites nostri infra tentoria sua delitescunt, et qui sibi festiname promittebant victoriam, ignavi et torpidi, et quasi convicti, contumelias sibi ab hostibus infra impune patiuntur." This letter was written after 12 October 1190, the date of Baldwin's arrival at Acre.

99. *Itinerarium2*, 1.40; Ibn Shaddād, 119–20.

100. *Estoire*, lines 3455–61.

101. Other losses in the vicinity compounded the problem. Ibn Shaddād, 120, mentions a report from Aleppo describing a separate detachment of westerners having been slaughtered in battle. The Muslims at Acre celebrated the news and it bolstered their morale.

102. *Itinerarium2*, 1.42. See also Coggeshall, 1.254; and *Anonymous2*, 254.

103. Ibn Shaddād, 121. *Anonymous1*, 3.cxx, lines 421–8, simply offers "militum numerositate."

104. *Eracles*, 5.10.149–50. Lists of names appear in *Estoire*, lines 3500–15; and *Itinerarium2*, 1.42. On crossbows, still valuable is Ralph Payne-Gallwey, *The Crossbow: Its military and sporting history, construction and use* (Reprint, Ludlow, 2007).

105. Ibn al-Athīr, 2.377; Ibn Shaddād, 120.

106. Popular and scholarly opinions of his career have swung to and fro across the centuries; for a review, see Robert Irwin, "Saladin and the Third Crusade: A case study in historiography and the historical novel," in *A Companion to Historiography*, ed. M. Bentley (London and New York, 1997), 139–52; as well as Hans Eberhard Mayer, *The Crusades*, trans. J. Gillingham (Oxford, 1988), 147; Cobb, *Race for Paradise*, 203–4; and Michael Ehrlich, "The Battle of Hattin: A chronicle of a defeat foretold?" *Journal of Medieval Military History* 5 (2007), 32. Gibb's argument that Saladin was not an outstanding strategist but nonetheless a good tactician seems on-point; still, even he admits that Saladin's men were themselves baffled by the crusader trenches. See Gibb, *Studies on the Civilization of Islam*, 98 and 104.

107. Ibn Shaddād, 120–1.

108. Ibn al-Athīr, 2.377.

109. Hamblin, "Saladin and Muslim military theory," 235.

## Chapter IV Autumn and winter, 1190

1. Ibn Shaddād, 130.

2. He is best known, rather, for his marriage in 1192 to Isabella, half-sister of Queen Sibylla of Jerusalem and widow of Conrad of Montferrat. Henry's father was a participant in the Second Crusade; see Theodore Evergates, *Henry the Liberal: Count of Champagne, 1127–1181* (Philadelphia, 2016), 16–33.

3. Ibn Shaddād, 123–5; 'Imād al-Dīn, 4.469. These were most likely rope-pulled "traction" trebuchets, not counterweight devices (*bildae*), because the latter do not appear to have been used by western armies until the early thirteenth century. See Rogers, *Latin Siege Warfare*, 265; Bachrach, "English artillery," 1421; and Peter Purton, *A History of*

*the Early Medieval Siege* (Woodbridge, 2009), 386–7. For their presence in eastern armies, dating to the mid-twelfth century, see DeVries and Smith, *Medieval Military Technology*, 126–7; and Hugh Kennedy, *Crusader Castles* (Cambridge, 1994), 107–8. Michael S. Fulton, "Anglo-Norman artillery in narrative histories, from the reign of William I to the minority of Henry III," *Journal of Medieval Military History* 14 (2016), 15, dissents and sees circumstantial evidence for counterweight devices at Acre. On the etymology of *trebuchet*, see William Sayers, "The name of the siege engine *trebuchet*: Etymology and history in medieval France and Britain," *Journal of Medieval Military History* 8 (2010), 189–96.

4. Ibn al-Athīr, 2.378 n.6.

5. On the Latin term for slings, *fundae*, see Bachrach, "English artillery," 1414–15.

6. Ibn Shaddād, 124–5. On the probable designs and compositions of fire arrows, see Robert Douglas Smith, *Rewriting the History of Gunpowder* (Nykøbing, 2010), 84–7.

7. One of these swimmers was caught with the nets of some Christian fishermen, who thereafter discovered the phials and delivered him to camp, where he was beheaded; see *Itinerarium2*, 1.55. Another, named ʿIsa, drowned while carrying three purses around his waist filled with sealed documents and 1,000 dinars; on this and the pigeons, see Ibn Shaddād, 124. The use of pigeons had been standardized by Nūr al-Dīn in 1172, when the birds were actually authorized to receive rations; see "On the pigeon post (1171–1172)," in *Islam: From the Prophet Muhammad*, 223–4.

8. Ibn Shaddād, 122–3; ʿImād al-Dīn, 4.469–70.

9. *Estoire*, lines 3689–94; *Itinerarium2*, 1.54. These accounts also suggest that the garrison sortied while many of the crusaders were away foraging. Piers D. Mitchell doubts the authenticity of this story; see *Medicine in the Crusades: Warfare, wounds and the medieval surgeon* (Cambridge, 2004), 176.

10. *Anonymous1*, 3.cxx, lines 409–12; Ibn al-Athīr, 378; Ibn Shaddād, 123–4. On the *botsha*, see Ehrenkreutz, "Saladin in naval history," 113. A *ghiara* was the equivalent of a sack of crops; see Sato Tsugitaka, *State and Rural Society in Medieval Islam: Sultans, Muqtaʿs and Fallahun* (Leiden, 1997), 70.

11. ʿImād al-Dīn, 4.476; Ibn Shaddād, 126–7; *Itinerarium2*, 97; *Itinerarium1*, 58.8.

12. *Estoire*, lines 3765–92; *Itinerarium2*, 1.58.

13. *Estoire*, lines 3793–812; *Itinerarium2*, 1.58.

14. Ibn Shaddād, 127–8.

15. Ibn Shaddād, 129–30.

16. *Estoire*, lines 3927–44; *Itinerarium2*, 1.60. A dromond was a large Byzantine-style warship; see in general John H. Pryor, *The Age of the Dromōn: The Byzantine navy, ca. 500–1204* (Leiden, 2006).

17. Ibn Shaddād, 132.

18. Ibn Shaddād, 127; *Itinerarium2*, 1.58.

19. Donald E. Queller and Thomas F. Madden, *The Fourth Crusade: The conquest of Constantinople*, 2nd ed. (Philadelphia, 1997), 122–4. For Villehardouin's account of the bridges, see F. Marzials (trans.), *Chronicles of the Crusades: Villehardouin and Joinville* (Reprint, Mineola, NY, 2007), 32–6.

20. Purton, *Early Medieval Siege*, 334.

21. R.L. Wolff, "The Fifth Crusade," in *A History of the Crusades*, ed. K. Setton and H.W. Hazard, 6 vols (Madison, 1969), 2.398–401. Oliver's own account is translated in Bird et al., *Crusade and Christendom*, 169–72.

22. Ibn Shaddād, 129–30 ("similar to the rod which is attached to a millstone"); *Estoire*, 85; *Itinerarium2*, 1.59; *Anonymous1*, 3.cxx–cxxi, lines 429–40.

23. *Estoire*, lines 3839–68; *Itinerarium2*, 1.59; *Anonymous1*, 3.cxxi, lines 441–60; Ibn Shaddād, 130.

24. Ibn Shaddād, 130. He claims the tip weighed 100 *qintars* (quintals), which is very roughly equivalent to 1,000 kilograms.

25. *Howden2*, 175.
26. *Itinerarium2*, 1.65; "Epistolae Cantuarienses," 328–9: "Turci nos obsident, quotidie provocaut, instanter impugnant. Milites nostri infra teutoria sua delitescunt, et qui sibi festinam promittebant victoriam, ignavi et torpidi, et quasi convicti, contemelias sibi ab hostibus infra impune patiuntur. Robur Saladini diebus augescit singulis; exercitus noster quotidie minuitur et deficit."
27. *Anonymous1*, 3.cxxi, lines 461–4.
28. Ibn Shaddād, 128–9; ʿImād al-Dīn, 4.478.
29. France, *Great Battles: Hattin*, 53–4.
30. On the latter, see Gibb, *Studies on the Civilization of Islam*, 104–5: "But when repeated success in the open field proved to be of no effect whatsoever in relieving the pressure on Acre, it was a natural reaction to slacken effort and to grumble against Saladin."
31. On his death, see Ibn al-Athīr, 2.380–1.
32. Ibn Shaddād, 132–5.
33. Ibn Shaddād, 135.
34. Ibn Shaddād, 133; Ibn al-Athīr, 2.384; ʿImād al-Dīn, 4.488–90.
35. On Fīq, see M.V. Guérin, *Description Géographique, Historique et Archéologique de la Palestine*, 3 vols (Paris, 1880), 1.314–16. Ibn al-Athīr, 2.385, tells the story differently, saying that Saladin had actually ordered Taqī al-Dīn to arrest Sanjar Shāh on his way from Hama to Acre.
36. The whole story is related at length in Ibn al-Athīr, 2.384–5; and Ibn Shaddād, 133–4.
37. For a detailed narrative of the conflict, see Ibn al-Athīr, 2.384–5.
38. On the naval aspects of the king's arrivals and departures in Sicily, see Charles D. Stanton, *Norman Naval Operations in the Mediterranean* (Woodbridge, 2011), 162–6.
39. See in general John Gillingham, "Richard I and Berengaria of Navarre," *Historical Research* 53:128 (1980), 157–73.
40. On these events, see the narratives in John Gillingham, *Richard I*, 132–9; and John W. Baldwin, *The Government of Philip Augustus: Foundations of French royal power in the middle ages* (Berkeley, 1986), 78.
41. Pryor, "Medieval siege of Troy," 107.
42. *Itinerarium2*, 1.61; *Howden1*, 2.134–5; *Estoire*, line 3955; Coggeshall, 1.255; *Anonymous1*, 3.cxxii, lines 485–8; Ibn al-Athīr, 2.378–9; Ibn Shaddād, 135.
43. Following Baldwin's death that same month, Hubert Walter distributed his estate to twenty knights and fifty sergeants in wages and gave the rest to the poor in camp; see Christopher Tyerman, *England and the Crusades, 1095–1588* (Chicago, 1988), 63.
44. *Estoire*, lines 3961–4 and 3975–7; *Itinerarium2*, 1.61; *Howden1*, 2.134–5; Ibn al-Athīr, 2.378; Ibn Shaddād, 138; ʿImād al-Dīn, 4.510. On Hubert Walter's military activities, see Lawrence G. Duggan, *Armsbearing and the Clergy in the History and Canon Law of Western Christianity* (Woodbridge, 2013), 26 and 65–6.
45. *Estoire*, lines 3981–2, is thus in error when writing "they headed straight for the Doc" ("Eht [les] vos errant dreit al / Doc").
46. Ibn Shaddād, 135–6; Ibn al-Athīr, 2.378.
47. *Itinerarium2*, 1.61; *Howden1*, 2.144; *Howden2*, 3.73. See also *Anonymous1*, cxxii–cxxiii, lines 489–500, which details the fighting but not the principals involved.
48. *Itinerarium2*, 1.61; *Estoire*, lines 3983–8.
49. ʿImād al-Dīn, 4.510: "Nos avant-gardes postés sur la colline d'El-ʾYadhyyah montèrent aussitot a cheval pour opérer une diversion et les assaillirent d'une grêle de flèches enflammées."
50. *Estoire*, lines 3997–4000: "E quant bataille ne troverent, / Vers Caïphas tot dreit tornerent, / Ou l'em dist qu'il aveit vitaille, / Dont al siege aveit meinte faille." *Itinerarium2*, 1.62, claims the crusaders were cheated out of a battle.

51. *Itinerarium2*, 1.62; *Estoire*, lines 4001–3. The account in *Anonymous1*, 3.cxxiii, lines 505–12, is vague. Today, the site is the En Afek Nature Reserve; En Afek is also the ancient site of Aphik mentioned in Judges 1.31.
52. Ibn al-Athīr, 2.379; Ibn Shaddād, 136; 'Imād al-Dīn, 4.511: "au centre droit."
53. Ibn al-Athīr, 2.379; *Estoire*, lines 4004–6; *Itinerarium2*, 1.62. On the role of drums and horns in Muslim attacks, see Nicolle, *Crusader Warfare*, 249–50.
54. Ibn al-Athīr, 2.379. On the fighting march, see Smail, *Crusading Warfare*, 156–65; John France, "Crusading warfare and its adaptation to eastern conditions in the twelfth century," *Mediterranean Historical Review* 15:2 (2000), 60–61; and Georgios Theotokis, "The square 'fighting march' of the crusaders at the Battle of Ascalon (1099)," *Journal of Medieval Military History* 11 (2013), 57–71.
55. Ibn Shaddād, 137; *Estoire*, lines 4007–9; *Itinerarium2*, 1.62; *Anonymous1*, 3.cxxiii, lines 513–16. 'Imād al-Dīn, 4.511: "et s'acquittèrent a leur égard des lois et coutumes de la guerre sainte."
56. Ibn Shaddād, 137.
57. *Estoire*, lines 4010–13; *Itinerarium2*, 1.62.
58. *Estoire*, lines 4029–32: "E li pelerin retornerent / Por repairier la dont tornerent, / Mais mul eürent ainceis entente / Qu'il venissent jusqu'a lor tentes." The contours of which I explore in depth in "Clausewitz's wounded lion: A fighting retreat at the siege of Acre, November 1190," in *Acre and its Falls*, ed. J. France (Brill, forthcoming). The march is also briefly discussed in Smail, *Crusading Warfare*, 161–2.
59. *Estoire*, lines 4024–8; *Itinerarium2*, 1.62.
60. The marshes were drained in the early twentieth century. For two visitor accounts of them, see Jacob Abbott, "Memoirs of the Holy Land," *Harper's New Monthly Magazine* 27:5 (1852), 291–2; and Malta Protestant College, *Journal of a Deputation sent to the East by the Committee of the Malta Protestant College, Part I* (London, 1849), 265.
61. *Itinerarium2*, 1.62; Ibn Shaddād, 137; 'Imād al-Dīn, 4.512; *Estoire*, lines 4040–6: "Que Deus ne fist neiff ne gresille, / Ne pluie en mai, quant il rosille, / Que chee plus menuement / Que li pilet espesement / En l'ost ausi tost ne cheïssent / Einz que noz genz d'illoc partissent." This stands *contra* Smail's narration, in which "the foot-soldiers protected the knights like a wall"; see *Crusading Warfare*, 161. Dismounted knights were a common feature in eleventh- and twelfth-century European warfare, although the image runs counter to the traditional importance attached to cavalry charges in the crusades. See Stephen F. Morillo, *Warfare under the Anglo-Norman Kings, 1066–1135* (Woodbridge, 1994), 156–9; and Matthew Bennett, "The myth of the military supremacy of knightly cavalry," in *Armies, Chivalry and Warfare: Proceedings of the 1995 Harlaxton Symposium*, ed. M.J. Strickland (Stamford, 1998), 309–10. Dismounted Templar knights are a rarer occurrence; indeed, there is not even a reference to infantry tactics in the Templar Rule; see Matthew Bennett, "*La Régle du Temple* as a military manual, or how to deliver a cavalry charge," in *Studies in Medieval History presented to R. Allen Brown*, ed. C. Harper-Bill and J.L. Nelson (Woodbridge, 1989), 7–20.
62. Ibn Shaddād, 137.
63. *Itinerarium2*, 1.62; Ibn al-Athīr, 2.379; Ibn Shaddād, 137.
64. Verbruggen, *Art of Warfare*, 89. On the unifying sign of the cross during the Third Crusade, see Robert W. Jones, *Bloodied Banners: Martial display on the medieval battlefield* (Woodbridge, 2010), 61. On rates of march in the region and the period, see John Haldon, "Roads and communications in the Byzantine Empire: Wagons, horses, and supplies," in *Logistics of Warfare in the Age of the Crusades*, 131–58.
65. 'Imād al-Dīn, 4.513: "mais les Francs continuaient à marcher lentement"; Lyons and Jackson, *Saladin*, 321; Kedar, "Plan for the battle of Arsūf/Arsur," 118.
66. *Itinerarium2*, 1.62; Ibn Shaddād, 137–8; 'Imād al-Dīn, 4.512–13: "mais les Francs demeuraient immobiles et comme fichés en terre, impassibles, silencieux."
67. *Estoire*, lines 4067–72: "They intended to destroy the bridge when the army came up and attacked them, but they were so thick on the bridge that the pilgrims did not know

how to cross, they saw them so piled up there" ("Ja veleient le pont abatre, / Quant l'ost s'envint sor els embatre, / Mais le pont si porpris aveient / Que le pelerin ne saveient / Par ont il peüssent passer, / Tant s'en i vindrent entasser").

68. *Estoire*, lines 4073–84; *Itinerarium2*, 1.62. Ibn Shaddād, 138, claims that Henry of Champagne and Conrad of Montferrat were injured in the fighting, two members of Saladin's royal guard were injured (Ayaz the Tall and Sayf al-Dīn Yāzkūj), and also that an unnamed, heavily armored crusader was captured and beheaded. However, his claim that the bridge had been cut the night before does not mesh with the other sources, and that of 'Imād al-Dīn, 4.513, is to be preferred. There is nothing left of the original bridge; on surviving crossings, see Andrew Petersen, "Medieval bridges of Palestine," in *Egypt and Syria in the Fatimid, Ayyubid and Mamluk Eras VI: Proceedings of the 14th and 15th International Colloquium Organized at the Katholieke Universitat Leuven in May 2005 and May 2006*, ed. U. Vermeulen and K. D'Hulster, Orientalia Lovaniensia Analecta (Leuven, 2010), 291–306.

69. *Anonymous1*, 3.cxxiii, line 519.

70. Ibn al-Athīr, 2.379; Ibn Shaddād, 138.

71. Ibn Shaddād, 138. Saladin received no response from Acre and had to abandon the plan.

72. Ibn Shaddād, 141–2.

73. Ibn al-Athīr, 2.379; Ibn al-Dīn, 139; 'Imād al-Dīn, 4.526–7. On the treasurer, see Baldwin, *Government of Philip Augustus*, 57.

74. Kedar believes it was October; see "Patriarch Eraclius," 204.

75. *Itinerarium2*, 1.63; *Estoire*, lines 4103–44; *Howden2*, 172–3.

76. On Baldwin's death and estate, see Gervase of Canterbury, "The historical works of Gervase of Canterbury," in *The Chronicle of the Reigns of Stephen, Henry II, and Richard I*, ed. W. Stubbs, 2 vols, Rolls Series (London, 1879–80), 1.488; *Howden1*, 2.142; *Ymagines*, 2.88; Coggeshall, 1.256; and *Anonymous2*, 256.

77. *Eracles*, 5.11.152, claims that Conrad had actively persuaded Philip and Hubert to support him. For more on the politics of the marriage, see Tyerman, *God's War*, 429–30; and also Hodgson, *Women, Crusading and the Holy Land*, 80 and 146.

78. *Estoire*, lines 4145–72. See also the similar account in *Itinerarium2*, 1.63.

79. For example in *Ymagines*, 2.86.

80. Ambroise launches into a general harangue about the marquis in *Estoire*, lines 4173–406. See also *Itinerarium2*, 1.64.

81. Ibn Shaddād, 140.

82. Ibn al-Athīr, 2.380; Ibn Shaddād, 141; 'Imād al-Dīn, 4.520.

83. Ibn al-Athīr, 2.380. Ralph of Diss copied a letter by Bishop Hubert Walter that reports the same; see *Ymagines*, 2.88–9.

84. *Howden2*, 175, is the only Christian source to narrate these events.

85. As such, I disagree with the assessment of Fulton, "Anglo-Norman artillery," 16, in which he claims "at no point did artillery create an aperture that could be stormed."

86. Ibn Shaddād, 142; 'Imād al-Dīn, 4.521.

## Chapter V  The siege concludes, 1191

1. Ibn Shaddād, 141–2.

2. For example, *Estoire*, lines 4235–6: "Lors maldisoient le marchis / Par qu[i] il esteient si aquis."

3. *Itinerarium2*, 1.66 ("Tunc Marchisum detestantur, / Subtracto solamine, / Per quem escis defraudantur / In famis discrimine"), 1.69 ("O tunc plebis vox plangentis, / Maledicentis Marchisi perfidiam, / Quod non curat tabescentis / Populi miseriam"), 1.74 ("Tunc Marchisum detestantur / Pacti transgressorium, / Cuique malum imprecantur, / Et vae peremptorium."), and 1.77 ("Quid Marchiso tunc optaret / Vox tot queritantium? / Quis non reum judicaret / Tot periclitantium!").

4. Ailes and Barber, *History of the Holy War*, 91 n.285.

5. Mitchell, *Medicine in the Crusades*, 1–2.

6. *Itinerarium2*, 1.68. Saladin's camp, on the other hand, supposedly contained 7,000 cook-shops, each one capable of preparing twenty-eight pots of food; each pot could hold nine sheep's heads. See Lyons and Jackson, *Saladin*, 329.

7. *Estoire*, lines 4223–36; *Itinerarium2*, 1.67 and 1.80. Ambroise claims an egg cost six deniers, which the *Itinerarium* renders as six pence; a chicken was likewise priced at twelve sous/shillings. Meat was also consumed during Lent, a sin for which the guilty confessed and did penance once the famine had subsided. With a stick, Hubert Walter administered three light blows on the penitents' backs; see *Estoire*, lines 4515–20; and *Itinerarium2*, 1.81.

8. *Estoire*, line 4367 ("Qu'il morouent, ça treis, ça quatre"); *Itinerarium2*, 1.76, 1.72, and 1.67: ("sicut volucres ad cadaver"); Coggeshall, 1.256.

9. There is a similar story in Albert of Aachen's account of the First Crusade, in which Robert of Flanders acquired a horse through begging; see Albert of Aachen, *Historia Ierosolimitana: History of the journey to Jerusalem*, ed. and trans. S. Edgington (Oxford, 2007), 4.55.

10. *Itinerarium2*, 1.71.

11. *Estoire*, lines 4273–309; *Itinerarium2*, 1.73.

12. *Estoire*, lines 4327–354; *Itinerarium2*, 1.75.

13. *Ymagines*, 2.88–9. On the issue see Conor Kostick, "Courage and cowardice on the First Crusade, 1096–1099," *War in History* 20:1 (2013), 32–49.

14. Ibn Shaddād, 142–3. He heard that the second attacks resulted in the capture of a nephew of Philip Augustus, but given that Henry of Champagne was already at Acre this report was false.

15. *Estoire*, lines 4232–325. Richard of Templo expounds on the problem by adding biblical verses, but he also hints that some of the wayward later returned to the Church; see *Itinerarium2*, 1.74.

16. Newburgh, 1.349; *Ymagines*, 2.82–3.

17. *Howden2*, 3.171; *Estoire*, lines 4407–56; *Itinerarium2*, 1.78; *Anonymous2*, 257. Howden chronicles the collection out of order, dating it to the famine of 1190, not 1191.

18. Ansbert, 93.20–1: "atrocissimus athleta dei factus et timor Sarracenorum."

19. Ibn Shaddād, 143.

20. Ibn Shaddād, 143; *Itinerarium2*, 1.70; Newburgh, 1.348–9. John Pryor has calculated that the crusaders would have required around 10,000 tons of provisions and 81,000 tons of water for the duration of the siege; see "Medieval siege of Troy," 108.

21. These accounts are dubious. Ibn Shaddād, 144, claims that Taqī al-Dīn was also present, which would have been impossible, given that he had left Acre on 2 March. Ibn al-Athīr, 386, on the other hand, claims that Saladin was at Shafar'am all spring.

22. *Estoire*, lines 4477–91; *Itinerarium2*, 1.79.

23. Ansbert, 97.9–16. *Ministeriales* were unfree knights; see Benjamin Arnold, *German Knighthood, 1050–1300* (Reprint, Oxford, 1999), 23–37.

24. 'Imād al-Dīn, 5.4; Ibn al-Athīr, 2.385. Saladin did not learn of his death until November; see Lyons and Jackson, *Saladin*, 343.

25. Rigord, 74. On Rigord, see Gabrielle M. Spiegel, *The Chronicle Tradition of Saint-Denis: A survey* (Brookline, 1978), 56–9.

26. *Eracles*, 5.13.156; *Estoire*, lines 4507–44; *Itinerarium2*, 3.4; *Howden2*, 3.196; *Ymagines*, 2.92; Newburgh, 1.349; Coggeshall, 1.257; Ibn al-Athīr, 386; Ibn Shaddād, 145–6. 'Imād al-Dīn, 5.6, gives the wrong date of 15 April. The latter claims incorrectly that Philip of Flanders arrived separately, and later than the king. On Mont Gisart, see Hamilton, *The Leper King*, 135–6; and Lyons and Jackson, *Saladin*, 122–4.

27. Rigord, 74.

28. *Eracles*, 5.14.156: "Merveille est de tant de prodes homes, qui ont esté en cestui siege, coment il se sont tant targé de prendre la."

29. Ibn al-Athīr, 2.387; Ibn Shaddād, 147; 'Imād al-Dīn, 5.10; Rigord, 74. On the Ox Spring Tower, see Ibn Shaddād, 150 n.3; on the terminology, see Bachrach, "English artillery," 1416–17.
30. *Eracles*, 5.14.157.
31. *Estoire*, lines 3620–55; *Itinerarium2*, 1.50: "O fides infirmiories sexus admirabilis! O zelus imitabilis mulieris, quae nec post mortem destitit operantibus cooperari, dum perseveravit etiam in moriente voluntas operandi." On the pious meaning of this event, see Hodgson, *Women, Crusading and the Holy Land*, 119.
32. Ibn Shaddād, 147 and 149.
33. *Eracles*, 5.14.157.
34. This was the remainder of the fleet contracted with Genoa by Duke Hugh of Burgundy, amounting to enough ships to carry 650 knights, 1,300 horses, and 1,300 squires; see Pryor, "Transportation of horses by sea," 20.
35. Ibn al-Athīr, 2.387; Ibn Shaddād, 147–9.
36. Rigord, 74; *Eracles*, 5.15.157.
37. *Howden2*, 3.207.
38. The *qāḍī* also later confirmed the French claim of wanting to wait for Richard's arrival; see Ibn Shaddād, 150–1.
39. Ibn Shaddād, 146, 148, and 150; *Itinerarium2*, 3.5; *Howden2*, 3.205; Rigord, 79.
40. Ibn al-Athīr, 2.386–7; Ibn Shaddād, 147. The latter claims that one of the ships – the sixth, if there was one – was a *ṭarīda* (*tarra'id*), a horse transport equipped with both oars and sails and having a larger load capacity; these were distinct from *safun*, which carried siege equipment, or general transports; see Pryor, "Transportation of horses by sea," 18–19 and 21.
41. Ibn al-Athīr, 2.387.
42. For a detailed account of the Cyprus campaign, see Gillingham, *Richard I*, 140–54. The Arabs viewed the conquest as treachery against the Byzantines; see Ibn al-Athīr, 2.387. Richard later sold the island to the Knights Templar, then took it back and gave it to Guy of Lusignan. See Peter W. Edbury, *The Kingdom of Cyprus and the Crusades, 1191–1374* (Cambridge, 1991), 28–9; and Jean Richard, "Les révoltes chypriotes de 1191-1192 et les inféodations de Guy de Lusignan," in *Montjoie*, 123–28. The writer Robert of Turnham, whose remembrances of the Third Crusade are recorded in the fourteenth-century Meaux chronicle, was left behind in Cyprus by Richard before the king proceeded to Acre. He must therefore be excluded as a witness source for Acre; see E. Bond (ed.), *Chronica monasterii de Melsa*, 3 vols, Rolls Series (London, 1868), 1.260.
43. *Eracles*, 5.27.169, incorrectly gives Egypt as the ship's departure point.
44. Ibn al-Athīr, 2.387; Ibn Shaddād, 151.
45. Devizes habitually romanticized Richard the Lionheart and often generalized complicated events at Acre in his *Cronicon de tempore regis Richardi primi*. His tone has been described as "bellicose, not pacific. He loves war, not peace"; see Gransden, *Historical Writing in England*, 248–9.
46. *Estoire*, lines 2149–80; *Itinerarium2*, 2.42; *Eracles*, 5.27.169; Devizes, 3.425; Newburgh, 1.352; *Ymagines*, 2.93–4. On the use of poisonous snakes and viper poison, see Adrienne Mayor, *Greek Fire, Poison Arrows, and Scorpion Bombs: Biological and chemical warfare in the ancient world* (New York, 2009), 75–92.
47. Rigord, 75; Ibn Shaddād, 151; *Howden2*, 3.207. See also the very brief mention of the dromond in *Giraldi Cambrensis opera*, 8.3.8.
48. *Itinerarium2*, 2.42.
49. *Howden2*, 3.206–7; *Eracles*, 5.27.170; Devizes, 3.425; *Estoire*, lines 2205–9; *Itinerarium2*, 2.42. The latter alone states that the Muslims first claimed to be French, then Genoese on further inquiry. For the legend, in which Richard personally kills nearly 1,600 Muslims, see Broughton, *Legends of King Richard I*, 103–4. On the different composite bows in Muslim armies, see D. Coetzee and L.W. Eysturlid (eds), *Philosophers of War:*

*The evolution of history's greatest military thinkers*, Volume I: *The Ancient to Pre-Modern World, 3000 BCE–1815 CE* (Santa Barbara, 2013), 227–9.

50. Ibn Shaddād, 150. *Howden2*, 3.207, mentions Greek Fire but seemingly in the context of it being dumped by the Muslims to keep it from falling into enemy hands.

51. *Estoire*, lines 2225–32; *Itinerarium2*, 2.42; *Ymagines*, 2.93. Presumably the ship used the old dual steering oars to maneuver, since stern-posted single rudders did not appear until the thirteenth century; see R.C. Anderson, *Oared Fighting Ships: From classical times to the coming of steam* (London, 1962), 59; and Pryor, *Geography, Technology, and War*, 120–1.

52. *Estoire*, lines 2255–9; *Ymagines*, 2.94; *Itinerarium2*, 2.42; *Howden2*, 3.207. On Richard's rams, see Anderson, *Oared Fighting Ships*, 59.

53. *Ymagines*, 2.94; cf. 1 Maccabees 6:43–6. Rigord, 75, claims a second Muslim ship was taken at Tyre at about the same time, but this is mentioned in no other sources.

54. *Eracles*, 5.27.170; *Itinerarium2* 2.42, 198; Ibn al-Athīr, 2.387; Ibn Shaddād, 151.

55. *Estoire*, lines 2327–8; *Itinerarium2*, 3.1.

56. Devizes, 3.426: "Rex inde progrediens venit ad Accaronis obsidionem, et exceptus est ab obsidentibus cum gaudio tanto, ac si esset Christus, qui revenisset in terram restituere regnum Israel. Rex Francorum praevenerat ad Accaronem, et magni habitus est ab indigenis; sed, superveniente Ricardo, ita delituit et sine nomine factus est, ut solet ad solis ortum suum luna lumen amittere."

57. *Estoire*, lines 2329–37; *Itinerarium2*, 3.2; 'Imād al-Dīn, 5.10; Ibn Shaddād, 151.

58. *Ymagines*, 2.94; Newburgh, 1.352. See also Coggeshall, 1.257.

59. *Eracles*, 5.26.169.

60. *Itinerarium2*, 3.3; *Howden2*, 3.207.

61. *Estoire*, lines 4563–84; *Itinerarium2*, 3.4.

62. Devizes, 3.426; *Howden1*, 2.171.

63. Gillingham, *Richard I*, 156–7 n.7.

64. On the house of Lusignan and its relations with the Angevin kings, see Sidney Painter, "The lords of Lusignan in the eleventh and twelfth centuries," *Speculum* 32:1 (1957), 42–3. Richard handed the prisoner Isaac into Guy's custody as well; see *Itinerarium2*, 2.41.

65. *Howden2*, 3.207–8; *Estoire*, lines 5033–59; Devizes, 3.428–9; Ibn Shaddād, 154.

66. Rigord, 74. Gervase of Canterbury, "The historical works," 1.489, briefly mentions the divisions in the camp. On Richard and Philip's military alliance in 1188–9, see Hosler, *Henry II*, 97–101.

67. For an extensive treatment of this illness, see Thomas Gregor Wagner and Piers D. Mitchell, "The illnesses of King Richard and King Philippe on the Third Crusade: An understanding of *arnaldia* and *leonardie*," *Crusades* 10 (2011), 23–44, and the copious medical studies cited within.

68. *Estoire*, lines 4645–86; *Itinerarium2*, 3.5.

69. *Estoire*, line 4676: "Biaus sire, Deus, com povre atente!" See also *Itinerarium2*, 3.5; Ibn al-Athīr, 2.387; and *Howden2*, 3.207.

70. The kings' respective illnesses were used by eyewitness authors to score political points; see Catherine Hanley, *War and Combat, 1150–1270: The evidence from Old French literature* (Cambridge, 2003), 76–9.

71. *Estoire*, lines 4687–729; *Itinerarium2*, 3.6.

72. Rigord, 77.

73. The date is given in Ibn Shaddād, 152. The number of stones that could be shot in such a fashion has often been debated. The most famous reference for the period is from the siege of Lisbon in October 1147, in which it is claimed that two mangonels hurled 5,000 stones in the space of ten hours. See D.W. David (ed. and trans.), *De expugnatione Lyxbonensi: The conquest of Lisbon* (Reprint, New York, 2001), 142–3. For a skeptical analysis of this rapidity of fire, see Fulton, "Anglo-Norman artillery," 8–9.

219

74. *Itinerarium2*, 1.32, reports the legend that the tower was so named because inside were minted the silver coins paid to Judas Iscariot in exchange for information leading to the arrest of Jesus in Matthew 26:14–15.

75. *Estoire*, lines 4731–802; *Itinerarium2*, 3.7; *Ymagines*, 2.94. There were nine *petrariae* in total; Fulton, "Anglo-Norman artillery," 13.

76. *Estoire*, lines 4781–6; *Itinerarium2*, 3.7.

77. Or what Ibn Shaddād, 155, calls "a man's height."

78. Rogers, *Latin Siege Warfare*, 226–7, believed it was the carriage holding the lever arm, not the arm itself, that was damaged. On the terminology related to Muslim catapult operators, see Rabei G. Khamisy, "Some notes on Ayyūbid and Mamluk military terms," *Journal of Medieval Military History* 13 (2015), 73–92.

79. *Estoire*, lines 3516–55; *Itinerarium2*, 1.47a: "Quis haec intelligens non pensaret magna opera Domini, cujus pro Se certantibus semper praesto est clementia?"

80. *Itinerarium2*, 3.7; Ibn Shaddād, 151–2; Devizes, 3.427. Elevated catapults were not common in the West, but were known. In 1141, Geoffrey Talbot put a *ballista* in the bell tower of Hereford Cathedral; see *Gesta Stephani*, ed. and trans. K.R. Potter (Oxford, 1976), 1.53.

81. Ibn Shaddād, 152–3.

82. Ibn Shaddād, 153–4.

83. *Howden1*, 2.172.

84. Ibn Shaddād, 154–5 and 160.

85. Ibn Shaddād, 156.

86. *Eracles*, 5.29.171; Ibn Shaddād, 153.

87. *Estoire*, lines 4803–32; *Itinerarium2*, 3.8. If Philip was indeed inside, that may explain Ibn Shaddād, 153, in which he claims that the king had been wounded.

88. Ibn Shaddād, 157.

89. *Estoire*, lines 4835–60; *Itinerarium2*, 3.9; Ibn Shaddād, 156–7. Richard of Templo incorrectly identifies the Muslim leader here as Taqī al-Dīn, not knowing that he had died back in April.

90. *Estoire*, lines 4861–902; *Itinerarium2*, 3.11; *Howden2*, 3.211; Devizes, 3.427; Rigord, 81; Ibn Shaddād, 158.

91. *Eracles*, 5.31.173; Devizes, 3.427; Rigord, 81; Ibn al-Athīr, 2.388; Ibn Shaddād, 158.

92. *Eracles*, 5.31.173; Ibn Shaddād, 158.

93. Ibn al-Athīr, 2.388.

94. *Howden2*, 3.211. The standard reference for the Second Crusade is now Jonathan Phillips, *The Second Crusade: Extending the frontiers of Christendom* (New Haven, 2007), and see 269–70 for the immediate aftermath of that war. On subsequent territorial losses, see chapters 9–11 in Malcolm Barber, *The Crusader States* (New Haven, 2012).

95. Devizes, 3.427; *Eracles*, 5.30.172.

96. Ibn Shaddād, 159.

97. Ibn al-Athīr, 2.388; Ibn Shaddād, 159.

98. *Eracles*, 5.30.172.

99. Ibn Shaddād, 159.

100. *Howden2*, 3.208–9.

101. Ibn Shaddād, 159; Ibn al-Athīr, 2.388.

102. Ibn Shaddād, 159; *Howden2*, 3.212. Ibn al-Athīr, 2.388, rather blames the members of the garrison, who spent much of the day packing their possessions and waited too long before sallying. There were spies on both sides. *Howden2*, 209, describes a Christian spy who lived in Acre and periodically sent messages in Hebrew, Greek, and Latin to the crusader camp. He never identified himself, even after the siege had concluded.

103. Ibn Shaddād, 159–60; Ibn al-Athīr, 2.388–9.

104. *Howden2*, 3.213–14.

105. *Howden2*, 3.119.
106. *Howden2*, 3.212; Ibn al-Athīr, 2.387–8.
107. *Estoire*, lines 4921–59; *Itinerarium2*, 3.14.
108. *Estoire*, lines 4960–81: "La n'aveit mestier armeüre, / Tant fust tenaz, fort ne seüre - / Dobles porpoinz, dobles haubercs - / Ne tenouent ne c'uns drap pers / Les quarels d'arb[a]leste a tur / Car trop erent de fort atur."
109. *Howden2*, 3.213–14; *Estoire*, lines 4982–5032; *Itinerarium2*, 3.14.

### Chapter VI Aftermath and repercussions

1. *Itinerarium2*, 3.13.
2. Indeed, "one of the longest ever recorded"; see Philippe Contamine, *War in the Middle Ages*, trans. M. Jones (Oxford, 1984), 101.
3. Ehrenkreutz, *Saladin*, 213–14.
4. *Estoire*, lines 5192–213; 'Imād al-Dīn, 5.28; Ibn al-Athīr, 2.389; *Howden2*, 3.214.
5. *Eracles*, 5.31.173.
6. The terms are laid out in Ibn al-Athīr, 2.389; Ibn Shaddād, 161; *Howden2*, 3.214; *Itinerarium2*, 3.17; Rigord, 81; *Ymagines*, 2.94. *Estoire*, lines 5192–213, corroborates the number of 2,000 only. The kings thus used prisoners to secure the surrender of a city, as Saladin himself had attempted to do with Tyre a few years earlier; see Yvonne Friedman, *Encounter between Enemies: Captivity and ransom in the Latin Kingdom of Jerusalem* (Leiden, 2002), 90.
7. *Estoire*, lines 5222–7. *Ymagines*, 2.94, concurs; Gervase of Canterbury, "The historical works," 1.490, gives no date, and the *Eracles*, 5.31.174, gives the 11th.
8. Ibn Shaddād, 163; Ibn al-Athīr, 2.389; *Howden2*, 3.214; *Itinerarium2*, 3.18.
9. Certainly this is the impression one gets in *Itinerarium2*, 3.16.
10. Rigord, 81; *Eracles*, 6.1.175; *Itinerarium2*, 3.18; Ibn Shaddād, 161.
11. *Itinerarium2*, 3.18.
12. Rigord, 81; Devizes, 3.427–8.
13. *Howden2*, 3.215; *Itinerarium2*, 3.18. These retainers were Hugh of Gournay (for Richard) and Drogo of Merlou (for Philip).
14. Jacoby, "Crusader Acre," 36–9.
15. Adrian Boas, *Archaeology of the Military Orders: A survey of the urban centres, rural settlements and castles of the military orders in the Latin East (c. 1120–1291)* (London, 2006), 222–3. Excavation work on the Hospitaller quarter has been extensive; see Boas, *Crusader Archaeology*, 37–41; and the summations in Eliezer Stern and Hanaa Abu-Uqsa, "New archaeological discoveries from crusader period Acre," and Yale Fuhrmann-Na'aman, "Conservation of the Knights Hospitaller compound," in *One Thousand Nights and Days: Akko through the ages*, ed. A.E. Killebrew and V. Raz-Romeo (Haifa, 2010), 41–4 and 60–5.
16. Joshua Prawer, *Crusader Institutions* (Oxford, 1980), 236.
17. Jacoby, "Crusader Acre," 24. On all these quarters, see David Jacoby, "Les communes italiennes et les Ordres militaires à Acre: aspects juridiques, territoriaux et militaires (1104–1187, 1191–1291)," in *État et colonisation au Moyen Age*, ed. M. Balard (Lyon, 1989), 193–214.
18. Kesten, *Acre*, 18–19 and 26–7. On the churches in the northeast quarter and elsewhere in the city, see Denys Pringle, *The Churches of the Crusader Kingdom of Jerusalem: A corpus*, Volume IV: *The Cities of Acre and Tyre with Addenda and Corrigenda to Volumes I–III* (Cambridge, 2009).
19. *Eracles*, 6.1.175.
20. *Itinerarium1*, 43.6. On the destruction, see *Ymagines*, 2.95; *Howden2*, 3.215. These prelates were principally the episcopal heads of Verona, Tours, Pisa, Aire, Salisbury, Évreux, Bayonne, Tripoli, Chartres, and Beauvais.

21. Their holdings were already extensive in the early twelfth century; for a summary, see Boas, *Crusader Archaeology*, 36.
22. *RRRH*, no. 1271. On this charter, see Jane Sayers, "English charters from the Third Crusade," in *Tradition and Change: Essays in honour of Marjorie Chibnall, presented by her friends on the occasion of her seventieth birthday*, ed. D. Greenway, C. Holdsworth, and J. Sayers (Cambridge, 1985), 199–200 [195–214].
23. *RRRH*, nos. 1311 and 1316. *Howden2*, 3.215, alludes to these grants.
24. *RRRH*, nos. 1280 and 1320. Genoese trade with Syria was lucrative and grew even more after 1191; see in general Eugene H. Byrne, "Genoese trade with Syria in the twelfth century," *American Historical Review* 25:2 (1920), 191–219.
25. *RRRH*, nos. 1314 and 1315.
26. *RRRH*, no. 1276.
27. *RRRH*, nos. 1272 (Pisans) and 1277 (Genoese).
28. *RRRH*, no. 1279. The commune of Marseille in Acre bought several forged charters in 1248 to bolster its claims in Acre; see Jacoby, "Crusader Acre," 22–3.
29. *RRRH*, no. 1285; *Eracles*, 5.3.141. Men from Bremen, Hamburg, and the Baltic region had built a wooden field hospital in the crusader camp in 1190; see Mitchell, *Medicine in the Crusades*, 59–60 and 90, and, on the Hospitaller facility in Acre, 80. On the Orders' property in the city, see David Jacoby, "Les communes italiennes," 193–214; Jonathan Riley-Smith, "The Knights of St. John in Jerusalem and Cyprus, c. 1050–1310," in *A History of the Hospital of St. John of Jerusalem*, ed. L. Butler, vol. 1 (New York, 1967); and in general David Matzliach, "The medical legacy of the Knights of St John and the Crusader Hospitals of Jerusalem and Acre" (MA Thesis, University of Manchester, 2012).
30. Jacoby, "Crusader Acre," 19.
31. *Howden2*, 3.123: "paupertate coacti ab eis."
32. Devizes, 3.428; Rigord, 82; Gervase of Canterbury, "The historical works," 514; Blasien, 36.54.29–30. On the meaning of this incident, see Gillingham, *Richard I*, 162–4. It surely contributed to Richard's plight when, on his return from the Holy Land, he was shipwrecked near Venice and was later captured in Vienna by Leopold's men.
33. *Estoire*, lines 5238–65.
34. Rigord, 77; *Itinerarium2*, 3.21. However, Richard of Templo expands on Ambroise's slight compliment of Philip's efforts to that point and praises the king, with the caveat that he still ought to have stayed, because much is required of one to whom much has been given (cf. Luke 12:48).
35. Ansbert, 100.1–5; Newburgh, 1.357; *Howden2*, 3.205. This view is echoed by Gilbert of Mons, who is our closest narrative source for Flanders in the period; see *Chronicle of Hainaut*, 140.
36. Jeffrey L. Singman, *Robin Hood: The shaping of the legend* (Westport, 1998), 131.
37. Rigord, 81.
38. *Howden2*, 3.216; *Ymagines*, 2.95.
39. On Harold's oath, see George Garnett, *Conquered England: Kingship, succession and tenure, 1066–1166* (Oxford, 2007), 7–9.
40. On Richard's use of archers, see Matthew Strickland and Robert Hardy, *The Great Warbow: From Hastings to the Mary Rose* (Stroud, 2005), 104–9.
41. *Estoire*, lines 5266–97; *Itinerarium2*, 3.21–2; *Howden1*, 2.183 and 2.186; *Howden2*, 3.125; Devizes, 3.429–30. Those left behind included Hugh of Burgundy and Henry of Champagne. Rigord, 81, claims that Philip took three other vessels prepared for him by the Genoese Ruffo da Volta. Hundreds of French elites died on the Third Crusade; Baldwin, *Government of Philip Augustus*, 80, writes: "Philip Augustus himself had survived, but he had left the major barons of his father's generation buried in the Syrian sands."

42. *Itinerarium2*, 3.18; Devizes, 3.427–8; *Anonymous1*, 3.cxxxv, lines 865–8; Ibn Shaddād, 161. John Pryor has provided a tidy summation of the Muslim reaction in "Medieval siege of Troy," 98.

43. Norman Housley, *Contesting the Crusades* (Oxford, 2006), 64; *Howden2*, 3.214–15.

44. Ibn Shaddād, 161 (cf. Koran 2.156) and 165.

45. Ibn Shaddād, 162.

46. *Howden2*, 3.215.

47. Ibn Shaddād, 162–3.

48. *Estoire*, lines 5098–191.

49. Ibn Shaddād, 161.

50. Ehrenkreutz, "Saladin in naval history," 111 and 115.

51. Ibn al-Athīr, 2.389; Ibn Shaddād, 109; Gibb, *Studies on the Civilization of Islam*, 104.

52. Lev, *Saladin in Egypt*, 132–3.

53. Ibn al-Athīr, 2.389; Ibn Shaddād, 162.

54. 'Imād al-Dīn, 5.32. Maalouf glosses over these details in a wholly sympathetic passage; see *Crusades through Arab Eyes*, 210.

55. *Estoire*, lines 5351–61 and 5480–506; *Itinerarium2*, 4.2; *Eracles*, 6.2.177; Rigord, 82; Devizes, 3.428

56. Ibn Shaddād, 163.

57. *Estoire*, lines 5386–405.

58. *Estoire*, lines 5488–9: "Quant cels qu[ë] a la mort livra / Ne rainst ne ne delivera."

59. Ibn al-Athīr, 2.390; Ibn Shaddād, 163.

60. Ibn al-Athīr, 2.389; Ibn Shaddād, 163.

61. Ibn Shaddād, 163.

62. *Eracles*, 6.2.177.

63. Ibn al-Athīr, 2.389.

64. Ibn Shaddād, 163.

65. *Howden1*, 2.187 and 2.188–9.

66. Thomas Asbridge has explored some of the possible reasons, which include cultural sensibilities and regard for the safety of the leaders; see "Talking to the enemy: The role and purpose of negotiations between Saladin and Richard the Lionheart during the Third Crusade," *Journal of Medieval History* 39:3 (2013), 278–9. On the subject in general, see Michael A. Köhler, *Alliances and Treaties between Frankish and Muslim Rulers in the Middle East: Cross-cultural diplomacy in the period of the crusades*, ed. K. Hirschler, trans. P.M. Holt (Leiden, 2013), 246–66.

67. Friedman, *Encounter between Enemies*, 91.

68. Rigord, 82.

69. Yaacov Lev, "Prisoners of war during the Fatimid-Ayyubid wars with the crusaders," in *Tolerance and Intolerance: Social conflict in the age of the crusades*, ed. M. Gervers and J.M. Powell (Syracuse, 2001), 23–4.

70. *Howden2*, 3.212–13 and 3.215; a similar negotiation took place a week later. One of these was probably the meeting related by Ibn Shaddād, 160–1.

71. *Estoire*, lines 5506–35; *Itinerarium2*, 4.4; *Eracles*, 6.3.177–8; 'Imād al-Dīn, 5.32–3; Ibn Shaddād, 165; Ibn al-Athīr, 2.390; Rigord, 82; Devizes, 3.428; *Ymagines*, 2.94; *Howden2*, 3.219; *Anonymous1*, 3.cxxxv, lines 861–4. A medical cleric, one Ralph Besace, was purportedly an eyewitness to Saladin's retributive act, having been sent by Richard to continue negotiations for the principals; see Mitchell, *Medicine in the Crusades*, 23.

72. 'Imād al-Dīn, 31.

73. "War crimes," Rome Statute of the International Criminal Court, https://www.icc-cpi. int/resource-library/Documents/RS-Eng.pdf (accessed 28 October 2016), 2.8.11–12.

74. Steven Runciman, *A History of the Crusades*, Volume III: *The Kingdom of Acre and the Later Crusades* (Reprint, Cambridge, 1999), 53–4; Jonathan Riley-Smith, *The Crusades:*

*A short history* (New Haven, 1987), 116; Lyons and Jackson, *Saladin*, 333; Tyerman, *God's War*, 456; Mayer, *The Crusades*, 146; Gillingham, *Richard I*, 169–71.

75. "Robin Hood (2010)," Internet Movie Database, www.imdb.com/title/tt0955308/quotes?ref_=ttpl_ql_trv_4/ (accessed 22 October 2016); text corrected by author.

76. For an overview of how Christian and Muslim contemporaries viewed the executions, see Gillingham, *Richard I*, 168–71.

77. These include stories about an angel ordering him to execute his prisoners and a supposed evening on which his cooks served severed Muslim heads for dinner; see Broughton, *Legends of King Richard I*, 56–7 and 104.

78. Devizes, 3.428; *Ymagines*, 2.94; Ibn Shaddād, 164; *Anonymous1*, 3.cxxxv, line 858.

79. Rigord, 82.

80. *Estoire*, lines 5506–12; Ibn Shaddād, 165.

81. Rigord, 82; *Itinerarium2*, 4.4.

82. *Eracles*, 6.3.178; *Itinerarium2*, 4.4; *Estoire*, line 5529; *Ymagines*, 2.94; *Anonymous1*, 3.cxxxvi, lines 889–92; Ibn Shaddād, 165. On the topic in general, see Susanna A. Throop, *Crusading as an Act of Vengeance, 1095–1216* (Farnham, 2011), but unfortunately she does not discuss Richard's behavior at Acre.

83. *Howden1*, 2.189; *Howden2*, 3.127–8; Gillingham, *Richard I*, 167.

84. John Gillingham, "Historians without hindsight: Coggeshall, Diceto and Howden on the early years of John's reign," *King John: New interpretations*, ed. S.D. Church (Woodbridge, 1999), 16–17.

85. *Howden2*, 3.131: "Ubi non multo temporis tractu elapso, reddita est domino regi Francorum et nobis civita Accon, salva vita Sarracenorum qui ad eam custodiendam et defendendam intus missi fuerant; pactione etiam ex parte Saladini plenius firmata, quod nobis Crucem Sanctam et mille et quingentos captivos vivos resignaret, diemque ad haec omnia persolvenda nobis constituit. Sed eodem termino exspirato, et pactione quam pepigerat penitus infirmata, de Sarracenis, quos in custodia habuimus, circa duo millia et sexcentos, sicut decuit, fecimus, exspirare; paucis tamen de nobilioribus retentis, pro quibus Sanctum Crucem et quosdam captivos Christianos sperabamus recuperaturos."

86. Maalouf, *Crusades through Arab Eyes*, 209. Maalouf's research is based nearly exclusively on Arabic primary sources, and there is no mention anywhere of Roger of Howden or his works.

87. *Eracles*, 5.31.173.

88. See in general David Wyatt, *Slaves and Warriors in Medieval Britain and Ireland, 800–1200* (Leiden, 2009), which, as the title implies, does not address the East; and also John Gillingham, "The treatment of the defeated, c. 950–1350: Historiography and the state of research," in *La conducción de la guerra en la Edad Media: Historiografía* (*Acta del Symposium Internacional celebrado en Cáceres, Noviembre 2008*), ed. Manuel Rojas (Cáceres, forthcoming). The major legal treatises for the Kingdom of Jerusalem are post-Third Crusade, dating from the later thirteenth century; for the difficulties this can present, see Adam M. Bishop, "Usāma ibn Munqidh and crusader law in the twelfth century," *Crusades* 12 (2013), 53–65.

89. Ibn Shaddād, 152–3 and 155–6.

90. *Itinerarium2*, 3.17: "ne forte jure belli incomprehensi haberentur exterminio, et probrosae mortis ludibrio; unde lex Mahumetica ab antecessoribus diligenter observata, quantum in eo esset, cassaretur."

91. Cook, *Understanding Jihad*, 61–2; Richard A. Gabriel, *Muhammad: Islam's first great general* (Norman, 2007), 101. For a broad view of justified killing of both Muslim and non-Muslims, see Khaled Abou El Fadl, "The rule of killing at war: An inquiry into the classical sources," *Muslim World* 89 (1999), 144–57.

92. Lyons and Jackson, *Saladin*, 187; Lev, "Prisoners of war," 12–14.

93. For a critique of the film in this light, see Jonathan Riley-Smith, "Truth is the first victim," *The Times*, 5 May 2005; for al-Fāḍil's remark, see 'Imād al-Dīn, "Les livres des deux jardins," 4.439.

94. Al-Qāḍī al-Fāḍil issued decrees to Saladin's subordinates and wrote letters to the sultan himself, and many of these are preserved in the writings of 'Imād al-Dīn and Abu Shāma. See M. Hilmy M. Ahmad, "Some notes on Arabic historiography during the Zengid and Ayyubid periods (521/1127–648/1250)," in *Historians of the Middle East*, ed. B. Lewis (London, 1962), 85–6; and Gibb, *Studies on the Civilization of Islam*, 93–4. On the pilgrim and infant, see Ibn Shaddād, 144–5 and 147–8. Summarizing the construct of Saladin-as-gentleman is France, *Great Battles: Hattin*, 132–3 and 140–2; for a sympathetic reading, see Hans Möhring, *Saladin: The sultan and his times, 1138–1193*, trans. D.S. Bachrach (Baltimore, 2008), 92–9. A general overview is Carole Hillenbrand, "The evolution of the Saladin legend in the west," in *Regards croisés sur le Moyen Âge arabe: Mélanges à la mémoire de Louis Pouzet s.j. (1928–2002)*, ed. A.-M. Eddé and E. Gannagé (Beirut, 2005), 497–512. For a revision of the Arabic memory, see Diana Abouali, "Saladin's legacy in the Middle East before the nineteenth century," *Crusades* 10 (2011), 175–89. Saladin's tolerance on the intellectual level has also been scrutinized; see Fozia Bora, "Did Salah al-Din destroy the Fatimids' books? An historiographical inquiry," *Journal of the Royal Asiatic Society* 24 (2014), 1–19.

95. France, *Great Battles: Hattin*, 111 and 103–4. For more on Saladin's various executions of prisoners, see Yves Gravelle, "Le problème des prisonniers de guerre pendant les croisades orientales, 1095–1192" (MA Thesis, University of Sherbrooke, 1999), 34–9.

96. Ehrenkreutz, *Saladin*, 202–3; Cook, *Understanding Jihad*, 45; *Arab Historians of the Crusades*, 138. On the connections between Sufism, Saladin, and military affairs in the period, see J. Spencer Cunningham, *The Sufi Orders in Islam* (Reprint, Oxford, 1998), 8–9 and 240–1.

97. Eamon Duffy, *Fires of Faith: Catholic England under Mary Tudor* (New Haven, 2009), 82.

98. Friedman, *Encounter between Enemies*, 90; *Estoire*, lines 5533–4: "E dont furent li cop vengié / De quarrels d'arb[a]laste a tor."

99. On the event, see John Gillingham, "Crusading warfare, chivalry, and the enslavement of women and children," in *The Medieval Way of War*, 140–1. Benjamin Kedar has written the best analysis of the Jerusalem accounts, which reveals that there was not one but two and perhaps three separate massacres there; see "The Jerusalem massacre of July 1099 in the western historiography of the crusades," *Crusades* 3 (2004), 15–75. On the embellishment of the Jerusalem massacre, see Thomas F. Madden, "Rivers of blood: An analysis of one aspect of the crusader conquest of Jerusalem in 1099," *Revista Chilena de Estudios Medievales* 1 (2012), 25–37.

100. Devizes, 3.428, claims that al-Mashṭūb was one of them. See also Alan Forey, "The military orders and the ransoming of captives from Islam (twelfth to early fourteenth centuries)," *Studia Monastica* 33 (1991), 259–79.

101. Lev, "Prisoners of war," 16. On the 1174 rebellion, see John D. Hosler, "Chivalric carnage? Fighting, capturing, and killing the enemy at the battles of Dol and Fornham in 1173," in *Prowess, Piety and Public Order in Medieval Society: Studies in honor of Richard W. Kaeuper*, ed. C.M. Nakashian and D.P. Franke (Leiden, 2017), 36–61. That said, crusader norms of ransoming their own prisoners were still rather undeveloped, even by the Third Crusade; see Yvonne Friedman, "The ransom of captives in the Latin Kingdom of Jerusalem," in *Autour de la Première Croisade*, 177–89. The question of ransom distinguishes this event from a similarly infamous episode, Henry V's execution of his French captives during the Battle of Agincourt in 1415. On that occasion, both sides fully expected to ransom their captives, whereas at Acre both Saladin and Richard had concluded that this was no longer possible. See Anne Curry, *Agincourt: A new history* (Stroud, 2005), 249.

102. An example of a failure to equate the two on religious terms is Philip Warner, *Sieges of the Middle Ages* (New York, 1994), 121–2.
103. Ibn Shaddād, 165.
104. *Estoire*, lines 5670–9: "La gent esteit trop peresçose, / Car la vile iert deli[ci]ose / De bons vins e de damiseles, / Dont il i aveit mult beles. / Les vins e les femmes hantouent, / E floement se delitouent, / Qu'en la vile aveit tant laidure / E [tant] pechié e tant luxure / Que li prodome honte aveient / De ço que li autre home faiseient."
105. *Howden1*, 2.188; *Itinerarium2*, 4.7.
106. *Eracles*, 6.7.182–3; *Itinerarium2*, 4.5; *Estoire*, lines 5690–1: "Qui laveient chiefs e dras linges / E d'espucer valeient singes."
107. *Itinerarium2*, 4.8. The identity of the count is unknown; see Ailes and Barber, *History of the Holy War*, 109–10 n.383.
108. *Estoire*, lines 5680–713; *Itinerarium2*, 4.9–10; Ibn al-Athīr, 2.390.
109. For two recent treatments, see Kedar, "Plan for the battle of Arsūf/Arsur," 117–32; and Michael Ehrlich, "The Battle of Arsur: A short-lived victory," *Journal of Medieval Military History* 12 (2014), 109–18.
110. On the murder, see Yuval Noah Harari, *Special Operations in the Age of Chivalry, 1100–1550* (Woodbridge, 2007), 102–4.
111. See David Jacoby, "Society, culture and the arts in crusader Acre," and Jaroslav Folda, "Before Louis IX: Aspects of crusader art at St. Jean d'Acre, 1191–1244," in *France and the Holy Land: Frankish culture at the end of the crusades*, ed. D.H. Weiss and L. Mahoney (Baltimore, 2004), 98–106 and 139, respectively; as well as, in general, Jacoby, "Aspects of everyday life in Frankish Acre," *Crusades* 4 (2005), 73–105. On the general rebuilding of the kingdom's power after Hattin and to the end of the crusade, see Stephen Donnachie, "Reconstruction and rebirth: The Latin Kingdom of Jerusalem, 1187–1233" (PhD Thesis, Swansea University, 2013).
112. David Jacoby, "Ports of pilgrimage to the Holy Land, eleventh–fourteenth century: Jaffa, Acre, Alexandria," in *The Holy Portolano: The sacred geography of navigation in the middle ages*, ed. M. Bacci and M. Rohde (Berlin, 2014), 56–59.
113. It has been developed into a museum; see "The Templar's tunnel," Secrets of Old Acre, www.akko.org.il/en/Old-Acre-The-Templars-Tunnel (accessed 28 October 2016).
114. For a condensed history and anthropology of the city from 1291 to the twentieth century, see Morton Rubin, *The Walls of Acre: Intergroup relations and urban development in Israel* (New York, 1974).
115. P. Crawford (ed. and trans.), *The "Templar of Tyre": Part III of the "Deeds of the Cypriots,"* Crusade Texts in Translation (Aldershot, 2003), 117.

### Conclusion

1. *Estoire*, lines 5594–7: "Por trestoz qui la mururent, / Et por trestoz qui s'i esmurent, / Por la grant gent e por la / Por qui l'ost Deu fud maintenue."
2. Although certainly not the 50,000 claimed in one of al-Qādī al-Fādil's letters, the figure is precise and not a fantasy; see 'Imād al-Dīn, "Les livres des deux jardins," 5.28. A comparable meeting-up might be at the siege of Damascus in 1148 during the Second Crusade, in which Louis VII of France, Conrad III of Germany, Baldwin III of Jerusalem, and Unur, atabeg of Damascus, all took part.
3. A similar question arises in the analysis of the commanders at the most famous siege of the middle ages; see Marios Philippides and Walter K. Hanak, *The Siege and the Fall of Constantinople in 1453: Historiography, topography, and military studies* (Farnham, 2011), 563.
4. See the analysis in Gibb, *Life of Saladin*, 66.
5. France, *Great Battles: Hattin*, 101.

6. David Hume, *The History of England: From the invasion of Julius Caesar to the revolution in 1688*, 6 vols (Reprint, Indianapolis, 1983), 1.10.
7. William Stubbs, *The Constitutional History of England*, 3 vols (Oxford, 1880), 1.575.
8. Sir Walter Scott, *Ivanhoe* (Reprint, London, 1920), xli. On Scott's valorizing, see C.A. Simmons, *Reversing the Conquest: History and myth in nineteenth-century British literature* (New Brunswick, 1990), 85.
9. Particularly Stubbs; See H.G. Richardson and G.O. Sayles, *The Governance of Mediaeval England from the Conquest to Magna Carta* (Edinburgh, 1963), 18.
10. John Gillingham, "Richard I and the science of warfare in the middle ages," in *War and Government in the Middle Ages: Essays in honour of J.O. Prestwich*, ed. J. Gillingham and J.C. Holt (Woodbridge, 1984), 90.
11. Smail, *Crusading Warfare*, 189; Tyerman, *God's War*, 470–1.
12. Philip's role is slowly receiving more credit; see, for example, James Naus, *Constructing Kingship: The Capetian monarchs of France and the early crusades* (Manchester, 2016), 125.
13. On the subject in general, see Kelly DeVries, "God and defeat in medieval warfare: Some preliminary thoughts," in *The Circle of War in the Middle Ages*, 87–97.
14. *Estoire*, line 3321; *Itinerarium2*, 1.38 and 1.62; Ansbert, 93.20–1. See Hosler, *John of Salisbury*, 126–31, for more on this motif.
15. Ibn Shaddād, 138.
16. *Estoire*, line 3101 ("De la gent Deu e de la chenaille") and lines 5225–6 ("Malgré le pople maleït / Que Deus de sa boche maldie").
17. *Howden2*, 3.131: "quae inimici crucis Christi hactenus ignominiose profanabant."
18. Ibn Shaddād, 138.
19. For example, David S. Bachrach, *Religion and the Conduct of War, c.300–1215* (Woodbridge, 2003), 135 n.121.
20. For example, a ten-year project, sponsored by Penn State University, is currently ongoing; see Total Archaeology @ Tel Akko, www.hominid.psu.edu/projects_labs/telakko (accessed 17 October 2016): for reports of its findings thus far, see Anne E. Killebrew and Brandon R. Olson, "The Tel Akko Total Archaeology Project: New frontiers in the excavation and 3D documentation of the past," in *Proceedings of the 8th International Congress on the Archaeology of the Ancient Near East, 30 April–4 May 2012, University of Warsaw, Volume 2*, ed. P. Bieliński et al. (Wiesbaden, 2014), 559–74; and Anne E. Killebrew and Jaime Quartermaine, "Total Archaeology @ Tel Akko: Excavation, survey, community outreach, and new approaches to landscape archaeology in 3D," in *Proceedings of the 9th International Congress on the Archaeology of the Ancient Near East, 9–13 June 2014, Basel, Volume 3*, ed. R.A. Stucky et al. (Wiesbaden, 2016), 491–502.
21. Maurice Hewlett, *The Life and Death of Richard Yea-and-Nay* (New York, 1901), 235–65, and 282 specifically.
22. M.D. Allen, *The Medievalism of Lawrence of Arabia* (University Park, 1991), 98. For his reference to Acre, see M. Brown (ed.), *T.E. Lawrence in War and Peace: An anthology of the military writings of Lawrence of Arabia*, new ed. (London, 2005), 105; and for his travels, the maps provided at "Maps," T.E. Lawrence Studies, www.telstudies.org/reference/maps.shtml (accessed 13 November 2016).

## Appendix A

1. David Jacoby, "Crusader Acre," 1.
2. "World Heritage Center," United Nations Educational, Scientific and Cultural Organization, http://whc.unesco.org/en/list/1042 (accessed 16 October 2016).
3. *Itinerarium2*, 1.32.
4. There are elements remaining from the latter, a section just north of the Gan HaMetsuda Festival Gardens.

5. Rafael Frankel, "The north-western corner of crusader Acre," *Israel Exploration Journal* 37:4 (1987), 256–61. Michael Ehrlich has argued to the contrary, that a wall did exist but was soon swallowed by the expansion of the town; see "Urban landscape development in twelfth-century Acre," *Journal of the Royal Asiatic Society*, Series 3 18:3 (2008), 258.

6. For Pietro Vesconte's map, which was drawn for the Venetian merchant Marino Sanudo's *Liber secretorum fidelium crucis super Terrae Sanctae recuperatione et conservatione* (c. 1306–21), see British Library, Add. MS 27376, f. 190r; other copies include Bodleian, MS Tanner 190, f. 207r; and Bibliotheca Apostolica Vaticana, MS Pal. Lat. 1362 pt. A, f. 9r. On Sanudo himself, see Julia Harte, "How one fourteenth-century Venetian remembered the crusades: The maps and memories of Marino Sanuto," *Penn History Review* 15:2 (Spring 2008), 9–17. For the map of Paulinus of Puteoli, which was drawn for Paolino Veneto (1320), see Bibliotheca Apostolica Vaticana, MS Vat. Lat. 1960, f. 268v. For the map in Matthew Paris' *Chronica maiora* (c. 1240–59), see British Library, Royal MS 14 C.vii, f. 4v; for an overview, see Suzanne Lewis, *The Art of Matthew Paris in the Chronica Majora* (Berkeley, 1987).

7. I have not yet been able to consult the essay by Adrian Boas, "The streets of Frankish Acre," in *Crusader Landscapes in the Medieval Levant: The archaeology and history of the Latin East*, ed. M. Sinibaldi, K.J. Lewis, B. Major, and J.A. Thompson (Cardiff, 2016).

8. On the gates, see Kesten, *Acre*, 26; Jonathan Riley-Smith, "Guy of Lusignan, the Hospitallers and the Gates of Acre," in *Dei gesta per Francos*, 113; and David Jacoby, "The *fonde* of Crusader Acre and its Tariff: Some new considerations," in *Dei gesta per Francos*, 282. The most accessible list of these gates is actually on a map in Boas, "Urban landscapes," 248.

9. Ibn Shaddād, 98 and 150; Pringle, "Town defences," 99.

10. Boas, *Crusader Archaeology*, 34–5, lists several of the gates by name.

11. Kedar, "Outer walls of Frankish Acre," 162.

12. Kedar, "Outer walls of Frankish Acre," 174–5.

13. *Itinerarium2*, 1.32.

14. For a survey of Acre's history from ancient Egypt to 1918, see N. Makhouly and C.N. Johns, *Guide to Acre*, 2nd ed. (Jerusalem, 1946), 1–64. On the dating of remains on the Toron (today, Tel Akko) to the Middle Bronze Age, see A. Druks, "Tel Akko – 1983," *Excavations and Surveys in Israel* 3 (1984), 1–2; and Moshe Dothan and A. Raban, "The sea gate of ancient Akko," *Biblical Archaeologist* 43:1 (1980), 35–9. For later periods, Dothan, "Akko: Interim excavation report first season, 1973/4," *Bulletin of the American Schools of Oriental Research* 224 (Dec. 1976), 1–48; and Arie Kindler, "Akko: A city of many names," *Bulletin of the American Schools of Oriental Research* 231 (Oct. 1978), 51–5.

15. Jacoby, "Aspects of everyday life in Frankish Acre," 83–4. For an interactive, thirteenth-century glimpse of Acre's proximity to other Holy Land sites, see the Matthew Paris map; "The Oxford Outremer Map," Fordham Medieval Digital Projects, https://medievaldigital.ace.fordham.edu/mapping-projects/oxford-outremer-map-project/ (accessed 28 October 2016).

## Appendix D

1. Rigord, 82; *Howden1*, 2.189–90; *Howden2*, 3.128; and *Ymagines*, 2.82, identify twenty-three other Muslims present, but due to their having rendered the names into Latinate forms I have thus far been unable to independently identify them. They may or may not correspond to some names already listed here. These are: Baldewinus, Benesemedin, Birenses, the treasurer Camardoli, Cerantegadin, Chorisin (perhaps a Kurdish leader, Chusterin), Coulin, Felkedin, Gemaladin, Gurgi, Hessedin Jordich (perhaps an emir from Aleppo), Joramenses, the writer Kahedin, Lice, Limathosius, Maruth, Migemal, Mirsalim, Mustop, Passelar, Rotasienses, Sefelselem (identified by William Stubbs as

"Saifol Islam, lord of Arabia"), and Suchar (perhaps Sunqur al-Ḥalabī or Sunqur al-Wishāqī).

2. Identified in Judith Bronstein, *The Hospitallers and the Holy Land: Financing the Latin East, 1187–1214* (Woodbridge, 2005), 147–8.

3. Stephen Bennett, "The crusading household of Richard I: Roger of Howden was right after all!" (working paper, 2012), www.academia.edu/1477586/The_Crusading_Household_of_Richard_I_-_Roger_of_Howden_was_right_after_all¬ (accessed 6 June 2016).

4. Constance B. Bouchard, *Sword, Miter and Cloister: Nobility and the church of Burgundy, 980–1198* (Ithaca, 1987), 198–9.

5. R. Röhricht (ed.), *Regesta regni Hierosolymitani* (Innsbruck, 1893), no. 697.

6. Signifies from P.W. Edbury (trans.). *The Conquest of Jerusalem and the Third Crusade: Sources in translation* (Aldershot, 1998).

7. Speculation by Stubbs in *Howden1*, 2.148 n.10.

8. Signifies Piers D. Mitchell, *Medicine in the Crusades: Warfare, wounds and the medieval surgeon* (Cambridge, 2004).

9. Identified in L. Dorez (ed.), *Chronique d'Antonio Morosini: extraits relatifs a l'histoire de France*, 3 vols (Paris, 1901), 3.57 n.4.

10. Both bishops are identified in Pius Bonifacius Gams, *Series episcoporum ecclesiae Catholicae* (Graz, 1957), 434.

11. Likely confused with the aforementioned Guy, butler of Senlis.

# BIBLIOGRAPHY

## Manuscripts

Bibliotheca Apostolica Vaticana, MS Pal. Lat. 1362 pt. A, f. 9r
Bibliotheca Apostolica Vaticana, MS Vat. Lat. 1960, f. 268v
Bodleian, MS Tanner 190, f. 207r
British Library, Add. MS 27376, f. 190r
British Library, Royal MS 14 C.vii, f. 4v

## Primary sources

Ailes, M. and M. Barber (ed. and trans.). *The History of the Holy War: Ambroise's Estoire de la Guerre Sainte*, 2 vols (Woodbridge, 2003).

Albert of Aachen. *Historia Ierosolimitana: History of the journey to Jerusalem*, ed. and trans. S. Edgington (Oxford, 2007).

Anonymous. "De expugnatione civitatis Acconensis," in *Chronica magistri Rogeri de Houedene*, ed. W. Stubbs, 3 vols, Rolls Series (London, 1868–71), 3.cvi–cxxxvi.

Anonymous. "Ein zeitgenössisches Gedicht auf die Belagerung Accons," in *Forschungen zur deutschen Geschichte*, ed. H. Prutz, vol. 21 (Göttingen, 1881), 449–94.

Anonymous. "Libellus de expugnatione terrae sanctae per Saladinum," in *Radulphi de Coggeshall Chronicon Anglicanum*, ed. J. Stevenson, Rolls Series (London, 1875), 209–62.

Bird, J., E. Peters, and J.M. Powell (eds). *Crusade and Christendom: Annotated documents in translation from Innocent III to the fall of Acre, 1187–1291* (Philadelphia, 2013).

Bond, E. (ed.). *Chronica monasterii de Melsa*, 3 vols, Rolls Series (London, 1868).

Brown, M. (ed.). *T.E. Lawrence in War and Peace: An anthology of the military writings of Lawrence of Arabia*, new ed. (London, 2005).

Chroust, A. (ed.). *Quellen zur Geschichte des Kreuzzuges Kaiser Friedrichs I*, Monumenta Germania Historica, Scriptores Rerum Germanicarum, New Series 5 (Berlin, 1928).

Crawford, P. (ed. and trans.). *The "Templar of Tyre": Part III of the "Deeds of the Cypriots,"* Crusade Texts in Translation (Aldershot, 2003).

David, D.W. (ed. and trans.). *De expugnatione Lyxbonensi: The conquest of Lisbon* (Reprint, New York, 2001).

Delaborde, H.F. (ed.). *Œuvres de Rigord et de Guillaume le Breton, historiens de Philippe-Auguste* (Paris, 1882).

al-Dīn, 'Imād. "Les livres des deux jardins: histoire des deux règnes, celui de Nour Ed-Dîn et celui de Salah Ed Dîn," in *Recueil des historiens des croisades, historiens Orientaux*, vol. 4 (Paris, 1898).

Dorez, L. (ed.). *Chronique d'Antonio Morosini: extraits relatifs a l'histoire de France*, 3 vols (Paris, 1901).

Edbury, P.W. (trans.). *The Conquest of Jerusalem and the Third Crusade: Sources in translation* (Aldershot, 1998).

Faris, Nabih Amin (ed. and trans.). *Arab Archery: An Arabic manuscript of about A.D. 1500, "A Book on the Excellence of the Bow & Arrow" and the description thereof* (Princeton, 1945).

Gabrieli, F. (ed. and trans.). *Arab Historians of the Crusades: Selected and translated from the Arabic sources* (Berkeley, 1984).

Gerald of Wales. "De principis instructione liber," in *Giraldi Cambrensis opera*, ed. G.F. Warner, 8 vols, Rolls Series (London, 1891).

Gerald of Wales. "Giraldus Cambrensis concerning the instruction of princes," in *The Church Historians of England*, trans. J. Stevenson, vol. 5:1 (London, 1858).

Gerald of Wales. "Itinerarium Kambriae," in *Giraldi Cambrensis opera*, ed. G.F. Warner, 8 vols, Rolls Series (London, 1891).

Gervase of Canterbury. "The historical works of Gervase of Canterbury," in *The Chronicle of the Reigns of Stephen, Henry II, and Richard I*, ed. W. Stubbs, 2 vols, Rolls Series (London, 1879–80).

Gilbert of Mons, *Chronicle of Hainaut*, trans. L. Napran (Woodbridge, 2005).

Hofmeister, A. (ed.). *Ottonis de Sancto Blasio chronica*, Monumenta Germania Historica, Scriptores Rerum Germanicarum (Hanover, 1912).

Howlett, R. (ed.). "Historia rerum Anglicarum," in *Chronicles of the Reigns of Stephen, Henry II, and Richard I*, 2 vols, Rolls Series (London, 1884–5).

Ibn Shaddād, Bahā' al-Dīn. *The Rare and Excellent History of Saladin by Bahā' al-Dīn Ibn Shaddād*, trans. D.S. Richards, Crusade Texts in Translation (Farnham, 2002).

Lewis, B. (ed. and trans.). *Islam: From the Prophet Muhammad to the Capture of Constantinople* (New York, 1974).

Loud, G.A. (trans.). *The Crusade of Frederick Barbarossa: The history of the expedition of the Emperor Frederick and related texts* (Farnham, 2013).

Marzials, F. (trans.), *Chronicles of the Crusades: Villehardouin and Joinville* (Reprint, Mineola, NY, 2007).

Meyer, H.E. (ed.). *Das Itinerarium peregrinorum: eine zeitgenössiche englische Chronik zum dritten Kreuzzug in ursprünglicher Gestalt* (Stuttgart, 1962).

Morgan, M.R. (ed.). *La Continuation de Guillaume de Tyr (1184–1197)* (Paris, 1982).

Nicholson, H.J. (trans.). *The Chronicle of the Third Crusade: The Itinerarium peregrinorum et gesta regis Ricardi*, Crusade Texts in Translation (Farnham, 1997).

Potter, K.R. (ed. and trans.). *Gesta Stephani* (Oxford, 1976).

Powell, J.M. (trans.). *The Deeds of Pope Innocent III, by an Anonymous Author* (Washington, DC, 2004).

Ralph of Coggeshall. *Radulphi de Coggeshall Chronicon Anglicanum, De expugnatione terrae sanctae libellus, Thomas Agnellus De morte et sepultura Henrici regis Angliae junioris; Gesta Fulconis filii Warini; Excerpta ex Otiis imperialibus Gervasii Tilebutiensis*, ed. J. Stevenson, 3 vols, Rolls Series (London, 1875).

Richard of Devizes, "The chronicle of Richard of Devizes," in *Chronicles of the Reigns of Stephen, Henry II, and Richard I*, ed. R. Howlett, 4 vols, Rolls Series (London, 1886).

Richard of Devizes, *The Chronicle of Richard of Devizes, concerning the Deeds of Richard I, king of England, and Richard of Cirencester's Description of Britain*, trans. J.A. Giles (London, 1841).

Richard of Holy Trinity. "Itinerarium peregrinorum et gesta regis Ricardi," in *Chronicles and Memorials of the Reign of Richard I*, ed. W. Stubbs, 2 vols, Rolls Series (London, 1864–5).

Richards, D.S. (trans.). *The Chronicle of Ibn al-Athīr for the Crusading Period from al-Mail fi'l-Ta'rikh*, Crusade Texts in Translation, 3 vols (Reprint, Farnham, 2010).

Riley-Smith, J. et al. *Revised regesta regni Hierosolymitani Database*, http://crusades-regesta.com

Roger of Howden. *The Annals of Roger de Hoveden*, trans. H.T. Riley, 2 vols (Reprint, New York, 1968).

Röhricht, R. (ed.). *Regesta regni Hierosolymitani* (Innsbruck, 1893).

Salloch, M. (ed.). *Die lateinische Fortsetzung Wilhelms von Tyrus* (Leipzig, 1934).

Scanlon, G.T. (ed. and trans.). *A Muslim Manual of War* (Reprint, Cairo, 2012).

Slack, C.K. (ed.). *Crusade Charters, 1138–1270*, trans. H.B. Feiss, Medieval and Renaissance Texts and Studies 197 (Tempe, 2001).

Stubbs, W. (ed.). *Chronica magistri Rogeri de Houedene*, 3 vols, Rolls Series (London, 1868–71).

Stubbs, W. (ed.). *Chronicles and Memorials of the Reign of Richard I*, 2 vols, Rolls Series (London, 1864–5).

Stubbs, W. (ed.). *Gesta regis Henrici secundi Benedicti abbatis*, 2 vols, Rolls Series (London, 1867).

Stubbs, W. (ed.). *Radulfi de Diceto decanis Lundoniensis opera historica*, 2 vols, Rolls Series (London, 1876).

William of Newburgh. *The History of English Affairs*, ed. and trans. P.G. Walsh and M.J. Kennedy, 2 vols (Oxford, 2007–11).

William of Newburgh. *The History of William of Newburgh*, trans. J. Stevenson (London, 1856).

## Unpublished studies

Bennett, Stephen. "The crusading household of Richard I: Roger of Howden was right after all!" (working paper, 2012), www.academia.edu/1477586/The_Crusading_Household_of_Richard_I_-_Roger_of_Howden_was_right_after_all_

Donnachie, Stephen. "Reconstruction and rebirth: The Latin Kingdom of Jerusalem, 1187–1233" (PhD Thesis, Swansea University, 2013).

Gravelle, Yves. "Le problème des prisonniers de guerre pendant les croisades orientales, 1095–1192" (MA Thesis, University of Sherbrooke, 1999).

Matzliach, David. "The medical legacy of the Knights of St John and the Crusader Hospitals of Jerusalem and Acre" (MA Thesis, University of Manchester, 2012).

## Electronic resources

"Historical UK inflation rates and calculator," http://inflation.stephenmorley.org/

Hodges, K. "List of price of medieval items," http://medieval.ucdavis.edu/120D/Money.html

"The Oxford Outremer Map," Fordham Medieval Digital Projects, https://medievaldigital.ace.fordham.edu/mapping-projects/oxford-outremer-map-project/

"Robin Hood (2010)," Internet Movie Database, www.imdb.com/title/tt0955308/quotes?ref_=ttpl_ql_trv_4

Rome Statute of the International Criminal Court, www.icc-cpi.int/resource-library/Documents/RS-Eng.pdf

Secrets of Old Acre, www.akko.org.il/en/Old-Acre-The-Templars-Tunnel
T.E. Lawrence Studies, www.telstudies.org
Total Archaeology @ Tel Akko, www.hominid.psu.edu/projects_labs/telakko
"World Heritage Center," United Nations Educational, Scientific and Cultural Organization, http://whc.unesco.org/en/list/1042

## Secondary studies

Abbott, Jacob. "Memoirs of the Holy Land," *Harper's New Monthly Magazine* 27:5 (1852), 291–2.

Abels, Richard. "'Cowardice' and duty in Anglo-Saxon England," *Journal of Medieval Military History* 4 (2006), 29–49.

Abels, Richard. "Cultural representation and the practice of war in the middle ages," *Journal of Medieval Military History* 6 (2008), 1–31.

Abels, Richard and Stephen Morillo. "A lying legacy? A preliminary discussion of images of antiquity and altered reality in medieval military history," *Journal of Medieval Military History* 3 (2005), 1–13.

Abouali, Diana. "Saladin's legacy in the Middle East before the nineteenth century," *Crusades* 10 (2011), 175–89.

Adler, M. *The Jews in Medieval Europe* (London, 1939).

Ahmad, M. Hilmy M. "Some notes on Arabic historiography during the Zengid and Ayyubid periods (521/1127–648/1250)," in *Historians of the Middle East*, ed. B. Lewis (London, 1962), 77–97.

Allen, M.D. *The Medievalism of Lawrence of Arabia* (University Park, 1991).

Anderson, R.C. *Oared Fighting Ships: From classical times to the coming of steam* (London, 1962).

Aristizábal, Lucas Villegas. "Revisión de las crónicas de Ralph de Diceto y de la gesta regis Ricardi sobre la participación de la flota angevina durante la Tercera Cruzada en Portugal," *Studia historica* 27 (2010), 153–70.

Arnold, Benjamin. *German Knighthood, 1050–1300* (Reprint, Oxford, 1999).

Asbridge, Thomas. "Talking to the enemy: The role and purpose of negotiations between Saladin and Richard the Lionheart during the Third Crusade," *Journal of Medieval History* 39:3 (2013), 275–96.

Aurell, Martin. "Les femmes guerrières (XIe et XIIe siècles)," in *Famille, violence et christianisation au Moyen Age: Mélanges offerts à Michel Rouche* (Paris, 2005), 319–30.

Bacharach, Jere L. "African military slaves in the medieval Middle East: The cases of Iraq (869–955) and Egypt (868–1171)," *International Journal of Middle East Studies* 13:4 (Nov. 1981), 471–95.

Bachrach, Bernard S. "Early medieval demography: Some observations on the methods of Hans Delbrück," in *The Circle of War in the Middle Ages: Essays on medieval and naval history*, ed. D.J. Kagay and L.J. Andrew Villalon (Woodbridge, 1999), 3–20.

Bachrach, Bernard S. "'A lying legacy' revisited: the Abels-Morillo defense of discontinuity," *Journal of Medieval Military History* 5 (2007), 153–93.

Bachrach, David S. *Religion and the Conduct of War, c.300–1215* (Woodbridge, 2003).

Bachrach, David S. "English artillery 1189–1307: The implications of terminology," *English Historical Review* 121:494 (2006), 1408–30.

Baldwin, John W. *The Government of Philip Augustus: Foundations of French royal power in the middle ages* (Berkeley, 1986).

Barber, Malcolm. "The Albigensian Crusades: Wars like any other?" in *Dei gesta per Francos: Etudes sur les croisades dédiées à Jean Richard*, ed. M. Balard, B.Z. Kedar, and J. Riley-Smith (Aldershot, 2001), 45–55.

Barber, Malcolm. *The Crusader States* (New Haven, 2012).

Bartlett, Robert. *Gerald of Wales, 1146–1223* (Oxford, 1982).

Bennett, Matthew. "*La Régle du Temple* as a military manual, or how to deliver a cavalry charge," in *Studies in Medieval History presented to R. Allen Brown*, ed. C. Harper-Bill and J.L. Nelson (Woodbridge, 1989), 7–20.

Bennett, Matthew. "The myth of the military supremacy of knightly cavalry," in *Armies, Chivalry and Warfare: Proceedings of the 1995 Harlaxton Symposium*, ed. M.J. Strickland (Stamford, 1998), 304–16.

Beshir, B.J. "Fatimid military organization," *Zeitschrift Geschichte und Kultur des Islamischen Orients* 55 (Jan. 1978), 37–49.

Bishop, Adam M. "Usāma ibn Munqidh and crusader law in the twelfth century," *Crusades* 12 (2013), 53–65.

Boas, Adrian. *Crusader Archaeology: The material culture of the Latin East* (London, 1999).

Boas, Adrian. "Some reflections on urban landscapes in the Kingdom of Jerusalem: archaeological research in Jerusalem and Acre," in *Dei gesta per Francos: Etudes sur les croisades dédiées à Jean Richard*, ed. M. Balard, B.Z. Kedar, and J. Riley-Smith (Aldershot, 2001), 241–60.

Boas, Adrian. *Archaeology of the Military Orders: A survey of the urban centres, rural settlements and castles of the military orders in the Latin East (c. 1120–1291)* (London, 2006).

Boas, Adrian. "The streets of Frankish Acre," in *Crusader Landscapes in the Medieval Levant: The archaeology and history of the Latin East*, ed. M. Sinibaldi, K.J. Lewis, B. Major, and J.A. Thompson (Cardiff, 2016).

Bora, Fozia. "Did Salah al-Din destroy the Fatimids' books? An historiographical inquiry," *Journal of the Royal Asiatic Society* 24 (2014), 1–19.

Bosworth, C.E. "Recruitment, muster, and review in medieval Islamic armies," in *War, Technology and Society in the Middle East*, ed. V.J. Parry and M.E. Yapp (London, 1975), 59–77.

Bouchard, Constance B. *Sword, Miter and Cloister: Nobility and the church of Burgundy, 980–1198* (Ithaca, 1987).

Bowlus, Charles R. "Tactical and strategic weaknesses of horse archers on the eve of the First Crusade," in *Autour de la Première Croisade: Actes du Colloque de la Society for the Study of the Crusades and the Latin East*, ed. M. Balard (Paris, 1996), 159–216.

Bradbury, Jim. *The Medieval Siege* (Woodbridge, 1992).

Bronstein, Judith. *The Hospitallers and the Holy Land: Financing the Latin East, 1187–1214* (Woodbridge, 2005).

Broughton, Bradford B. *The Legends of King Richard I Coeur de Lion: A study of sources and variations to the year 1600* (The Hague, 1966).

Buck, Andrew D. *The Principality of Antioch and its Frontiers in the Twelfth Century* (Woodbridge, 2017).

Byrne, Eugene H. "Genoese trade with Syria in the twelfth century," *American Historical Review* 25:2 (1920), 191–219.

Cahen, Claude. "Un traité d'armurerie composé pour Saladin," *Bulletin d'études orientales* 12 (1947–8), 103–63.

Chevedden, Paul E. "The hybrid trebuchet: The halfway step to the counterweight trebuchet," in *On the Social Origins of Medieval Institutions: Essays in honor of Joseph F. O'Callaghan*, ed. D.J. Kagay and T.M. Vann (Leiden, 1998), 179–222.

Chevedden, Paul E. "The Islamic view and the Christian view of the crusades: A synthesis," *History* (2008), 181–200.

Christides, V. "Navies, Islamic," in *Dictionary of the Middle Ages*, ed. J. Strayer, 13 vols (New York, 1987), 9.76.

Christie, Niall. *Muslims and Crusaders: Christianity's wars in the Middle East, 1095–1382, from the Islamic sources* (New York, 2014).

Cobb, Paul M. *The Race for Paradise: An Islamic history of the crusades* (Oxford, 2014).

Coetzee, D. and L.W. Eysturlid. *Philosophers of War: The evolution of history's greatest military thinkers*, Volume I: *The Ancient to Pre-Modern World, 3000 BCE–1815 CE* (Santa Barbara, 2013).

Contamine, Philippe. *War in the Middle Ages*, trans. M. Jones (Oxford, 1984).

Cook, B.J. "The bezant in Angevin England," *Numismatic Chronicle* 159 (1999), 255–75.

Cook, David. *Understanding Jihad* (Berkeley, 2005).

Crosby, Alfred W. *Throwing Fire: Projectile technology through history* (Cambridge, 2002).

Cunningham, J. Spencer. *The Sufi Orders in Islam* (Reprint, Oxford, 1998).

Curry, Anne. *Agincourt: A new history* (Stroud, 2005).

Cushing, Dana. *A German Third Crusader's Chronicle of his Voyage and the Siege of Almohad Silves, 1189 AD/Muwahid Xelb, 585 AH: De itinere navali* (Antimony Media, 2013).

Dajani-Shakeel, Hadia. "*Jihād* in twelfth-century Arabic poetry: A moral and religious force to counter the crusades," *Muslim World* 66 (1976), 96–113.

Damian-Grint, Peter. *The New Historians of the Twelfth-Century Renaissance: Inventing vernacular authority* (Woodbridge, 1999).

Dennis, George T. "Byzantine heavy artillery: The Helepolis," *Greek, Roman, and Byzantine Studies* 39 (1998), 99–115.

DeVries, Kelly. "God and defeat in medieval warfare: Some preliminary thoughts," in *The Circle of War in the Middle Ages: Essays on medieval military and naval history*, ed. D.J. Kagay and L.J.A. Villalon (Woodbridge, 1999), 87–97.

DeVries, Kelly and Robert Douglas Smith. *Medieval Military Technology*, 2nd ed. (Toronto, 2012).

Dothan, Moshe. "Akko: Interim excavation report first season, 1973/4," *Bulletin of the American Schools of Oriental Research* 224 (Dec. 1976), 1–48.

Dothan, Moshe and A. Raban. "The sea gate of ancient Akko," *Biblical Archaeologist* 43:1 (1980), 35–9.

Dotson, John E. "Ship types and fleet composition at Genoa and Venice in the early thirteenth century," in *Logistics of Warfare in the Age of the Crusades*, ed. J.H. Pryor (Aldershot, 2006), 63–75.

Druks, A. "Tel Akko – 1983," *Excavations and Surveys in Israel* 3 (1984), 1–2.

Duffy, Eamon. *Fires of Faith: Catholic England under Mary Tudor* (New Haven, 2009).

Duggan, Lawrence G. *Armsbearing and the Clergy in the History and Canon Law of Western Christianity* (Woodbridge, 2013).

Edbury, Peter W. *The Kingdom of Cyprus and the Crusades, 1191–1374* (Cambridge, 1991).

Edbury, Peter W. *John of Ibelin and the Kingdom of Jerusalem* (Woodbridge, 1997).

Edbury, Peter W. "The Lyon Eracles and the Old French continuations of William of Tyre," in *Montjoie: Studies in crusade history in honour of Hans Eberhard Mayer*, ed. B.Z. Kedar, J. Riley-Smith, and R. Hiestand (Aldershot, 1997), 139–53.

Edbury, Peter W. "New perspectives on the Old French continuations of William of Tyre," *Crusades* 9 (2010), 107–13.

Eddé, Anne-Marie. "Kurdes et Turcs dans l'armée ayyoubide de Syrie du nord," in *War and Society in the Eastern Mediterranean, 7th–15th Centuries*, ed. Y. Lev (Leiden, 1996), 225–36.

Edgington, Susan. "The doves of war: The part played by carrier pigeons in the crusades," in *Autour de la Première Croisade: Actes du colloque de la Society for the Study of the Crusades and the Latin East*, ed. M. Balard (Paris, 1996), 167–75.

Ehrenkreutz, A.S. "The place of Saladin in the naval history of the Mediterranean Sea in the middle ages," *Journal of the American Oriental Society* 75:2 (1955), 100–16.

Ehrenkreutz, A.S. *Saladin* (Albany, 1972).

Ehrlich, Michael. "The Battle of Hattin: A chronicle of a defeat foretold?" *Journal of Medieval Military History* 5 (2007), 16–32.

Ehrlich, Michael. "Urban landscape development in twelfth-century Acre," *Journal of the Royal Asiatic Society*, Series 3 18:3 (2008), 257–74.

Ehrlich, Michael. "The Battle of Arsur: A short-lived victory," *Journal of Medieval Military History* 12 (2014), 109–18.

Eickhoff, Ekkehard. *Friedrich Barbarossa im Orient: Kreuzzug und Tod Friedrichs I* (Tübingen, 1977).

Evergates, Theodore. *Henry the Liberal: Count of Champagne, 1127–1181* (Philadelphia, 2016).

Fadl, Khaled Abou El. "The rule of killing at war: An inquiry into the classical sources," *Muslim World* 89 (1999), 144–57.

Fahmy, Aly Mohamed. *Muslim Sea Power in the Eastern Mediterranean, from the Seventh Century to the Tenth Century A.D.* (New Delhi, 1966).

Farmer, D.L. "Some price fluctuations in Angevin England," *Economic History Review* 9:1 (1956), 34–43.

Folda, Jaroslav. "Before Louis IX: Aspects of crusader art at St. Jean d'Acre, 1191–1244," in *France and the Holy Land: Frankish culture at the end of the crusades*, ed. D.H. Weiss and L. Mahoney (Baltimore, 2004), 138–57.

Forey, Alan. "The military orders and the ransoming of captives from Islam (twelfth to early fourteenth centuries)," *Studia Monastica* 33 (1991), 259–79.

Forey, Alan. "Henry II's crusading penance for Becket's murder," *Crusades* 7 (2008), 153–64.

France, John. *Victory in the East: A military history of the First Crusade* (Cambridge, 1994).

France, John. *Western Warfare in the Age of the Crusades, 1000–1300* (Ithaca, 1999).

France, John. "Crusading warfare and its adaptation to eastern conditions in the twelfth century," *Mediterranean Historical Review* 15:2 (2000), 49–66.

France, John. *Perilous Glory: The rise of western military power* (New Haven, 2011).

France, John. *Great Battles: Hattin* (Oxford, 2015), 102–4.

France, John. "'Crusading' warfare in the twelfth century," in *The Crusader World*, ed. A.J. Boas (London and New York, 2016), 68–83.

France, John. "Egypt, the Jazira and Jerusalem: Middle Eastern tensions and the Latin states in the twelfth century," in *Crusader Landscapes in the Medieval Levant: The archaeology and history of the Latin East*, ed. M. Sinibaldi, K.J. Lewis, B. Major, and J.A. Thompson (Cardiff, 2016), 145–56.

Franke, Daniel P. "Crusade, empire, and the process of war in Staufen Germany, 1180–1220," in *The Crusader World*, ed. A.J. Boas (London and New York, 2016), 128–43.

Frankel, Rafael. "The north-western corner of crusader Acre," *Israel Exploration Journal* 37:4 (1987), 256–61.

Freed, John B. *Frederick Barbarossa: The prince and the myth* (New Haven, 2016).

Friedman, Yvonne. "The ransom of captives in the Latin Kingdom of Jerusalem," in *Autour de la Première Croisade: Actes du Colloque de la Society for the Study of the Crusades and the Latin East*, ed. M. Balard (Paris, 1996), 177–89.

Friedman, Yvonne. *Encounter between Enemies: Captivity and ransom in the Latin Kingdom of Jerusalem* (Leiden, 2002).

Fuhrmann-Na'aman, Yale. "Conservation of the Knights Hospitaller compound," in *One Thousand Nights and Days: Akko through the ages*, ed. A.E. Killebrew and V. Raz-Romeo (Haifa, 2010), 60–5.

Fulton, Michael S. "Anglo-Norman artillery in narrative histories, from the reign of William I to the minority of Henry III," *Journal of Medieval Military History* 14 (2016), 1–31.

Gabriel, Richard A. *Muhammad: Islam's first great general* (Norman, 2007).

Gams, Pius Bonifacius. *Series episcoporum ecclesiae Catholicae* (Graz, 1957).

Garnett, George. *Conquered England: Kingship, succession and tenure, 1066–1166* (Oxford, 2007).

Gertwagen, Ruthy. "The crusader port of Acre: Layout and problems of maintenance," in *Actes du Colloque de la Society for the Study of the Crusades and the Latin East (Clermont-Ferrand, 22–25 juin 1995)*, ed. M. Balard (Paris, 1996), 553–81.

Gertwagen, Ruthy. "Harbours and facilities along the Eastern Mediterranean sea lanes to Outremer," in *Logistics of Warfare in the Age of the Crusades*, ed. J.H. Pryor (Aldershot, 2006), 95–118.

Gertwagen, Ruthy. "A chapter on maritime history: Shipping and nautical technology of trade and warfare in the medieval Mediterranean, 11th–16th century," in *Maritimes Mittelalter: Meere als Kommunikationsräume*, ed. M. Borgolte and N. Jaspert (Ostfildern, 2016), 109–48.

Gibb, Hamilton A.R. "The Arabic sources for the life of Saladin," *Speculum* 25:1 (1950), 58–72.

Gibb, Hamilton A.R. *Studies on the Civilization of Islam*, ed. S.J. Shaw and W.R. Polk (Boston, 1962).

Gibb, Hamilton A.R. "The Aiyūbids," in *A History of the Crusades*, Volume II: *The Later Crusades, 1189–1311*, ed. H.W. Hazard, K.M. Setton, and R.L. Wolff (Madison, 1969), 693–714.

Gibb, Hamilton A.R. *The Life of Saladin, from the Works of 'Imad ad-Din and Baha' ad-Din* (Oxford, 1973).

Gillingham, John. "Richard I and Berengaria of Navarre," *Historical Research* 53:128 (1980), 157–73.

Gillingham, John. "Richard I and the science of warfare in the middle ages," in *War and Government in the Middle Ages: Essays in honour of J.O. Prestwich*, ed. J. Gillingham and J.C. Holt (Woodbridge, 1984), 78–91.

Gillingham, John. "Roger of Howden on Crusade," in *Richard Coeur de Lion: Kingship, chivalry and war in the twelfth century* (London, 1994), 141–53.

Gillingham, John. *Richard I* (New Haven, 1999).

Gillingham, John. "Historians without hindsight: Coggeshall, Diceto and Howden on the early years of John's reign," *King John: New interpretations*, ed. S.D. Church (Woodbridge, 1999), 1–26.

Gillingham, John. "Two Yorkshire historians compared; Roger of Howden and William of Newburgh," *Haskins Society Journal* 12 (2002), 20–5.

Gillingham, John. "Crusading warfare, chivalry, and the enslavement of women and children," in *The Medieval Way of War: Studies in medieval military history in honor of Bernard S. Bachrach*, ed. G.I. Halfond (Aldershot, 2015), 133–51.

Gillingham, John. "The treatment of the defeated, c. 950–1350: Historiography and the state of research," in *La conducción de la guerra en la Edad Media: Historiografía (Acta del Symposium Internacional celebrado en Cáceres, Noviembre 2008)*, ed. Manuel Rojas (Cáceres, forthcoming).

Gransden, Antonia. *Historical Writing in England c. 550 to c. 1307* (London, 1974).

Guérin, M.V. *Description Géographique, Historique et Archéologique de la Palestine*, 3 vols (Paris, 1880).

Haldane, Douglas. "The fire-ship of Al-Sālih Ayyūb and Muslim use of 'Greek fire,'" in *The Circle of War in the Middle Ages: Essays on medieval and naval history*, ed. D.J. Kagay and L.J. Andrew Villalon (Woodbridge, 1999), 137–44.

Haldon, John. "Roads and communications in the Byzantine Empire: Wagons, horses, and supplies," in *Logistics of Warfare in the Age of the Crusades*, ed. J.H. Pryor (Aldershot, 2006), 131–58.

Haldon, John and M. Byrne. "A possible solution to the problem of Greek fire," in *Byzantinische Zeitschrift begründet von Karl Krumbacher*, ed. H.-G. Beck et al. (München, 1977), 91–9.

Haldon, John, Andrew Lacey, and Colin Hewes. "'Greek fire' revisited: Recent and current research," in *Byzantine Style, Religion and Civilization: In honour of Sir Steven Runciman*, ed. E.M Jeffreys (Cambridge, 2006), 290–325.

Hamblin, William J. "Saladin and Muslim military theory," in *The Horns of Hattin: Proceedings of the Second Conference of the Society for the Study of the Crusades and the Latin East, Jerusalem and Haifa 2–6 July 1987*, ed. B.J. Kedar (Jerusalem and London, 1992), 228–38.

Hamilton, Bernard. *The Leper King and his Heirs: Baldwin IV and the crusader Kingdom of Jerusalem* (Cambridge, 2000).

Hamilton, Bernard. "The crusades and northeast Africa," in *Crusading and Warfare in the Middle Ages, Realities and Representations: Essays in honour of John France*, ed. S. John and N. Morton (Farnham, 2014), 167–79.

Handyside, Philip. *The Old French William of Tyre* (Leiden, 2015).

Hanley, Catherine. *War and Combat, 1150–1270: The evidence from Old French literature* (Cambridge, 2003).

Harari, Yuval Noah. "Eyewitnessing in the accounts of the First Crusade: The *Gesta Francorum* and other contemporary narratives," *Crusades* 3 (2004), 77–99.

Harari, Yuval Noah. *Special Operations in the Age of Chivalry, 1100–1550* (Woodbridge, 2007).

Harte, Julia. "How one fourteenth-century Venetian remembered the crusades: The maps and memories of Marino Sanuto," *Penn History Review* 15:2 (Spring 2008), 9–17.

Hewlett, Maurice. *The Life and Death of Richard Yea-and-Nay* (New York, 1901).

Hill, Donald R. "Trebuchets," *Viator* 4 (1973), 99–114.

Hillenbrand, Carole. *The Crusades: Islamic perspectives* (New York, 2000).

Hillenbrand, Carole. "The evolution of the Saladin legend in the west," in *Regards croisés sur le Moyen Âge arabe: Mélanges à la mémoire de Louis Pouzet s.j. (1928–2002)*, ed. A.-M. Eddé and E. Gannagé (Beirut, 2005), 497–512.

Hirschler, Konrad. *Medieval Arabic Historiography: Authors as actors*, Routledge Studies on the Middle East (Abingdon, 2006).

Hirschler, Konrad. "The Jerusalem conquest of 492/1099 in the medieval Arabic historiography of the crusades: From regional plurality to Islamic narrative," *Crusades* 13 (2014), 37–73.

Hodgson, Natasha R. *Women, Crusading and the Holy Land in Historical Narrative* (Woodbridge, 2007).

Hosler, John D. "Henry II, William of Newburgh, and the development of English anti-Judaism," in *Christian Attitudes towards the Jews in the Middle Ages: A casebook*, ed. M. Frassetto (New York, 2007), 167–82.

Hosler, John D. *Henry II: A medieval soldier at war, 1147–1189* (Leiden, 2007).

Hosler, John D. *John of Salisbury: Military authority of the twelfth-century renaissance* (Leiden, 2013).

Hosler, John D. "Identifying King Stephen's artillery," *Journal of Conflict Archaeology* 10:3 (2015), 192–203.

Hosler, John D. "Chivalric carnage? Fighting, capturing, and killing the enemy at the battles of Dol and Fornham in 1173," in *Prowess, Piety and Public Order in Medieval Society: Studies in honor of Richard W. Kaeuper*, ed. C.M. Nakashian and D.P. Franke (Leiden, 2017), 36–61.

Hosler, John D. "Knightly ideals at the siege of Acre, 1189–1191," in *Chivalric Identity in the High Middle Ages*, ed. X. Baecke, D. Crouch, and J. Deploige (Leuven, forthcoming).

Hosler, John D. "Clausewitz's wounded lion: A fighting retreat at the siege of Acre, November 1190," in *Acre and its Falls*, ed. J. France (Brill, forthcoming).

Housley, Norman. *Contesting the Crusades* (Oxford, 2006).

Hoyland, Robert G. *In God's Path: The Arab conquests and the creation of an Islamic empire* (Oxford, 2015).

Hume, David. *The History of England: From the invasion of Julius Caesar to the revolution in 1688*, 6 vols (Reprint, Indianapolis, 1983).

Irwin, Robert. "Saladin and the Third Crusade: A case study in historiography and the historical novel," in *A Companion to Historiography*, ed. M. Bentley (London and New York, 1997), 139–52.

Isaac, Steven. "Cowardice and fear management: The 1173–74 conflict as a case study," *Journal of Medieval Military History* 4 (2006), 50–64.

Jacoby, David. "Crusader Acre in the thirteenth century: Urban layout and topography," *Studi medievali*, 3rd ser. 20:1 (1979), 1–46.

Jacoby, David. "Montmusard, suburb of crusader Acre: The first stage of its development," in *Outremer: Studies in the history of the crusading Kingdom of Jerusalem presented to Joshua Prawer*, ed. B.Z. Kedar, H.E. Mayer, and R.C. Smail (Jerusalem, 1982), 205–17.

Jacoby, David. "Les communes italiennes et les Ordres militaires à Acre: aspects juridiques, territoriaux et militaires (1104–1187, 1191–1291)," in *État et colonisation au Moyen Age*, ed. M. Balard (Lyon, 1989), 193–214.

Jacoby, David. "The *fonde* of Crusader Acre and its Tariff: Some new considerations," in *Dei gesta per Francos: Etudes sur les croisades dédiées à Jean Richard*, ed. M. Balard, B.Z. Kedar, and J. Riley-Smith (Aldershot, 2001), 277–93.

Jacoby, David. "Society, culture and the arts in crusader Acre," *France and the Holy Land: Frankish culture at the end of the crusades*, ed. D.H. Weiss and L. Mahoney (Baltimore, 2004), 97–137.

Jacoby, David. "Aspects of everyday life in Frankish Acre," *Crusades* 4 (2005), 73–105.

Jacoby, David. "Ports of pilgrimage to the Holy Land, eleventh–fourteenth century: Jaffa, Acre, Alexandria," in *The Holy Portolano: The sacred geography of navigation in the middle ages*, ed. M. Bacci and M. Rohde (Berlin, 2014), 51–72.

Jones, Robert W. *Bloodied Banners: Martial display on the medieval battlefield* (Woodbridge, 2010).

Kedar, Benjamin Z. "The Patriarch Eraclius," in *Outremer: Studies in the history of the crusading Kingdom of Jerusalem presented to Joshua Prawer*, ed. B.Z. Kedar, H.E. Mayer, and R.C. Smail (Jerusalem, 1982), 177–204.

Kedar, Benjamin Z. "A western survey of Saladin's forces at the siege of Acre," in *Montjoie: Studies in crusade history in honour of Hans Eberhard Mayer*, ed. B.Z. Kedar, J. Riley-Smith, and R. Hiestand (Aldershot, 1997), 113–22.

Kedar, Benjamin Z. "The outer walls of Frankish Acre," *Atiqot* 31 (1997), 157–80.

Kedar, Benjamin Z. "The Jerusalem massacre of July 1099 in the western historiography of the crusades," *Crusades* 3 (2004), 15–75.

Kedar, Benjamin Z. "Prolegomena to a world history of harbour and river chains," in *Shipping, Trade and Crusade in the Medieval Mediterranean: Studies in honour of John Pryor*, ed. R. Gertwagen and E. Jeffreys (Farnham, 2012), 3–37.

Kedar, Benjamin Z. "King Richard's plan for the battle of Arsūf/Arsur, 1191," in *The Medieval Way of War: Studies in medieval military history in honor of Bernard S. Bachrach*, ed. G.I. Halfond (Aldershot, 2015), 117–32.

Kennedy, Hugh. *Crusader Castles* (Cambridge, 1994).

Kesten, A. *Acre: The old city, survey and planning* (Tel Aviv, 1962).

Khamisy, Rabei G. "Some notes on Ayyūbid and Mamluk military terms," *Journal of Medieval Military History* 13 (2015), 73–92.

Killebrew, Anne E. and Brandon R. Olson, "The Tel Akko Total Archaeology Project: New frontiers in the excavation and 3D documentation of the past," in *Proceedings of the 8th International Congress on the Archaeology of the Ancient Near East, 30 April–4 May 2012, University of Warsaw, Volume 2*, ed. P. Bieliński et al. (Wiesbaden, 2014), 559–74.

Killebrew, Anne E. and Jaime Quartermaine, "Total Archaeology @ Tel Akko: Excavation, survey, community outreach, and new approaches to landscape archaeology in 3D," in *Proceedings of the 9th International Congress on the Archaeology of the Ancient Near East, 9–13 June 2014, Basel, Volume 3*, ed. R.A. Stucky et al. (Wiesbaden, 2016), 491–502.

Kindler, Arie. "Akko: A city of many names," *Bulletin of the American Schools of Oriental Research* 231 (Oct. 1978), 51–5.

Köhler, Michael A. *Alliances and Treaties between Frankish and Muslim Rulers in the Middle East: Cross-cultural diplomacy in the period of the crusades*, ed. K. Hirschler, trans. P.M. Holt (Leiden, 2013).

Kostick, Conor. "Courage and cowardice on the First Crusade, 1096–1099," *War in History* 20:1 (2013), 32–49.

Lambton, A.K.S. "Reflections on the Iqṭā," in *Arabic and Islamic Studies in Honour of Hamilton A.R. Gibb*, ed. G. Makdisi (Leiden, 1965), 358–76.

Lapina, Elizabeth. "'Nec signis nec testis creditur': the problem of eyewitnesses in the chronicles of the First Crusade," *Viator* 38 (2007), 117–39.

Latham, R.E. (ed.). *Revised Medieval Latin Word List from British and Irish Sources* (Reprint, Oxford, 1994).

Lev, Yaacov. *Saladin in Egypt* (Leiden, 1999).

Lev, Yaacov. "Prisoners of war during the Fatimid-Ayyubid wars with the crusaders," in *Tolerance and Intolerance: Social conflict in the age of the crusades*, ed. M. Gervers and J.M. Powell (Syracuse, 2001), 11–27.

Lev, Yaacov. "Infantry in Muslim armies during the crusades," in *Logistics of Warfare in the Age of the Crusades*, ed. J.H. Pryor (Aldershot, 2006), 185–207.

Lewis, Bernard. *Race and Slavery in the Middle East: An historical inquiry* (Oxford, 1990).

Lewis, Suzanne. *The Art of Matthew Paris in the Chronica Majora* (Berkeley, 1987).

Lyons, Malcolm C. and D.E.P. Jackson. *Saladin: The politics of the holy war* (Cambridge, 1982).

Maalouf, Amin. *The Crusades through Arab Eyes*, trans. J. Rothschild (New York, 1984).

Mack, Merav. "A Genoese perspective of the Third Crusade," *Crusades* 10 (2011), 45–62.

Madden, Thomas F. "Rivers of blood: An analysis of one aspect of the crusader conquest of Jerusalem in 1099," *Revista Chilena de Estudios Medievales* 1 (2012), 25–37.

Makhouly, N. and C.N. Johns. *Guide to Acre*, 2nd ed. (Jerusalem, 1946).

Malta Protestant College. *Journal of a Deputation sent to the East by the Committee of the Malta Protestant College, Part I* (London, 1849).

Markowski, Michael. "Richard Lionheart: Bad king, bad crusader?" *Journal of Medieval History* 23:4 (1997), 351–65.

Mayer, Hans Eberhard. *The Crusades*, trans. J. Gillingham (Oxford, 1988).

Mayor, Adrienne. *Greek Fire, Poison Arrows, and Scorpion Bombs: Biological and chemical warfare in the ancient world* (New York, 2009).

Micheau, François. "Ibn al-Athīr," in *Medieval Muslim Historians and the Franks in the Levant*, ed. A. Mallett (Leiden, 2015), 52–83.

Mitchell, Piers D. *Medicine in the Crusades: Warfare, wounds and the medieval surgeon* (Cambridge, 2004).

Möhring, Hans. *Saladin: The sultan and his times, 1138–1193*, trans. D.S. Bachrach (Baltimore, 2008).

Morillo, Stephen F. *Warfare under the Anglo-Norman Kings, 1066–1135* (Woodbridge, 1994).

Morillo, Stephen F. "Expecting cowardice: Medieval battle tactics reconsidered," *Journal of Medieval Military History* 4 (2006), 65–73.

Murray, Alan V. "'Mighty against the enemies of Christ': The relic of the True Cross in the armies of the Kingdom of Jerusalem," in *The Crusades and their Sources: Essays presented to Bernard Hamilton*, ed. J. France and W.G. Zajac (Aldershot, 1998), 217–38.

Murray, Alan V. "Finance and logistics of the crusade of Frederick Barbarossa," in *In Laudem Hierosolymitani: Studies in crusades and medieval culture in honour of Benjamin Z. Kedar*, ed. I. Shagrir, R. Ellenblum, and J. Riley-Smith (Aldershot, 2007), 357–68.

Naus, James. *Constructing Kingship: The Capetian monarchs of France and the early crusades* (Manchester, 2016).

Neocleous, Savvas. "The Byzantines and Saladin: Opponents of the Third Crusade?" *Crusades* 9 (2010), 87–106.

Nesbitt, John W. "The rate of march of crusading armies in Europe," *Traditio* 19 (1963), 167–81.

Nicholson, Helen. "Women on the Third Crusade," *Journal of Medieval History* 23:4 (2013), 335–49.

Nicholson, R.L. *Joscelyn III and the Fall of Crusader States, 1134–1199* (Leiden, 1973).

240

Nicolle, David. *Crusader Warfare*, Volume II: *Muslims, Mongols and the Struggle against the Crusades* (London, 2007).

Oman, Charles. *A History of the Art of War in the Middle Ages*, Volume I: *378–1278 AD* (Reprint, London, 1998).

Painter, Sidney. "The lords of Lusignan in the eleventh and twelfth centuries," *Speculum* 32:1 (1957), 27–47.

Painter, Sidney. "The Third Crusade: Richard the Lionheart and Philip Augustus," in *A History of the Crusades*, Volume II: *The Later Crusades, 1189–1311*, ed. K. Setton, R.L. Wolff, and H.W. Hazard (Madison, 1969), 45–85.

Partington, J.R. *A History of Greek Fire and Gunpowder* (Cambridge, 1960).

Partner, Peter. "Holy war, crusade and *jihād*: An attempt to define some problems," in *Autour de la Première Croisade: Actes du Colloque de la Society for the Study of the Crusades and the Latin East*, ed. M. Balard (Paris, 1996), 333–43.

Payne-Gallwey, Ralph. *The Crossbow: Its military and sporting history, construction and use* (Reprint, Ludlow, 2007).

Perry, Guy. "'Scandalia . . . tam in oriente quam in occidente': the Briennes in East and West, 1213–1221," *Crusades* 10 (2011), 63–77.

Petersen, Andrew. "Medieval bridges of Palestine," in *Egypt and Syria in the Fatimid, Ayyubid and Mamluk Eras VI: Proceedings of the 14th and 15th International Colloquium Organized at the Katholieke Universitat Leuven in May 2005 and May 2006*, ed. U. Vermeulen and K. D'Hulster, Orientalia Lovaniensia Analecta (Leuven, 2010), 291–306.

Philippides, Marios and Walter K. Hanak, *The Siege and the Fall of Constantinople in 1453: Historiography, topography, and military studies* (Farnham, 2011).

Phillips, Jonathan. "The Latin East: 1098–1291," in *The Oxford History of the Crusades*, ed. J. Riley-Smith (Reprint, Oxford, 2002), 111–37.

Phillips, Jonathan. *The Second Crusade: Extending the frontiers of Christendom* (New Haven, 2007).

Prawer, Joshua. *Crusader Institutions* (Oxford, 1980).

Pringle, Denys. "Town defences in the crusader Kingdom of Jerusalem," in *The Medieval City Under Siege*, ed. I.A. Corfis and M. Wolfe (Woodbridge, 1995), 69–121.

Pringle, Denys. *The Churches of the Crusader Kingdom of Jerusalem: A corpus*, Volume IV: *The Cities of Acre and Tyre with Addenda and Corrigenda to Volumes I–III* (Cambridge, 2009).

Pryor, John H. "Transportation of horses by sea during the era of the crusades: Eighth century to 1285 A.D.," *The Mariner's Mirror* 68 (1982), 9–27.

Pryor, John H. *Geography, Technology, and War: Studies in the maritime history of the Mediterranean, 649–1571* (Cambridge, 1988).

Pryor, John H. "The *Eracles* and William of Tyre: An interim report," in *The Horns of Hattin: Proceedings of the Second Conference of the Society for the Study of the Crusades and the Latin East, Jerusalem and Haifa 2-6 July, 1987*, ed. B.Z. Kedar (Jerusalem and London, 1992), 270–93.

Pryor, John H. "Digest," in *Logistics of Warfare in the Age of the Crusades*, ed. J.H. Pryor (Aldershot, 2006), 275–92.

Pryor, John H. *The Age of the Dromōn: The Byzantine navy, ca. 500–1204* (Leiden, 2006).

Pryor, John H. "A medieval siege of Troy: The fight to the death at Acre, 1189–1191 or the tears of Ṣalāḥ al-Dīn," in *The Medieval Way of War: Studies in medieval military history in honor of Bernard S. Bachrach*, ed. G.I. Halfond (Aldershot, 2015), 97–115.

Purton, Peter. *A History of the Early Medieval Siege* (Woodbridge, 2009).

Queller, Donald E. and Thomas F. Madden. *The Fourth Crusade: The conquest of Constantinople*, 2nd ed. (Philadelphia, 1997).

Richard, Jean. "Les révoltes chypriotes de 1191–1192 et les inféodations de Guy de Lusignan," in *Montjoie: Studies in crusade history in honour of Hans Eberhard Mayer*, ed. B.Z. Kedar, J. Riley-Smith, and R. Hiestand (Aldershot, 1997), 123–8.

Richards, D.S. "A consideration of two sources for the life of Saladin," *Journal of Semitic Studies* 25:1 (1980), 46–65.

Richards, D.S. "Biographies of Ayyubid sultans," in *Ayyubid Jerusalem: The holy city in context, 1187–1250*, ed. R. Hillebrand S. Auld (London, 2009), 441–55.

Richardson, H.G. and G.O. Sayles. *The Governance of Mediaeval England from the Conquest to Magna Carta* (Edinburgh, 1963).

Richter-Bernburg, Lutz. "'Imād al-Dīn al-Iṣfahānī," in *Medieval Muslim Historians and the Franks in the Levant*, ed. A. Mallett (Leiden, 2015), 29–51.

Riley-Smith, Jonathan. "The Knights of St. John in Jerusalem and Cyprus, c. 1050–1310," in *A History of the Hospital of St. John of Jerusalem*, ed. L. Butler, vol. 1 (New York, 1967).

Riley-Smith, Jonathan. *The Crusades: A short history* (New Haven, 1987).

Riley-Smith, Jonathan (ed.). *The Atlas of the Crusades* (New York, 1991).

Riley-Smith, Jonathan. "Guy of Lusignan, the Hospitallers and the Gates of Acre," in *Dei gesta per Francos: Etudes sur les croisades dédiées à Jean Richard*, ed. M. Balard, B.Z. Kedar, and J. Riley-Smith (Aldershot, 2001), 111–15.

Riley-Smith, Jonathan. *The First Crusade and the Idea of Crusading* (Reprint, London, 2003).

Riley-Smith, Jonathan. "Truth is the first victim," *The Times*, 5 May 2005.

Rodger, N.A.M. *Safeguard of the Sea: A naval history of Britain, 660–1649* (New York, 1997).

Rogers, Clifford J. *Soldiers' Lives throughout History: The middle ages* (Westport, 2007).

Rogers, Clifford J. "Constables," in *The Oxford Encyclopedia of Medieval Warfare and Military Technology*, ed. C. Rogers (Oxford, 2010).

Rogers, R. *Latin Siege Warfare in the Twelfth Century* (Oxford, 1992).

Rubenstein, Jay. "In search of a new crusade: A review essay," *Historically Speaking* (April 2011), 25–7.

Rubin, Morton. *The Walls of Acre: Intergroup relations and urban development in Israel* (New York, 1974).

Runciman, Steven. *A History of the Crusades*, Volume III: *The Kingdom of Acre and the Later Crusades* (Reprint, Cambridge, 1999).

Sayers, Jane. "English charters from the Third Crusade," in *Tradition and Change: Essays in honour of Marjorie Chibnall, presented by her friends on the occasion of her seventieth birthday*, ed. D. Greenway, C. Holdsworth, and J. Sayers (Cambridge, 1985), 195–214.

Sayers, William. "The name of the siege engine *trebuchet*: Etymology and history in medieval France and Britain," *Journal of Medieval Military History* 8 (2010), 189–96.

Scott, Sir Walter. *Ivanhoe* (Reprint, London, 1920).

Simmons, C.A. *Reversing the Conquest: History and myth in nineteenth-century British literature* (New Brunswick, 1990).

Singman, Jeffrey L. *Robin Hood: The shaping of the legend* (Westport, 1998).

Sivan, Emmanuel. *L'Islam et la Croisade: Idéologie et propagande dans les réactions Musulmanes aux croisades* (Paris, 1968).

Smail, R.C. "The predicaments of Guy of Lusignan, 1183–87," in *Outremer: Studies in the history of the crusading Kingdom of Jerusalem presented to Joshua Prawer*, ed. B.Z. Kedar, H.E. Mayer, and R.C. Smail (Jerusalem, 1982), 159–76.

Smail, R.C. *Crusading Warfare, 1097–1193*, 2nd ed. (Cambridge, 1995).

Smith, Robert Douglas. *Rewriting the History of Gunpowder* (Nykøbing, 2010).

Spiegel, Gabrielle M. *The Chronicle Tradition of Saint-Denis: A survey* (Brookline, 1978).

Spufford, Peter. *The Handbook of Medieval Exchange*, Royal Historical Society Guides and Handbooks (London, 1986).

Stanton, Charles D. *Norman Naval Operations in the Mediterranean* (Woodbridge, 2011).

Stern, Eliezer and Hanaa Abu-Uqsa, "New archaeological discoveries from crusader period Acre," in *One Thousand Nights and Days: Akko through the ages*, ed. A.E. Killebrew and V. Raz-Romeo (Haifa, 2010), 40–8.

Strickland, Matthew and Robert Hardy, *The Great Warbow: From Hastings to the Mary Rose* (Stroud, 2005).

Stubbs, William. *The Constitutional History of England*, 3 vols (Oxford, 1880).

Sweetenham, Carol. "What really happened to Eurvin de Créel's donkey? Anecdotes in sources for the First Crusade," in *Writing the Early Crusades: Text, transmission and memory*, ed. M. Bull and D. Kempf (Woodbridge, 2014), 75–88.

Tarver, W.T.S. "The traction trebuchet: A reconstruction of an early medieval siege engine," *Technology and Culture* 36:1 (Jan. 1995), 136–67.

Theotokis, Georgios. "The square 'fighting march' of the crusaders at the Battle of Ascalon (1099)," *Journal of Medieval Military History* 11 (2013), 57–71.

Throop, Susanna A. *Crusading as an Act of Vengeance, 1095–1216* (Farnham, 2011).

Tsugitaka, Sato. *State and Rural Society in Medieval Islam: Sultans, Muqta's, and fallahun* (Leiden, 1997).

Tyerman, Christopher. *England and the Crusades, 1095–1588* (Chicago, 1988).

Tyerman, Christopher. *The Invention of the Crusades* (London, 1998).

Tyerman, Christopher. *God's War: A new history of the crusades* (Cambridge, 2006).

Unger, Richard W. "Difficult sources: Crusader art and the depiction of ships," in *Shipping, Trade and Crusade in the Medieval Mediterranean*, ed. R. Gertwagen (New York, 2012), 85–104.

Verbruggen, J.F. *The Art of Warfare in Western Europe during the Middle Ages, from the Eighth Century to 1340*, trans. S. Willard and Mrs. R.W. Southern, 2nd ed. (Woodbridge, 1997).

Wagner, Thomas Gregor and Piers D. Mitchell, "The illnesses of King Richard and King Philippe on the Third Crusade: An understanding of *arnaldia* and *leonardie*," *Crusades* 10 (2011), 23–44.

Warner, Philip. *Sieges of the Middle Ages* (New York, 1994).

Wolff, R.L. "The Fifth Crusade," in *A History of the Crusades*, ed. K. Setton and H.W. Hazard, 6 vols (Madison, 1969), 2.376–428.

Wyatt, David. *Slaves and Warriors in Medieval Britain and Ireland, 800–1200* (Leiden, 2009).

# INDEX